FEM
AGGRESSION

FEMALE AGGRESSION

Helen Gavin and
Theresa Porter

WILEY Blackwell

This edition first published 2015
© 2015 John Wiley & Sons, Ltd.

Registered Office
John Wiley & Sons, Ltd, The Atrium, Southern Gate, Chichester, West Sussex, PO19 8SQ, UK

Editorial Offices
350 Main Street, Malden, MA 02148-5020, USA
9600 Garsington Road, Oxford, OX4 2DQ, UK
The Atrium, Southern Gate, Chichester, West Sussex, PO19 8SQ, UK

For details of our global editorial offices, for customer services, and for information about how
to apply for permission to reuse the copyright material in this book please see our website
at www.wiley.com/wiley-blackwell.

The right of Helen Gavin and Theresa Porter to be identified as the authors of this work has been
asserted in accordance with the UK Copyright, Designs and Patents Act 1988.

Library of Congress Cataloging-in-Publication Data

Gavin, Helen.
    Female aggression / Helen Gavin, Theresa Porter.
        pages   cm
    Includes bibliographical references and index.
    ISBN 978-0-470-97547-3 (hardback : alk. paper) – ISBN 978-0-470-97548-0 (paper : alk. paper)
    1. Aggressiveness.   2. Women–Psychology.   3. Sex differences (Psychology)
    I. Porter, Theresa.   II. Title.
    BF575.A3G38 2015
    155.3′338232–dc23
                                                            2014020563

A catalogue record for this book is available from the British Library.

Cover image: © Apostrophe / Shutterstock

Set in 11/13.5pt Bembo by SPi Publisher Services, Pondicherry, India
Printed and bound in Malaysia by Vivar Printing Sdn Bhd

1   2015

Contents

Preface

We met several years ago at an interdisciplinary conference where we were both presenting different papers on the same topic: the sexual abuse of children by women. Our post-conference contacts evolved into a discussion about child murder, then a journal article on infanticide, followed by more discussions and more articles. At one point, we decided that we wanted to address the widespread problem of aggressive and violent behaviour by women in a more comprehensive way. We noted that, over the last twenty years, a variety of texts has been published, each addressing a single topic of female aggression, including:

- *When Women Kill* (Mann, 1996)
- *Sexually Aggressive Women* (Anderson & Struckman-Johnson, 1998)
- *Woman-to-Woman Sexual Violence* (Girshick, 2002b)
- *Aggression, Antisocial Behavior and Violence among Girls* (Putallaz & Bierman, 2004)
- *Gender Inclusive Treatment of Intimate Partner Violence* (Hamel, 2005)
- *Why Mothers Kill* (McKee, 2006)
- *Female Sexual Offenders* (Gannon & Cortoni, 2010)

Each of these texts was a landmark publication in its own right, calling attention to the problems and consequences of specific arenas of aggression by women. What was missing, however, was a comprehensive review and analysis of aggression by women in multiple areas, a single volume that looked at all aspects of murder, rape and abuse by women.

We also agreed that the topic of female aggression has earned its own place within the literature. For a multitude of reasons, female behaviour, including aggressive behaviour, is consistently reported within the context of direct comparison with male behaviour. Historically, reports of female aggression have been described only in comparison to male aggression (i.e., women are less aggressive than men). By setting women's aggression only within the context of male behaviour, the implication is that aggression is typical of men and unusual for women. This trivializes the problem of women's aggression and the experiences of victims of that aggression. We view women's aggression as an important societal problem and a topic worthy of study on its own, rather than simply a footnote to male aggression.

It is our hope that this text will become a useful reference for behavioural scientists interested in the topic of human aggression, one that stimulates interdisciplinary research on the topic. We also hope that professionals within law enforcement, policy development and psychology will also find this volume useful as they move beyond simple awareness of women's aggression as an unrecognized public health issue and towards changes to address and prevent these behaviours.

Acknowledgements

We would like to acknowledge all those at Wiley Blackwell who helped bring this work to fruition, including Andrew Peart and Karen Shield. We would like to thank the librarians and researchers without whose work this book would have been far more difficult. We also would like to thank our respective families and friends for their continued support and enthusiasm for our work.

1

Theories, Research and Misconceptions about Female Aggression

Read the newspapers or watch TV and we view a world that is clearly violent. In many places, news agencies report on conflict, war, ethnic cleansing and torture. Every week it seems that there is another young man stabbed to death on the streets of a major city, and sportsmen or celebrities are in court accused of monstrous sexual assaults. What the majority of these news stories have in common is that they are about men and male aggression. There is an unvoiced popular belief that this violence is male, or originated by men. If this seems a strange thing to point out, try to imagine how these events would be reported if the perpetrators were female.

Introduction

Aggression is defined as intra-species behaviour carried out with the intent to cause pain or harm (Tremblay, Hartup, & Archer, 2005). This definition covers the forms of aggression identified as aggression between nations or states, adopted by the Unite Nations General Assembly in 1974, but it also applies to the interpersonal violence that affects our everyday lives. The behaviour can be physical, mental or verbal, and should not be confused with assertiveness or anger. Aggression can also be classified as hostile (usually regarded as having an emotional or retaliatory context) or instrumental (predatory or goal oriented). Dependent on the theoretical position, a definition of aggression can vary from the above. For example,

Female Aggression, First Edition. Helen Gavin and Theresa Porter.
© 2015 John Wiley & Sons, Ltd. Published 2015 by John Wiley & Sons, Ltd.

Buss and Perry (1992) suggest that we can separate out the acts of verbal and physical aggression and define them as the motor components of behaviour that involve harm to others. Hostile aggression is regarded as spontaneous, motivated by anger, in comparison to instrumental aggression, which is deliberate, planned and targeted towards the attainment of a goal (Ramirez, 2009). This dichotomous definition is questioned by some, as the reactive emotional goal may be to inflict pain on another, but is a handy description that distinguishes some types of behaviour or motivations from others. This dichotomy is commonly encountered when describing aggression in women. According to Barratt et al. (1999), aggression can be classified in terms of the cause of the motivation, i.e., it can be premeditated (proactive), impulsive (reactive) or medically (biologically) based. The common element in all the arguments is that they are behaviourally based, but some also include the terms 'anger' and 'hostility' interchangeably with 'aggression', which appear to be emotional (internal) in nature and hence not directly observable. This complexity is also reflected in the different forms of measurement for aggression (Suris et al., 2004).

This lack of definitional clarity is possibly due to the range of theoretical positions underlying all of the research in aggression. This range can be loosely defined as psychological theories (from psychodynamic positions to cognitive and behavioural models to social origins of behaviour, and societal factors inherent in aggression) and biological perspectives (including evolutionary theories, genetic causes, chemical contributions and neurological outcomes). This chapter introduces these positions and relates them to the study of female aggression.

Aggression and Women

It is accepted that men are more likely to express their aggression in ways that are physically violent, and that women will behave in indirect ways, being less capable of exerting the same physical force. This somewhat simplistic viewpoint is reflected in every major theoretical perspective on aggression; comparative, evolutionary, biological, psychological and social models all reiterate that men/males are the aggressors. Women are viewed as only using aggression in passive, submissive or emotional ways. This book sets out to examine this position and to explore theories and research about female aggression, its motives and outcomes, possibly exposing a few myths on the way.

Physical aggression among and by girls and women has become more prevalent. This is evident in women's sports, media aimed at or including women, and the criminal and juvenile justice systems (e.g., UK Home Office, 2012; US Bureau of Justice Statistics, 2014). Psychological theories provide a basis for examining a society that values aggression and the consequences of that (erroneous) placement of worth. If society that accepts male aggression and violence becomes accepting of female aggression, then rising rates of female-perpetrated violence must be the consequence. Conversely, women's violence and aggression may be leaving the domestic sphere, where it has been relatively invisible, and entering the public arena.

Female aggression is a fact of life, but one that is only lately being addressed by mainstream social and behavioural sciences. There is a wealth of animal research that examines female aggression, but applying these findings to human behaviour or emotional response is difficult at best. Studies on rodents, or red-fronted lemurs, or even our genetically closest primates concentrate on female aggression as the result of events that concern animals, such as competition for mates or food, or the protection of offspring. Such research must also be careful to curtail any interpretation that could open itself to criticism of anthropomorphizing behaviour. When we do find aggression studies on humans, it is almost as if the peculiar lens of comparative psychology must be applied here, as researchers seem happy to compare female behaviour to that exhibited in the male, rather than as behaviour in its own right. The literature on the topic seems to view aggression by women or girls as either a pale copy of male aggression, or specific to certain situations, such as alcohol abuse or domestic violence. There is also a tacit assumption that female aggression has the same motivations and form of expression as male aggression. There is little acknowledgement in the literature that viewing female aggression as poorly expressed imitative behaviour of male aggression minimizes and trivializes women's behaviour, anger, perspectives and viewpoints. In 2005, Richardson reviewed thirty years of research on gender differences in aggressive behaviour. She found that the assumption that females were not aggressive could not be supported, as studies did, in effect, demonstrate the opposite. Women in laboratory studies did respond to provocation and could not be described as passive. The conclusion is that the major point of difference is not in the form of aggression, but the relationship between aggressors, or aggressor and victim.

Incidents of violence in which women are the victims has reached high proportions, not least because it is now more likely to be reported to, and followed up by, police. However, there is evidence to suggest that reports of the violence and its prevalence are given in sexualized terms (rape or sexual assault, or assault on the woman as object of hate) or in relation to intimate partner violence. Sexual or domestic violence is not the only aggression that women receive, but reports give the impression that it is. For example, in a ten-country study linking women's health and violence against women conducted by the World Health Organization (2010), the statistics are presented in terms of reported physical or sexual violence by a husband or partner (ranging between 15% and 71%, dependent on country) and non-consensual sex. There is little acknowledgement of the female recipient of violence that is not linked to rape/sexual assault or wife beating (domestic or intimate partner violence). It is as if these are the only types of victimization that women experience. Similarly, in the United States, the Centers for Disease Control estimate more than five million women suffer intimate-partner victimizations annually, with around 1,300 of these resulting in the death of the woman. Such figures are horrific, but also serve to hide other forms of violence, and give the impression that women are always passive recipients. Neither of the two above studies acknowledges that women can be perpetrators of the same aggression. In fact, research has established that intimate partner violence is bi-directional and that such aggression is more highly correlated with substance abuse than with either ethnicity or gender (Sullivan et al., 2009). This also is true when considering all other forms and level of violence. Olson and Lloyd (2005) suggest that less severe or 'minor' cases of aggression, including those within intimate relationships, are relatively equal across men and women. A possible source of understanding why female aggression is seen as less prevalent than male aggression might be the definition of aggression and the conflating of types of violence. In Olsen and Lloyd's study, women reported they had initiated aggression in 54 per cent of the events they discussed, although there was a confused or confusing view of what 'starting aggression' meant. Some women defined this as getting angry, or thought asking their partner to talk about issues of conflict was a form of aggression, and an initiation of conflict in itself. Moreover, 63 per cent of conflicts contained only verbal aggression linked to the dynamics of conflict and communication in the relationship. Thus, these women define aggression as a complex issue, beyond (and before) the striking of blows. Women in this study also identified a range of motives for aggression, with 'rule' violation by the male partner and their own desire to gain attention or the male's compliance as the most likely reasons, together with psychological factors. This complex set of motives for initiating aggression is supported by a study by Hettrich and O'Leary (2007), in which 32 per cent of their sample of female college students who were in a relationship admitted they used physical aggression against their partners. Additionally, they reported that they used it more than their male partners, with anger at partners and poor communication being cited as reasons. However, they also reported that their male partners as more sexually coercive than they were and they were more dissatisfied with their relationships than the women who did not report using or experiencing violence within them. Hence, women appear to use aggression in particular ways within relationships, including as a way of expressing dissatisfaction or anger rather than simply as a means to harm another. These findings, however, still do not consider female aggression outside the immediate familial setting. Perhaps a consideration of criminal activity that involves aggressive acts might shed some light on this.

Violent Crime and Women

Aggression and violence are inseparable from crime, and the fear of crime influences a great deal of our behaviour and perception of others. It also influences research and practice in criminal psychology and other allied disciplines, and hence policy within justice systems. Women do commit crimes, and always have. However, there is a particular phenomenon surrounding conviction of female offenders, referred to as Chivalric Justice (Iacovetta & Valverde, 2002). This includes the circumstances of women receiving lesser sentences than men for the same kinds of crime. For example, the issue of sole female child molester generates responses of disbelief rather than the revulsion produced by male paedophiles (Gavin, 2010). Such an offender is also less likely to receive a custodial sentence than her male counterpart. This chivalric position is reflected in media reporting of crime by women. Grabe and Kamhawi (2006) observed what they noted as a patriarchal chivalry in news coverage of crime carried out by women alone, but that the reporting is much harsher when women collaborate with men; they term the last the Bonnie and Clyde effect.

The complementary reaction to female offenders is one expressed in the 'evil woman hypothesis', the view that women who offend outside normative gender roles are doubly deviant (Mellor & Deering, 2010). This is particularly evident when considering women who participate in sexual murder with a male partner (Gavin, 2010). Moors Murderer Myra Hindley, for example, is seen as much more 'evil' and culpable than Ian Brady, as she was, after all, a woman, and women do not kill children.

In most places around the world, at least those in which we can view statistics with confidence, crime rates are falling in proportion to population figures, seen clearly in the report of agencies such as the UK Home Office (2012) and the US Bureau of Justice Statistics (2014). The only crime that appears to be growing is violent crime perpetrated by female offenders, although many postulate that this is a result of changes in reporting and arresting behaviour rather than any increase in female violence per se (Schwartz, Steffensmeier, & Feldmeyer, 2009). Similarly, there is a possibility that the perceived change in offences and arrest rates are an artefact of policy changes that reflect cultural changes in the perception of gender roles and gendered behaviour. There is still an overwhelming difference in the number of incidents attributed to men/boys and women/girls, but the increase in observed female violence does bear scrutiny. Moore (2007) contends that the ways in which young male and female offenders exhibit aggression are very similar, and that this is bound up with constantly changing views of masculinity and femininity. This is particularly important to address in the light of the falling-off in the rate of male-perpetrated violent crime, which is attributed to policies targeting this behaviour. This would suggest that female aggression needs a different focus in research and practice to that addressing male behaviour. There is evidence to suggest that, whilst parental aggression, antisocial peers and academic problems can be associated with aggressive behaviour in youths of both sexes, there are considerable differences in social and psychological factors related to aggression by women. These include levels of mental illness (usually depression) and physical or sexual victimization (Leschied, Cummings, Van Brunschot, Cunningham, & Saunders, 2000). Further distinguishing factors may be due to differences in impulsivity or the readiness to take risks (Campbell & Muncer, 2009). Studies that examine these issues suggest that, if the pertinent variables are subtracted from the analysis, disparity in aggression and resultant behaviour is not simply due to sex differences. Moreover, the significant sex differences in rates of depression may be due to oversimplified diagnostic criteria, and 'male-typed' depression being overlooked because the distinguishing features are not included as critical factors (Möller–Leimkühler & Yücel, 2010). Hence, mental illness may not be the distinguishing sex-linked factor it appears to be in violent crime, but other issues may need to be accounted for. Readiness and willingness to participate in risky or criminal behaviour might be a core issue in the likelihood of aggressive behaviour from males and females. For example, Russell and Baenninger (1996) concluded that personal characteristics, such as irritability and religiosity, contribute more than sex to the reported likelihood to commit undetected murder. Therefore, interventions designed to prevent violence in young women and girls should take these questions into account in addition to those associated with male violence.

Further issues surround the definition of gender difference itself, together with other social and individual factors that affect it. Richardson and Hammock (2007) concluded that gender role is the better predictor of aggression than gender, and the effect becomes less distinctive when the type of aggression (direct versus indirect) is taken into account. This might be accounted for by differential paths of socialization of boys and girls, and the development of social skills in respect of socially accepted gender role expression. For example, Gavin and Hockey (2010) demonstrated that young men with one or more offences in their history are more likely to make an aggressive response in situations where the socially accepted behaviour would be conciliatory. It has yet to be established how the ways in which women process such problems might differ. In addition, Farrington (2005) examined a large range of individual and socially derived risk factors that might lead to the development of delinquency in boys, including violence. As yet, no such study on the impact of developmental or psychological factors has been undertaken on women or girls, despite the awareness of increasing crime rates for women/girls, and the challenge to readily accepted assumption of gender differences in crime, arrest and conviction (Farrington, Loeber, & Welsh, 2010).

It is clear, therefore, that the ways in which female aggression is observed need to be different to the ways in which male aggression is addressed. It is also clear that this topic is only just beginning to be tackled by feminist, social, psychological and medical interpretations of the human discourse. If we examine the various theories of aggression, it is difficult to determine how each addresses female aggression and violence, if at all. The presumption that male behaviour equates to all human behaviour continues to exist within aggression theory and research.

Theories of Aggression

Theories based on biological difference

If female aggressive behaviour, and its motivations and prevalence are truly different to male aggression, then biological models that address differences between the sexes should be compellingly convincing. For example, the theories of evolutionary biology and psychology posit a position in which the differential evolution of men and women is due to natural selection for the continuation of genetic material. Additionally, biological differences between the sexes suggest that aggression is simply not an advantageous behaviour for women, as they are more at risk of being hurt. However, things are just not that simple.

Evolution   Evolutionary biology is a theory of the development of characteristics of different species in response to specific environmental needs. Darwinist evolutionary theory suggests that there are four basic mechanisms by which evolutionary change occurs: mutation, migration, genetic drift and natural selection. Mutation is a natural or induced change in genetic material that is passed to offspring. Migration is the movement of individuals from one population to another. Genetic drift is the chance survival of certain characteristics from one generation to the next. Natural selection is the ability of individual with an advantageous mutation to survive to produce offspring. These mechanisms alter the frequency of different genes in a population, which results in descendants with modification, i.e., the transmission of genetic material producing particular traits from parent to offspring, known as heredity. If genes can mutate, producing variations in the characteristic they control that are favourable to the organism, the mutation is reproduced, and hence genetic material survives via natural selection. Hence, there is a differential reproduction of genetic variations in a population resulting in individuals whose fitness is greater, having more offspring than individuals of lesser fitness. This means there is a change in gene frequencies within the population over time.

This biological theory of evolution and selection has its counterparts within psychology. Evolutionary psychology attempts to explain psychological traits as evolutionary adaptations, that is, as the functional products of natural or sexual selection. The argument is that much of human behaviour is generated by evolutionary adaptations that combat problems in human environments. For example, the mental capacities for acquiring language are almost universal, but humans do not inherit the capacity for reading and writing. Natural selection, in both biological and psychological terms, suggests that organisms are in competition with other members of their species, for food, territory and sexual mates. Humans, psychologically speaking, also have the universal disposition for cooperation and empathy, amongst other things, hence evolutionary psychology is an extension of the theory that encompasses the human capacity to experience and act on emotion. Evolutionary theory can therefore explain aggression because it is universally experienced and has not been adapted out of human responses. Violence may be useful because it can increase chances of gaining resources, survival and reproductive success. These can be behaviours such as the higher likelihood of male animals to protect mates when females are in short supply (Cashdan, 1996). According to this position, natural selection does not simply shape the behaviour, but also determines what the nature of the response will be. Thus gender-based violence is explained, as females, being weaker, require protection from males other than the mate. However, if females are protected, and males receive reward (in terms of reproductive success) for doing so, why are females aggressive? Indeed, why are females becoming more, not less, visibly aggressive and violent? This is not explained in traditional theories of evolutionary biology or psychology. A major criticism of evolutionary theories is that they are very much androcentric, that is, they consider all reasons for adaptation and selection from the male point of view. There are alternative theories of evolution, those that consider a different set of reasons for why we arrived at the position we have. These will be considered in detail in the next chapter.

If traditional evolutionary theories are not a complete explanation for female aggression and its difference to male aggressive behaviour, then might there be more persuasive arguments from other related biological positions? Integral to the idea of evolutionary survival is the transmission of genetic material, thereby suggesting that the explanation for aggression may be within the genes themselves.

Genetics Biology's 'magic bullet' of the twentieth and twenty-first centuries was the surge in understanding genetics and the increasing use of DNA analysis. As such, the unlocking of the genetic code seemed to offer the possibility of identifying a violent or a criminal gene. It has been noted that the overwhelming majority of (violent) crimes are perpetrated by men, at least those that are detected. Most people have 46 chromosomes, and a person's sex is determined by the X and Y chromosomes. Genetic women usually have two X chromosomes and genetic men have an XY pair. In a condition known as 47: XYY syndrome, occurring in around 1/1000 male births (Torniero et al., 2011), males are born with an additional Y chromosome, i.e., XYY, and this has led some to think that such men are 'extra-masculine' and more prone to sexual aggression. However, these individuals are not necessarily linked to higher levels of aggression or violent crime (Jones, 2006). XYY syndrome may provide the circumstances for aggressive behaviour, but it is more likely that social circumstances in combination with the anomaly determine how behaviour manifests itself. What interest in this syndrome does highlight is the idea that aggressive and/or violent behaviour is the province of the 'masculine' individuals, and the more masculine, the more aggressive. It also strengthens the argument that aggression has a biological cause.

Other genetic characteristics can be examined in terms of the transmission of criminality and/or aggressive tendencies. Empirical studies of identical twins with identical genetic characteristics, or children within a family but not biologically related, such as those adopted into the family, are an excellent way to search for any evidence for the relationship between genes and behaviour. In this way, any biological contribution or social, environmental influences can be investigated. The traditional twin study is an experiment provided by nature; there are identical (monozygotic MZ) twins and fraternal (dizygotic DZ) twins, with differing levels of similarity in genetic material. DZ twins have no more similarity than any other siblings, but are born at the same time; therefore, it is assumed they experience the same things as they mature. MZ pairs share identical genetic material, if all characteristics are due to genetic influence, then we can expect to see twice as much similarity in the MZ twins as the DZ twins. Deviations from the similarity are then assumed to be due to environmental influences. Research clearly shows that violent children often come from violent families, suggesting the existence of some form of familial transmission of aggression. These comparisons do show that consistency between behavioural aspects of an individual is significantly higher in identical twins. Although this is compelling evidence, however, it does not rule it out the social influences because there is a high likelihood of similar treatment in familial and social environments, particularly of identical twins – they are the same age, go to the same school; parents often dress them identically and so on. A much more persuasive argument would be derived if identical twins reared apart demonstrated the same level of identical behaviour seen in those brought up together. The rarity of this situation means using a case study approach, but with enough cases, a database of information can be compiled to such an extent that rigorous research questions are tested. The largest study of this kind is the Minnesota study of twins reared apart (MISTRA) started in 1979 (Bouchard et al., 1990). This intensive study determined that at least 70 per cent of the variance in IQ was due to genetic factors, i.e., twins have very similar levels of IQ whether separated or together, and there is a high probability that they will have similar IQs in comparison to their separated siblings. There was also a significant level of similarity in a wide range of other anthropometric and psycho-physiological factors, and psychological and social behaviours, to the same levels of similarity seen in monozygotic twins reared together. What has not been clearly established, however, is whether this extends to criminal and offending behaviours. However, there is an interesting possibility that it might relate to other forms of aggression, such as that directed inwards, as in the case of suicide. In 2003, Brent et al. reported on a study to examine whether there was familial transmission of suicide and whether this was related to impulsive aggression. They found that the children of suicide attempters showed a higher risk of suicide attempt, with an earlier age onset than those in families with no history of suicide attempts. A history of impulsive aggression was the most powerful predictor of early age of suicide attempt. This study did not examine twins as the sample did not contain them, but it demonstrates that a familial examination of aggression is fruitful.

The contrasting examination is of children who are genetically dissimilar but were brought up in the same parental and familiar environment. Studies of children who were adopted at birth (or very young) means that the occurrence of any characteristics can be compared between adopted and biological parents. Genetic influences on the characteristic can be inferred from any similarity between child and biological parent and the environmental influences from similarity between adoptee and adoptive parent.

For adopted children and any criminal tendencies, Beaver (2011) reports that adopted children with at least one biological parent who had been arrested, especially for violent offences, are more likely to enter the juvenile justice system multiple times than adoptees whose biological parents have not been arrested. This suggests that the criminality of the biological parent is more likely to predict the child's delinquent behaviour than that of the adoptive parent, although Klahr, McGue, Iacono and Burt (2011) assert that a conflictive adoptive environment may also contribute.

There are criticisms of twin and adoption studies. Firstly, there is an assumption of equal environments across families; secondly, the representativeness of samples is questionable (Rutter, 2005). Assuming equal environments means assuming that any influence will remain constant, i.e., that identical and fraternal twins, or other siblings, share identical environments as well as biological characteristics. This assumption cannot be made, particularly in terms of behavioural characteristics. In addition, it has been demonstrated that multiple births carry more risk of obstetric problems; children whose mothers suffer birth complications are routinely excluded from studies that are not exceptionally longitudinal in nature. Similarly, twins often exhibit mild delays in language development; these pairs are again excluded. Problems with adoption studies are of a similar nature, in that adoptive families are selected using very strict criteria and represent a very small sample of the home environment in which children are raised (Moffit, 2005).

The genetics of aggression provides a convincing line of reasoning, but it is only a partial explanation. Genetic make-up determines not just physical and possibly psychological make-up; the influence extends to the biochemistry of sex.

The biochemistry of aggression   Testosterone is an androgen, a hormone that has major involvement in the development of sexual characteristics and organs in male animals, but also has effects on female development and behaviour. In both males and females, testosterone is produced by the adrenal glands, with some released from the ovaries in females. The release is much slower in females, while in men it is made by Leydig cells in the testis, and is secreted into the bloodstream in spurts, which means that levels can change significantly within minutes. Testosterone has clear masculinizing and anabolic effects in both sexes, but the high level in men appears to affect aggression, a possible reason for the difference in level and type of aggression from each sex. Animal experiments demonstrate that castration reduces aggression in male mice, for example (Wagner, Beuving, & Hutchinson, 1980), but does not eliminate it. Such findings lead to the conclusion that high levels of testosterone are necessary but not sufficient to trigger aggression. Castrated animals, rated as non-aggressive before removal of the testes, cannot be made aggressive by injections of testosterone, whereas initially aggressive-rated mice do return to prior levels of aggression.

As always, animal studies can be criticized for their limited application in humans. Human data is derived from non-experimental studies, which also have their problems due to the lack of direct observation. Studies on hormone levels in male and female prisoners do seem to suggest that testosterone does encourage social dominance, competitiveness and impulsiveness, all of which facilitate aggressive behaviour.

There are two hypotheses about the effect of testosterone. The basal model suggests that testosterone causes changes in dominance behaviour, whereas the reciprocal model posits the idea that testosterone changes as dominance changes. This clearly has implications for a sex difference model of aggression. If females are submissive and hence low in aggression due to low ranking in hierarchies, then the basal model would suggest it may be a result of lack of testosterone, or the lack of ability to quickly release it into the blood stream at crucial moments. However, if individual women are raised in dominance, according to the reciprocal model, their testosterone levels should be rising too. No conclusive data has been found to suggest either model is correct, as injecting non-aggressive but ambitious women with testosterone would not be viewed as an ethical study.

In addition to endogenous hormones, the study of the influence of neurotransmitters on aggression also follows an animal-model paradigm. Neurotransmitters are chemicals that allow the transmission of signals between neurones. The chemicals are released into the synaptic cleft, the gap between neurones. The molecules can then bind to receptor proteins within the postsynaptic cell, which causes a change in the electrical state of the cell. This change in electrical state can either excite the cell, passing along the chemical message, or inhibit it. Excess molecules are taken back up by the presynaptic cell and reprocessed. One neurotransmitter of particular interest in aggression is serotonin (also called 5-hydroxytryptamine, or 5-HT). The neurones in the brain that release serotonin are found in small dense collections called Raphe nuclei in the medulla, pons and midbrain. Serotonergic neurones have axons that project to many different parts of the brain; therefore serotonin affects many different behaviours. 5-HT receptors mediate both excitatory and inhibitory neurotransmission. Animal models show that increases in the availability of serotonin reduces aggression. This increase is facilitated by increasing the activity at neurotransmitter sites with drugs such as 5-HT agonists (drugs that stimulate the action); this has been shown to reduce several different types of aggression (Nelson & Trainor, 2007). There are several types of drugs that inhibit the 5-HT receptors. Inhibiting the reuptake of serotonin allows higher levels in the system; the famous Prozac is one such drug that acts in this way. A second class of drugs are known as monoamine oxidase inhibitors or MAO inhibitors. Monoamine oxidase (MAO) is an enzyme that causes serotonin, dopamine and noradrenaline inactivation. MAO inhibitors prevent inactivation of monoamines within a neuron, causing excess neurotransmitter to diffuse into the synaptic space. Brunner et al. (1993) conducted a study on a large extended family, finding a mutation in the structural gene for MAO that appeared to be associated with aggressive behaviour among the males. They were reported to have selective MAO deficiency, again with an association with impulsive aggression, at least within circumstances of socio-emotional hypersensitivity (Eisenberger et al., 2007). However, there were no such deficiencies or aggressive behaviour reported in the female members of the family.

The final class of drugs are those that interfere with the ability of synaptic vesicles to store monoamines, again displacing serotonin. Such drugs include amphetamines. Animal experimentation shows clearly that 5-HT inhibitors do reduce some forms of aggression, or prevent its escalation (Takahashi, Quadros, de Almeida, & Miczek, 2011), although de Boer and Koolhaas (2005) did question the simple linkage between such serotonin increase and the reduction in all forms of aggression. There are suggestions that the more likely action is on certain forms of female aggression such as defensive and offensive postpartum aggression for the protection of offspring against male intruders, at least in rodents (da Veiga, Miczek, Lucion, & de Almeida, 2011).

Extending these findings to humans is again not very clear, but it is known that there are reduced concentrations of 5-HT and 5-HIAA (a metabolite of 5-HT) in the brains of suicide victims, particularly those involving violent suicide methods, suggesting a link between suicidal and dominance/homicidal-related behaviours. If this linkage appears tenuous, it may be illuminated by the 2005 finding of Dumais et al. that a violent form of suicide was an indicator of a lifetime of aggression and impulsivity. However, these results only seem to explain male violent suicide. Whilst hanging is the favoured form of suicide for both sexes, male suicides are much more likely to use firearms, particularly in Switzerland (Värnik et al., 2008), whereas women will use a much less violent and messy method. The question remains as to why reduced concentrations of 5-HT would lead to violent suicide in men and not in women, leading to the supposition that there are many more factors acting here than simply the opportunity to access and use serotonin and its biological pathways.

Nelson and Trainor (2007) suggest that aggression is the result of impaired recognition of social cues and enhanced impulsivity, and that these are mediated by biological signals at the molecular level. This hypothesis is credible, but difficult to test. Further findings make the issue even more complex. The release of the hormone prolactin from the pituitary gland is controlled by serotonin, and its levels in the bloodstream can be used to determine changes in serotonin levels. The action of the 5-HT agonists is to allow serotonin to be released, increasing the level of prolactin. However, there is no linear relationship between the dose of a drug and the amount of prolactin across individuals, showing a highly variable response to either the drug or the serotonin levels. In 1996, Coccaro, Berman, Kavoussi and Hauger showed that violent male patients, given fenfluramine, showed negative correlation between measures of irritability and impulsive aggression (on the Buss-Durkee Hostility Inventory) and prolactin concentration. Those with high levels of aggression showed an attenuated response to fenfluramine, suggesting that they had reduced serotonergic activity, consistent with low serotonin activity being associated with increased aggressive and impulsive behaviours. It is as yet unknown if such findings be extrapolated to violent women. We cannot know, as no studies have been carried out, but once again the assumption is that the reduced serotonin may have a different effect on women.

Other biochemical models are those linking ingested chemicals and their effects on the body and emotions. One of the world's most popular and widely available drugs is, of course, alcohol, which can increase aggression due to a disinhibitory effect. But few studies have demonstrated that alcohol increases aggression in women, and those that do concentrate on the aggression in interpersonal or domestic settings. However, in these studies, it has been shown that the aggression–inducing effect of alcohol is less pronounced in women (Giancola et al., 2009). Light may be cast on this finding when the issue of physical size and the effect of alcohol on aggression are examined. In 2010, DeWall et al. established that larger/ heavier men were more likely to become aggressive after ingesting alcohol. They suggested that this is not necessarily a physical difference, but more to do with a cognitive acceptance of larger men as more aggressive anyway, and who should be avoided when they are drunk. In other words, larger physical size permits men (but not women) to think that they can inflict costs on others if they find themselves in conflictive situations. This in turn increases the likelihood that they will escalate to aggression, together with a feeling of self-importance and entitlement to special treatment, which, when threatened, results in aggression. Support for this position comes from Vandello, Ransom, Hettinger and Askew (2009), who demonstrated that men misperceived aggression as more expected or socially desirable, possibly a learned gender behaviour. Additionally, men perceive aggression as attractive to women. All of these misperceptions were highly correlated with lower self-esteem and a weaker gender identification. The conclusion may be drawn that male aggression is related to perceived social inadequacies, an area of research that has yet to be explored fully.

These findings do have implications for the way in which female aggres-sion is manifested, and why it might be different to, rather than simply less than, that exhibited by males. The effect of testosterone is an important issue, and clearly shows different actions in men and women, but the other issues should be taken into account along with it. For example, high levels of depression are seen disproportionately in women (Gavin, 2010) with the difference in rates starting around puberty. The effects of depression can be reduced, or at least masked, by SSRIs such as fluoxetine (Prozac). However, if low serotonin leads to higher levels of aggression in males, why does it lead to depression in females? Perhaps some forms of interaction between the body's biochemical and neurochemical status is implicated.

Neurochemical transmission in the body is an important factor to address, but broader questions of neurology also need to be considered.

The neurology of aggression   One of the major regions of the brain that contributes to the modulation of aggression is the limbic system, consisting of the hippocampus, amygdala, septal area, nucleus accumbens, ventral striatum and parts of the prefrontal and anterior cingulate cortices.

Siegel and Victoroff (2009) showed evidence that aggression stimulated by defence against a threat (real or perceived) is associated with activity in the sympathetic nervous system. This leads to impulsivity and has little cortical involvement. Predatory attack behaviour, on the other hand, that which is planned, has high cortical involvement. It requires activation of the lateral hypothalamus, in contrast to defence, which shows activation of the medial hypothalamus and midbrain. Both forms of aggression are, however, controlled by components of the limbic system, which requires sensory inputs from the cerebral cortex and monoaminergic inputs from the brainstem reticular formation.

The prefrontal cortex has been identified as the area that inhibits antisocial behaviour, with this area being up to 15 per cent smaller in people who have abnormally aggressive responses to stimuli (Raine, Lenz, Bihrle, Lacasse, & Colletti, 2000). A seminal study by Bard and Mountcastle (1948) showed that cats with lesions in the hypothalamus appeared to have suffered a break in the link between the subcortical structures and the cortical areas needed for inhibition, and the cats showed difficulty controlling attack behaviour. Later studies (e.g., Flynn & Wasman, 1960) found that electrical stimulation of the lateral hypothalamus elicits predatory aggression in cats, whereas stimulation of the medial hypothalamus elicited attack behaviour. More modern, human studies are not as clear-cut. For example, removal or excision of the amygdala will reduce violent behaviour, but it has a flattening effect on all emotions. Conversely, temporal lobe epilepsy involving the amygdala can lead to more violent behaviour, not less. This seemingly anomalous action can be clarified by looking at the amygdala's involvement in other emotions. The central nucleus of the amygdala receives sensory information associated with fear response (LeDoux, 1994) because it receives input from the thalamus, the hippocampus and the cortex. However, as the thalamus transmits to the amygdala without the cortex being involved, it is a very rapid communication, without cognitive interferences. This means that any stimulus that induces fear can be responded to very quickly, without thinking about it. The second pathway involved here is the transmission from thalamus to cortex to amygdala. This is slower, but it is at this point that cognitive appraisal of the stimuli takes place. Hence, the quick pathways allow for the response to the stimuli to be set in motion quickly, but the cortex will decide on the actual behaviour, with the hippocampus involvement being the addition of memory. So, when a tiger leaps, the body gets ready to run, but the cortex returns the message 'we are in the zoo and there is very thick glass in the way.' It is clear, therefore, that in addition to internal biochemical or neural processes, there are external and cognitive factors to be taken into account regarding aggression.

Environmental factors

Arousal   There have been various attempts to show a link between physical arousal and aggression. Again, the findings are not clear-cut. It is thought that there is a correlation between viewing violent media, which leads to greater autonomic arousal, and that higher levels of aggression will follow. This has been shown to not be the case, even when the media is highly immersive (Goodson, Pearson, & Gavin, 2010). The Excitation-Transfer Theory suggests that high physical arousal (either exercising or viewing pornographic material, etc.) leads to high aggression because the arousal is misattributed to the provocation, not the arousing stimulus.

Heat   There are documented links between increasing temperature and increasing levels of violence. Police officers are told to expect higher incidence rates and even riots in the hotter seasons (Anderson, Anderson, Dorr, DeNeve, & Flanagan, 2000). This effect has been demonstrated in laboratory studies, with subjects increasing aggressive acts (giving electric shocks to others) with increasing temperature, but in extreme heat the number of acts decreased. This is not supported by violent crime incidence statistics, however, as Anderson and Bushman (2002) found that incident rates increased with no decrease in extreme temperature.

Crowding   A higher density of people leads to higher levels of violence, but only when the crowding is with those not expected to be in close proximity, such as would be acceptable in families. Personal space issues are thought to be the trigger here, and these do exhibit clear cultural and gender differences. Noise is also highly correlated with overcrowding. Noise is unwanted sound, and it can lead to negative effects, in some cases aggressive effects. It can be classed as intrusive and have detrimental effects on health, as well as provoking hostility (Gavin, 2006).

Sleep   Heat, noise and other environmental factors can have severe effect on sleep patterns, and there are various research findings that relate sleep patterns to disorders, including those involving antisocial behaviour. Lindberg et al. (2008) found that this was associated with decreased amounts of slow-wave sleep (SWS), the stage of sleep that has the most effect on physical well-being. However, the most aggressive male patients had increased SWS, which may indicate specific brain pathology or a delay in the normal development of sleep patterns. Later studies showed this was the same for female homicidal offenders with antisocial personality disorder. This seems to suggest that there is a fundamental difficulty in the development of sleep patterns which is gender-neutral, and which prevents the SWS stage from working effectively.

Biological models do provide some information on the issues of aggression and the different ways in which male and female aggression is expressed. It is clearly a very complex set of issues and it is unlikely that biology provides the overarching theory to address this. More holistic models may provide these key additional points.

Psychological models

Psychological models of aggression provide a broader perspective than biology alone. If women's aggression is different to men's, then biology plays some part, but the complexity of responses to aggressive-producing stimuli is not necessarily only biological. As seen above, the internal justification of large men to act aggressively when drunk means there are psychological factors both social and cognitive to take into account.

Cognition and aggression   Cognitive psychology suggests that we respond to our environment in ways that are learned, and this behaviour then becomes part of our everyday repertoire and directs the ways in which we remember and make decisions. There are three major positions within cognitive psychology that attempt to apply this perspective to aggression.

Cognitive neo-association theory suggests that encountering negative events on a routine basis produces and encourages thoughts, expressive motor reactions, memories and physiological reactions linked with emotive response that are productive either of fight or flight. These negative events include frustration, loud noises, uncomfortable temperatures and other noxious experiences/stimuli. In addition to the association of the stimuli with negative experience, memory acts to link the emotion to behaviour that results, so that future response is also predicated (Collins & Loftus, 1975). Cognitive neo-association theory suggests that when the memory of a learned association between a negative stimulus and resultant emotion and behaviour is activated, this triggers activation in related concepts. So having learned that a loud bang can mean gunshots, the idea of shots triggers the memories of specific responses to guns. Cognitive neo-association theory also includes higher-order cognitive processes, such as the appraisal of a situation and attributions of beliefs. In other words, people may make an appraisal of emotions experienced and consider the consequences of action.

Alternatively, social learning theory posits that aggressive reactions are learned in the same way as any other complex social behaviour, through experience and/or observation and imitation. This behaviour is then either positively reinforced, meaning it will persist, or negatively reinforced and will be extinguished. In the early studies of aggression in children, Bandura and colleagues clearly demonstrated that children will learn to be aggressive and even destructive from adult role models, and that this effect was independent of the sex of the children or their adult models. It seems strange then that later research did not follow up on this, and the majority of these studies were male focused only. Any studies including girls, or focusing on them, concluded that aggression in female children was relational in nature. There have been studies that demonstrate aggression in girls, particularly those such as that of Crick (1995) who suggested that children use aggression as a means to socially damage peers, but that boys used physical aggression to damage a male peer's relational image, while girls used relational aggression to the same ends. If the aspect of physicality is removed, then many conclude that few differences exist between the frequency of aggression in boys and girls (Bowie, 2007). This does not explain the rising frequency of the use of physical aggression in girls reported in official statistics. In the light of these figures, Cohen, Hsueh, Russell and Ray (2006) emphasize the importance of examining the broader social context of aggression. The framework of the social learning theory (SLT) may offer this context. Early social learning models suggested that all individuals have the capability for aggression, but that there must be an opportunity to learn it, together with internal and external situations that reinforce and maintain it. Observation of aggression and imitating it is the source of learning, with the models being family, peers, and so on (direct modelling), community models, such as those within a neighbourhood, and media sources. Once the behaviour is learnt, individuals will expand on a repertoire of behaviours and act out aggression in innovative ways, but which are related to the source. An important issue within Bandura's work was media, which are more pervasive now than in the 1970s. Bandura suggested that the violent and aggressive forms of (American) media to which children have access are an important aspect of developing and learning aggression. This is due not only to media providing a source of learning, but also because media act to reduce natural restraint of aggression and decreases sensitivity to violence. Moise and Huesmann (1996) found a relationship between viewing violent media and physical aggression in girls, as this increased when they identified with a violent female character. Furthermore, Smith and Thomas (2000) reported that girls were aware of the negative effect that television had on their peers; although this may be representative of a third-person effect (Gavin, 2001), it also implies that it could have a negative effect on every individual. Aggressive female characters are becoming more popular in children's television and films (Bent, Porter, & Gavin, 2014), as well as those shows aimed at adolescents and adults. Studies on the effect of violent media are still inconclusive, but the number of hours spent viewing television and so on is much higher than it has ever been, and boys and girls are exposed to the same level of aggression, violence and 'evil', although it has been found that girls read more than boys (Smith & Thomas, 2000). If exposure is similar, then the resulting tendency to aggression may be the same but simply expressed differently. An interesting difference might lie in the way in which aggressive female role models affect the individual. Greenwood (2007) showed that identification with and/or idealization (wishful identification) of a favourite female action hero was associated with aggressive tendencies in young women. However, behavioural identification (perceived similarity) was not associated with behavioural or affective aggression and was inversely related to relational aggression. Werner and Crick (2004) suggest that, traditionally, aggressive responses in girls were of the relational kind, in which gossip and back-stabbing was the norm, but that the tendency for girls to use physical violence is increasing. Research also suggests that feelings of anger potentially leading to aggression are correlated with feelings of alienation, such as loneliness, isolation and peer rejection (Smith & Thomas, 2000), and this means that girls who are aggressive tend to escalate to physical violence more readily when feeling rejected. If girls place higher value on their relationships than boys do, then negative aspects of those relationships can lead to delinquent behaviours

(Henderson & King, 1998). This is particularly evident in those who are less socially adept, as Björkqvist, Österman, and Kaukiainen (2000) found a significant correlation between social intelligence and the ability to resolve conflict by negotiation rather than aggression. This is further compounded by the inability to interpret social cues correctly (Bowie, 2007).

A further alternative comes from script theory. Scripts are collections of related concepts in memory, which involve links, and action strategies. Huesmann (1998) suggested that observing violence in the media leads to the learning of aggressive scripts. Scripts are sets of highly associated concepts that involve goals and action plans (Schank & Abelson, 1977), which form a unitary component in semantic memory. They become well rehearsed and form expectations and intentions involving important social behaviours. As scripts define situations and guide behaviour, in that an individual selects a script that relates to the event and assumes a role within it, it is learnt and utilized later, with the link becoming even stronger because multiple rehearsals create additional links to other concepts in memory, thus increasing the number of paths by which it can be activated. Observing others' behaviour is a secondary form of rehearsal and this also strengthens the links. Therefore, according to Anderson and Bushman (2002), children who watch violent media acquire knowledge of aggressive scripts, and linking to memory strengthens these associations. This link has yet to be fully documented, but there is evidence to suggest (Gavin & Hockey, 2010) that young men do have internalized scripts that are aggressive in nature, even though they understand the resultant behaviour may not be the most socially desirable choice. It remains unclear if young women also have similar aggressive internalized scripts. As mentioned above in the effect of environmental factors, the excitation transfer theory is also concerned with how physiological arousal is dispelled. If that arousal is excitation leading to anger, then it may extend beyond the time in which the stimulus is available. Hence, the anger and subsequent aggression may be misdirected.

In addition, the social interaction theory (Tedeschi & Felson, 1994) proposes that aggression has social influences that are reinforced by high reward and high self-esteem. Acting aggressively can result in tangible reward, and hence will never be negatively reinforced. Aggressive behaviour is thus seen as socially influenced behaviour in that someone uses coercive actions to produce some change in another's behaviour. This can mean obtaining something of value (theft or robbery), acts of retribution or to gain desired social and self identities. This suggests that the aggressor is making conscious decisions directed by the expected rewards and costs; hence, the motivations are the attainment of higher-level goals.

This leaves us with a very complex position in trying to understand aggression, that there is an internalized set of behaviours expressed in highly personalized ways dependent on experience. Anderson and Bushman (2002) attempted to condense all the above positions into a general aggression model (GAM) which they proposed brings a unifying framework to the study of aggression. They suggests that such a model has value in that it can explain more issues within aggression, as no one person or group has a single motive for acting aggressively, and hence the development of interventions will be more effective.

GAM incorporates much of the work on cognition in terms of how internalized states and knowledge develop from experience and learning. However, the model presents ways in which subtypes of knowledge are important. These subtypes are: perceptual schemata, which are used to identify phenomena encountered by an individual (objects or acts); and person schemata, the beliefs about phenomena encountered, including people and behavioural scripts, the information about behaviour. The model is also novel as it includes the influence of emotion on cognition, as the knowledge structures also contain what they term 'experiential affect nodes'. If a node relating to, for example, anger is activated, this emotion is experienced, compared to internal knowledge about the event, and the appropriate behavioural script is then activated.

This model, based in cognitive psychological theories of learning, memory and decision-making, is open to the possibility of obtaining empirical evidence. Some areas have already been studied, such as the internalized aggressive scripts of young men (Gavin & Hockey, 2010) or Björkqvist et al.'s (2000) examination of social intelligence and conflict resolution. However, the major point of cognitive psychology is still that it is reliant on the supposition of an internalized state that cannot be observed. Experimental psychology cannot hope to examine that any more easily than theoretical positions that are wholly based upon the unobservable parts of the mind.

Psychodynamics and aggression   Psychodynamic theory has subsumed some of the components of a theoretical position in physics known as thermodynamics. The law of thermodynamics are theoretical, but accepted as rules by which the world operates. Thermodynamics rules are applied to the exchange of energy and the way that this exchanges acts upon the systems containing it. Hence, a closed system, containing anything but a vacuum, when acted upon by energy perhaps in the form of heat, changes its state to one of high energy, and this energy must be expended or exchanged in some way. This is applied to psychological systems (or human minds) by considering the concept of psychic energy, or psychological energy, first suggested by Von Brucke in 1874. He suggested that humans (and indeed all living things) are energy systems that need to conform to the conservation of energy. One of von Brucke's students was Sigmund Freud who developed this idea further. Freud argued that both the first and second laws of thermodynamics apply to mental processes, and that there was a mental energy that functioned within these laws, with the id being the source of the psychic energy powering the psychological system. Therefore, if the human mind is a system in which there is psychological energy of some form, it must be reactive to the pressure of external energy in the same way as any other system. External forces can be positive or negative, and this leads us to the frustration-aggression hypothesis (Berkowitz, 1989; Dollard, Miller, Doob, Mowrer, & Sears, 1939), a component of psychodynamic theory.

Frustration-aggression   Frustration is the state that occurs when circumstances interfere with a goal, and as such is an external source of negative energy, according to psychodynamic theory, and acts upon the mind in a particular way. Frustration can lead to aggression and can be caused by several different things. For example, relative deprivation theory suggests that if an individual thinks that s/he is not receiving the rewards s/he deserves, frustration can result. Alternatively, cue-arousal theory would argue that frustration leads to anger, not always expressed in aggressive acts. Such theoretical positions are termed social cognition, and social psychology also has explanations to offer. For example, sense of identity and self can be lost in a large group. Individuals take on the identity of the group; hence, a mob can be more aggressive than any of its members. This is known as de-individuation, and a group can behave in more aggressive and violent ways that any of its members would if alone. During August 2011, the United Kingdom saw evidence of this when a peaceful vigil for a young man shot by police officers whilst under covert surveillance turned into rioting and looting in Tottenham, London, followed by groups looting in other cities across the country. Much of this was reported as 'mob mentality' but there were two distinct behaviours. The first was the rioting, the facing-down of police in riot gear, throwing stones and other missiles, burning vehicles. Almost exclusively male in content, these mobs were violent towards the representation of authority. The second was the looting, in which women were quite visibly active. This is a less violent, although still illegal activity. Does this represent a dichotomy and a different sense of purpose in the violence of the two genders? This has yet to be explored, although media sources are reporting and questioning the behaviours (Castella & McClatchey for the BBC, 2011). As the BBC reported on its own press videos, rioters covered their faces and behaved recklessly, setting fire to buildings and cars, including police vehicles. Some even set fire to homes in which people were sleeping. The other behaviour was seen when newspapers printed pictures of people, their faces for the most part uncovered, walking out of shops with expensive electrical goods or clothes in their hands. They posed for pictures and posted them on social networking sites. Unfortunately for them, the police downloaded these too. As Pitts (2009) points out, there is an issue of numbers here, as one man cannot make a riot on his own. There is a point when the crowd realizes it is in control, not the authorities, represented here by the police. The second issue of looting, he suggests, provides a sense of power to people who do not have any. This of course suggests that the looting is being carried out by people who are somehow disenfranchised, but the pictures do not necessarily bear this supposition out.

Nevertheless, frustration–aggression theories are convincing. The suggestion is that people behave aggressively towards others when goals are impeded. The frustration–aggression model is based on the physical laws mentioned above; these are applied to hydraulics where pressure means that something has to be vented. Hence, building frustration and hostility must have an outlet. Carlsmith, Wilson and Gilbert (2008) suggested the idea that venting aggression relieves frustration. In other words, revenge has a clear utility for the health of the person seeking it. In reality, it does not, and we arrive once again at the conclusion that interpersonal aggression is a complex social phenomenon that is not really explained by one theoretical position.

Psychodynamic theories do offer alternatives to the strictly biological or cognitive position. Freudian psychology suggests the issue of aggression as instinct, a primary drive that Freud termed destructive and which he named

Thanatos. This is in conflict with the drive for life and survival (Eros). In addition to this conflict, displacement means that self-destructive energy is directed outwards, and self-aggressive drives are turned into aggressive acts against others. This tendency for aggression is mediated by catharsis, in which watching violent events or engaging in mild displays of anger diminishes the aggressive urge.

Psychodynamic positions are interesting, but also contain somewhat intangible elements that are difficult for scientific minds to accept. They are very difficult to examine in any rigorous manner. Popper (1959) pointed out that nothing could, even in principle, falsify psychoanalytic/ psychodynamic theories, and suggested that they have more in common with primitive myths than with genuine science. Perhaps that is a little too far; psychodynamic theory, and its application in psychiatry and psychoanalysis, has as its chief source of strength, and the principal basis on which its claim to scientific status is grounded, a capability to accommodate and explain every form of human behaviour. This, in scientific terms, is its critical weakness, for it cannot be genuinely predictive. Nevertheless, psychoanalysis works when applied in various settings, so it has utility even if it is, as some claim, unscientific, so psychodynamic theory must have some value, even if its core elements cannot be examined via experimentation. Therefore, the question remains of how to evaluate theories of aggression in terms of utility of learning about it in order to minimize its effects.

Measuring aggression

This chapter started with a set of arguments about what aggression actually is. This confusion or, at best, lack of agreement makes studying aggression a minefield of controversies, and also makes the measurement and treatment of it problematic. The choice of definition and theoretical perspective naturally influences any policy or clinical decisions to be made. It also counteracts any study of the aggression of women, as many measures of aggression do not take into account any social, psychological or biological influence of gender.

Methods of studying and measuring aggression occupy a large range. Each type of measurement also carries a particular process by which it is administered and calculated. These range from self-reports, which rely on the respondent's memory, honesty and ability to reflect on past behaviour, to laboratory measures, which can only hope to capture the present behaviour, to observation by an independent source, which can be biased by the observers' use of report mechanisms. Additionally, all of these measures and methods include time frames, replying the idea that personality and behavioural characteristics are immutable and transcend time, which is debatable. It is worth examining, however, some of the more commonly used measurements of aggression, as many of these will appear in the research about aggression.

Self-report measures Several questionnaires on hostility and aggression have been developed for clinical use. The Aggression Questionnaire (Buss & Perry, 1992), the Buss–Durkee Hostility Inventory (Buss & Durkee, 1957) and the Cook–Medley Hostility Scale (Cook & Medley, 1954) are probably the most popular and enduring. All questionnaires that ask about difficult behaviours or feelings can suffer from social desirability, and these are no exceptions, relying as they do on self-rating of something that is antisocial. There is a complication here, however, as those for whom social approval is less desirable may be the most hostile, and hence a measure to reduce such bias may be counterproductive.

Observer ratings Observer scales, in which episodes or acts of aggressive behaviour are recorded, include the Overt Aggression Scale (OAS; Yudofsky, Silver, Jackson, Endicott, & Williams, 1986), Social Dysfunction and Aggression Scale (SDAS; Wistedt et al., 1990), and Staff Observation Aggression Scale (SOAS; Palmstierna & Wistedt, 1987). As the last implies, these are again all for use in clinical settings, but may be affected by an observer's exposure to aggression.

Projective tests Projective assessment also includes some aggression measures, usually included after the tests have been developed and approved, and established in clonal experimental settings. For example, Wanamaker and Reznikoff (1989) used several pictures of the Thematic Apperception Test (TAT) to assess aggression levels. However, McCrae and Costa (1989) question the reliability and validity of such techniques.

Laboratory measures Instruments designed to be used in controlled settings are varied, from EEG to cognitive measures.

They can also include direct measures of physiological activity, such as assays for blood levels of various biochemical agents mentioned above. As with all laboratory settings, these measures are subject to questions of ecological validity.

Interview measures Some clinical tools include interviews, some of which are unstructured in nature and open to a good deal of bias if used by inexperienced interviewers. The alternative is a tool such as the Structured Clinical Interview for the DSM-IV (SCID-IV; First, Spitzer, Gibbon, & Williams, 1997), which, as its name suggests, allows for very little exploration of side issues. Also used are the Abusive Violence Scale (Hendrix & Schumm, 1990), Intermittent Explosive Disorders Module (Coccaro, 1998), Life History of Aggression (Coccaro, Berman, & Kavoussi, 1997) and Suicide and Aggression Scale (Korn et al., 1992).

As already outlined, these tests are usually employed with clinical populations and there is an issue of generalizability across other types of sample, as the scoring level may be too high in the latter. Additionally, those using them in clinical settings need to be assured that the test can predict the potential for risk and dangerousness. In order to incorporate all of these issues, it is difficult to see how the measurement of aggression (and its concomitant concepts of hostility and violence risk, etc.) can be carried out in women, particularly in non-clinical populations. The issue exercising the minds of policy makers today is the rise in violence in women outside of any question of psychopathology; this is the rise in delinquency and the issue of underlying aggressive tendencies in general, not in the psychiatric hospital, but in the streets of our cities.

The following chapters will discuss various aspects of women's aggression in the light of these theoretical positions.

2

The Evolution of Aggression

The idea that all life is descended from a common ancestor and that complex creatures descend from simpler is very old, and can be found in ancient writings such as those of Anaximander, the Greek philosopher who lived in the sixth century BC (Couprie, Hahn, & Gerard, 2003). However, we do not have to look quite that far back to examine modern, more scientific thought on the origin of our species, nor its paradoxical and seemingly unstoppable quest to destroy itself.

Darwinism and Sociobiology

Modern evolutionary theory is based on the writings of Charles Darwin, and it adds more scientific knowledge to the understanding of the process of descent. The process of this change is genetic mutation, and those mutations that are beneficial to an organism will survive to the next generation. The process by which beneficial mutations survive is known as natural selection. This refers to the preservation of a functional advantage that enables a species to compete better for food, territory, mates and so on, and leads to the elimination of inferior species gradually over time. Evolutionary biology concentrates on the physical aspects of species and how they have adapted over time. Evolutionary psychology, on the other hand, focuses on behaviour that demonstrates psychological adaptations to recurring problems. Hence, it attempts to identify how emotional and cognitive adaptations have evolved. A genetic mutation has no hope of

Female Aggression, First Edition. Helen Gavin and Theresa Porter.
© 2015 John Wiley & Sons, Ltd. Published 2015 by John Wiley & Sons, Ltd.

being successfully passed to the next generation without some accompanying behaviour that allows it to aid in the reproductive success of the organism and the survival of its offspring. In dimorphic organisms, those that have developed two sexes of different forms, these behaviours relate to sexual selection, as well as all the other changes needed to survive, such as gathering food, finding shelter and so on. Psychological adaptations are specialized for the environment of evolutionary adaptedness, or EEA (Gaulin & McBurney, 2003). Hence, humans have evolved adaptations related to mating. In males, this means adaptations which assist them to compete for females; in females, it means adaptations allowing choice of mate and behaviour designed to enable offspring to survive. Males are adapted to fight for the privilege of having females choose them for their mates. In non-human animals, this competition can be very fierce, if not fatal. In humans, this behaviour is no longer tolerated, and such inhibition of aggression against competitors for female preference has led to very complex behaviour around human mate selection (to say the least) and investment in offspring. How can we explain the massive industries that we find in the western world, dedicated to attracting a mate, keeping him and then making sure he stays around to look after his young? Why has the balance of female mate selection turned into females vying to appear attractive in the male gaze, when predominantly, for non-humans, it is female animals who need to be impressed by the male's aggressive acts?

Humans have very few offspring in comparison to other mammals, but invest large amounts of time and resources in caring for them. If you doubt that, just take a trip round your local branch of Mothercare or Babies R Us (a US store). This is costly in biological terms (as well as financial ones in our society) and means that a female must choose a mate wisely, one that can afford this investment in children. It also means she must be able to attract mates in order for her to have the possibility of selection, and have some way of keeping the chosen mate loyal to her. Hence we see the complex behaviours we call dating, courting, betrothal and marriage. We have also evolved complex adjunct activities that have become inseparable from these behaviours. We call this fashion and beauty care.

How did we arrive at the point of all this when our primate cousins just, well, get on with it? Why are we so different? And why are we so naked?

The Naked Ape – Was She in the Jungle or the Sea?

According to evolutionary theory, the psychological and biological adaptations are inextricably linked. A major hypothesis in the twentieth century was concerned with why and how humans became bipedal, the only primate to do so, and why we became hairless, again unlike all of the primates. The so-called 'Savannah theory' suggested that, as the population of early humans grew, they needed to expand and so outgrew the forested regions. Moving in to the grasslands (savannah) meant that humans that stood up to see further gained an advantage in hunting, and this ability was passed on through natural selection. In addition, long-range hunting in hot regions meant that males needed to sweat to achieve homeostasis so the shedding of hair was beneficial. Hence, humans evolved into hunting, omnivorous creatures that needed to adapt to the environment in such a way that the males could move quickly and capture food. Females waited in the home territory for males to return from hunting and received whatever was left after the males had had their fill. Females adapted to this by ensuring males stayed with them and provided for them and their offspring by becoming more attractive and available for sex. So hunting males were dominant and females simply became the adjunct to this and a handy place to keep babies while they grew viable enough to survive outside the womb.

Does anyone else think this sounds strange? As you can probably tell from this, most of the influential writers in evolutionary theory in the twentieth century were male. Female writers were not quite as taken with the savannah hypothesis. If males shed their hair in order to sweat in the hunting ground, why would females shed hair too? It does not seem feasible to suggest that they needed to. Also, why would giving less food to females and young be advantageous? Surely it was in the males' vested interests to keep mates and offspring healthy and well fed. It would also mean that potential and current mates would be attracted to them because they could provide this food. Also, why would only adaptations beneficial to the male be those that perpetuated and not any that helped a female who needed to care for offspring? For example, in the *Naked Ape* (1967), Desmond Morris suggested that human females developed rounded breasts and buttocks as sexual signalling devices, and that pair bonding (and its counterpart, sexual jealousy) evolved so that hunters out on the savannah knew that their mates were not having sex with other males.

In 1972, one woman writer did indeed think this was a bit odd, and decided to see if there was an alternative. There is, and it has nothing to do with intelligent design, creationism or table scraps. Elaine Morgan's book *The Descent of Woman* championed the alternative hypothesis, that of the aquatic ape, and the alternative perspective, that of the female (note, this is not the feminist). First proposed by Hardy in 1960, and later elaborated upon by Morgan, this hypothesis was, originally, completely censured by the scientific community, although it did attract attention. In this position, the evolution of human nakedness and bipedalism is explained as adaptation to an aquatic lifestyle, with female layers of fat, which contribute to the rounded breasts and buttocks, being needed for warmth, for babies to hold onto and for sitting for long periods on a pebble beach whilst babies were being fed. There are some heavy criticisms of this position, such as the high cost of maintaining body temperature in relatively small hairless creatures (Rantala, 2007). Whilst not fully accepted as a viable position amongst evolutionary theorists, it does demonstrate that evolutionary theory is a matter of best interpretation of evidence, and that there is the potential for alternative explanations. This potential for alternative positions can be seen when examining the evolution of aggression.

The Evolution of Aggression and the Archaeology of War

Humans, as a species, do have a violent past; this can be seen in archaeological, anthropological and comparative data. Skeletal remains show the marks of weapons (Lambert, 2002); not all such injuries and deaths could have been accidental. Traumatic injuries in ancient bones illustrate, in ways historical records cannot, that interpersonal violence has been present in all forms of social organizations (Walker, 2001). This is demonstrated by studies of societies that are classified as 'traditional', i.e., those that live without modern technology, or economic and social organization. For example, the Yąnomamö are an indigenous people of the Amazon rainforest who led a life completely without contact with the modern world until the 1960s. According to Chagnon (2000), 25 per cent of Yąnomamö males die in a violent manner, usually homicide; the tribes are described as ferocious and warlike. Often this violence is turned on the womenfolk, with particularly unpleasant and sometimes fatal punishments for transgressions such as sexual infidelity.

This account of perpetual warfare has been revised as Ferguson (2001) concluded warfare was the result of western influence, not a lack of it; however, the fact remains that there is still ubiquitous violence within societies that are living at subsistence levels. The argument revolves around the question of whether violence has evolved among the Yạnomamö because of competition resulting from a lack of nutritional resources in their territory. So, did we evolve to be violent and naturally aggressive? Archaeology and anthropology suggests that half of us did anyway, the male half. Anatomy bears this out; male humans have high upper-body strength in comparison to females, and other bodily divergence unaccounted for by sexual differences. Such an adaptation would seem to have led larger males to be competitively successful in intersexual competition for both food and mates. Several other types of aggression are seen as functional adaptation: defence against attack, negotiating status in hierarchical societies (another form of competition for resources and for mates); deterrence from future aggression, deterrence from infidelity and reduction of resources to be expended on offspring that is not genetically related to the aggressor. The last is seen as an explanation for infanticide by a step-parent (see chapter 7). Whether these forms of aggression are direct adaptations or by-products of another is difficult to determine (Schmitt & Pilcher, 2004). It is also true that aggression and violence are not necessarily indiscriminate: they are usually context-dependent in some way. The examination of violence, particularly fatal violence, often distinguishes between the intrasexual and the intersexual.

Intersexual vs Intrasexual Aggression

The majority of homicides are committed by men upon men and are a result of real or perceived threats to either self or status. These tend to escalate from some trivial argument and are termed provocations (Goetz, 2010). The combatants are usually young males, and death occurs when neither will acquiesce; the problems are more apparent today because homicidal weaponry is much more prevalent than in any other time; brandishing a stick is less likely to result in death than shooting a gun. Non-lethal means of maintaining or gaining status are more productive than lethal ones as the status needs to have someone for acknowledgement and a dead recipient of the effect of status is of little use. As such, both homicide and non-lethal violence indicate a psychological position sensitive to status hierarchy and threats to status. This means that the altercations are usually between individuals who are very similar in status, with one challenging the other – challenges from individuals whose status is far beneath the challenged are ignored. This can be examined experimentally too; in 2009, Griskevicius et al. had participants read scenarios involving status competition (e.g., competition for a promotion) or mating competition (going on a date with a desirable member of the opposite sex) or neutral scenarios. They found that men who read the scenarios about competition and dating were more likely to respond aggressively to a trivial insult, but only when observers were other men. Aggression was modified in front of women. Female participants behaved very differently. Status and mating motives did not increase women's direct aggression, but indirect aggression, such as gossiping, was increased. These findings do indicate that there is a high context-specificity to violence and aggression, mediated by gender.

Intersexual violence is seen as having different motivations to intrasexual. Across animal species, it appears to represent a punishment for behaviour that conflicts with the interests of the aggressor (Clutton-Brock, 2007), particularly threats to an individual's fitness, i.e., the probability of survival and reproductive success. This may explain human violence that is directed at women, if recurrent threats to men's fitness by women led to natural selection for the aggressor's survival. This is a very controversial suggestion, as it provides an evolutionary process for the development of intimate-partner violence, but it must be stressed that this is not condoning it. However, it is interesting to note that the most likely motive for such violence would have been infidelity, a sure way of reducing the reproductive success of an individual male, and that this issue, sexual jealousy, is still one major reason for domestic violence committed by either sex. Of course, sexual jealousy can be the precursor to lethal violence. Serran and Firestone (2004) note that, although uxoricide and mariticide would seem to carry high costs in any culture, it is possible that benefits may be perceived as higher. This suggests that intimate-partner violence and murder may be premeditated, and not killing in an explosive rage. Buss and Duntley (2008) suggested that many instances of lethal domestic violence could be indicative of evolved psychological mechanisms designed to motivate killing a female partner when discovering sexual infidelity. This is termed the homicide adaptation hypothesis and refers to evolved mechanisms in which the costs and benefits of lethal violence are considered and that uxoricide is the desired outcome.

Whilst it is evident that evolution can explain why humans have evolved to use aggression and violence, it does not explain why we are extremely aggressive to our own species and others despite being far from the best equipped anatomically to express violence. We do not naturally have claws and sharp teeth; we are more likely to become lunch than to kill it. In our route to aggress, we often need additional equipment: weapons. Evolutionary theory also does not explain why there is a large sex difference in both the anatomical capacity to aggress and the number of violent acts carried out by male and female humans. This difference is observed even during childhood, when the physical capacity for hurting another person is not too different between girls and boys. If the sex differences are not culturally influenced, then the biological influence would be greater and girls would be as aggressive as boys until anatomical differences were apparent. However, the sex difference is substantial even in pre-school ages (Bjorklund & Pellegrini, 2000), peaking between two and three years of age, and declining in early school ages, suggesting an influence of learning in order to inhibit physical aggression (Archer, 2004). Gendered learning then takes over in order to increase the difference, along with increases in testosterone and sexual interest in the opposite sex. Hess and Hagen (2006) also point out that at this time the forms of aggression start to differ in terms of the expression by girls and by boys. Girls start to escalate their use of indirect aggression at the same time as the increase in use of direct and physical aggression by boys, but boys also use indirect aggression. An evolutionary hypothesis that pressures for sexual selection acting on post-pubescent children and young adults for this difference is inconclusive, as the measures of indirect aggression are all self-report. Few studies have examined this experimentally, although Bjorklund and Pellegrini's study showed greater tendency for women to use indirect aggression when exposed to the same aggression-evoking stimulus as men.

Therefore, we have evolutionary models suggesting aggression has developed in humans in order to ensure success in securing resources and mates for survival of individuals and offspring. This also encompasses explanations of sex difference in the use of direct, physical aggression, but not necessarily the use of indirect aggression. This explains intrasexual male aggression and intersexual male-on-female aggression, but not female-on-male or female intrasexual aggression. If threats to dominance in males are met with aggression, how can we explain female–female fighting? Campbell (1995) suggests that there are similar reasons for female aggression against other females, namely accusations of promiscuity. Thus, female–female aggression is therefore instigated by threats to reputation rather than dominance, as labelling a woman as promiscuous leads to uncertainty of paternity and a threat to acquisition of mates. Long-term investment in a female with a high likelihood of infidelity due to early promiscuity is risky for the male. However, an accusation of promiscuity is difficult to disprove and silencing the accuser may be the only effective way of restoring reputation. Cashdan (2003) suggests that this holds cross-culturally, with female intrasexual violence being the result of the need to defend reputation in order to enhance the likelihood of acquiring a valuable mate. In addition, Snyder et al. (2011) demonstrated that female preference for aggressive dominance and physical capacity in a potential mate is a natural consequence of the need for protection of self and offspring. However, this is tempered by the likelihood of being on the receiving end of a partner's aggression. Therefore, these preferences vary in proportion to the woman's perception of her own vulnerability. If a woman sees herself as needing more protection, she will favour aggressive dominance and physical formidability in a mate. This vulnerability can be expressed in measurement of the fear of crime, which is seen to be a high predictor of women's preference for aggressive and physically dominant men.

Conclusion

Evolutionary theories should always be approached with a sceptical mind; there is little tangible evidence beyond bones and archaeological artefacts and some, albeit rigorous, speculation. However, once the androcentric positions are surmounted, there are some very compelling arguments for the development of aggression and the sex difference found in it. Male aggression is seen as necessary for securing resources and mates for the survival of this and the next generation, hence males require the dominance and status that goes along with this. All forms of male violence can be pictured in this way, from hand-to-hand combat to all-out world war. Female aggression, on the other hand, is seen as the protection of reputation in order to remain attractive to potential mates who will protect a woman and provide resources and desirable genetic material.

This is a very cold and objective view of something that can cause huge physical and emotional pain to people. Women are no less guilty of perpetrating major acts of aggression and violence, whether emotionally driven or premeditated. In the next few chapters, we will explore some of the forms of aggression that girls and women can carry out and see whether indeed the evolution of aggression has changed along with changes in female status.

3

Indirect Aggression

Although aggression is defined as intra-species behaviour carried out with the intent to cause pain or harm (Tremblay, Hartup, & Archer, 2005), western society has long focused on physical aggression as 'true' aggression, with indirect aggression generally ignored or viewed as unimportant. This perspective is problematic since all aggression is designed to cause harm and engender the dominance of one member over another. To say that indirect aggression is not really aggression is similar to the idea that oral sex is not really sex, despite having some of the same motivations as other forms of sexual behaviour.

Archer and Coyne (2005) define indirect aggression as an alternative strategy to direct aggression. Like overt or physical aggression, the aim of indirect aggression is to harm the victim, often by damaging the victim's social status or self-esteem. Different terms have been used to describe indirect aggression, including relational aggression or social aggression. As Archer and Coyne have shown, these terms all describe the same essential behaviours by the perpetrators. Indirect aggression can include reputation-destroying gossip, threats, insults, ostracizing or excluding behaviour, and breaking of confidences. Most forms of indirect aggression are devious; they allow the perpetrator to deny any harmful intent and to claim that the victim misunderstood. In this way, indirect aggression is safer for the perpetrator than direct physical aggression, which cannot as easily be disavowed. Research on indirect aggression is a relatively new area of investigation compared to research on physical aggression, and it initially focused on schoolchildren, where peer ratings of aggression were found to

Female Aggression, First Edition. Helen Gavin and Theresa Porter.
© 2015 John Wiley & Sons, Ltd. Published 2015 by John Wiley & Sons, Ltd.

be more accurate than teacher estimates. There has also been research on adults, although this is a more difficult population to study in naturalistic settings. It was clear from the beginning of such research that self-report measures for perpetration of indirect aggression could not be used because many people were reticent to admit to engaging in such behaviours (Archer & Coyne, 2005).

Indirect Aggression in Girls and Teens

Indirect aggression appears to develop in children alongside the development of communication skills. In toddlers, direct aggression is observed, including snatching toys, pushing, biting, and so on (Underwood, 2003). As children begin to develop verbal skills, they are able to engage in less direct forms of aggression (Archer & Coyne, 2005). By the early teens and puberty, girls routinely choose the option of utilizing indirect rather than direct aggression (Bjorkqvist, Lagerspetz, & Kaukianen, 1992). This holds true internationally; a study comparing children from Finland, Israel, Poland and Italy found that, regardless of nationality and ethnic group, indirect aggression was the preferred method of aggression by the pre-teen years (Osterman et al., 1998). By this age, girls have not only developed strong verbal skills but also a degree of social intelligence. They are more able at this age to assess and analyse social situations, set social goals and engage in behaviours to achieve those goals in socially tolerable ways (Kaukiainen et al., 1999). For example, a 14-year-old girl who is interested in holding social dominance over her peers can utilize anonymous gossip against potential rivals, knowing that any attempts to publicly slander or physically assault rivals would hold the possibility of being sanctioned (Owens, Shute, & Slee, 2000; Pronk & Zimmer-Gembeck, 2010).

By puberty, girls have also learned the social norms that discourage their use of direct physical aggression (Richardson, 2005). In lieu of physical aggression, indirect aggression by girls (and, later, by women) is tolerated and even sanctioned in society. This is seen in the differential gender socialization parents engage in with their daughters and sons (Underwood, 2003). Traditionally, daughters have been encouraged to focus on relationships and interpersonal connectedness (Letendre, 2007). By emphasizing the importance of 'being nice' and maintaining relationships, parents teach girls that relational disruption is bad, leaving the way open for indirect aggression as a tool for both dealing with aggressive desires and maintaining the social facade of 'niceness'. Parents are not the only source of normalization of indirect aggression in girls. For example, a study of British television programmes found that indirect aggression is more likely to be displayed by female characters (Coyne & Archer, 2004). These programmes reaffirm the social norms that women simultaneously may not utilize physical aggression and may utilize indirect aggression. Teen-oriented media including *Skins, Mean Girls, Daria*, and *Heathers* all showcase the phenomena of indirect aggression by teenage girls.

Ultimately, indirect aggression can be very difficult for those who are victimized. Studies of teenagers show that victims of indirect aggression experience depression, anxiety and a loss of self-esteem (Owens et al., 2000). Victims often report that the experience is more harmful than physical violence, disproving the old adage 'Sticks and stones may break my bones but words can never hurt me' (Archer & Coyne, 2005; Gavin, 2011). Further, indirect aggression can also lead to direct aggression. For example, negative gossip regarding the supposed 'dishonourable' behaviour of young women has led to murder (a.k.a. 'honour killings') in some cultures (Glazer & Ras, 1994). In these cases, the 'honour' refers to one's reputation for either upholding or defying sociocultural standards of behaviour, including chastity. For example, if a teenage girl's rivals pass gossip that she has been witnessed socializing with a young man without a chaperone, the implication is that she has been unchaste and the culture-bound shame of this may inspire the males in her family to expiate the shame by killing her. Whether or not the victim actually engaged in the accused behaviours becomes irrelevant as the gossip takes on a life of its own (Awwad, 2001). In this way, the 'male' crime of honour killing is instigated (intentionally or not) by the 'female' aggression of malicious gossip. As Barthes states 'Gossip is "death by language"' (cited in Chesler, 2009, p. 152).

Women and Indirect Aggression

Indirect aggression is not something girls outgrow as they enter womanhood. Social norms against physical aggression increase with age, leaving the use of physical aggression to come under the rubric of 'loss of self-control' (Chesler, 2009). Further, the cost of physical aggression increases with age, including the dangers to oneself (Walker, Richardson, & Green, 2000). As an individual ages, being physically violent can become more physically painful. Indirect aggression also takes on even more subtle forms in adulthood, including the use of 'rational-appearing' aggression such as the manipulation of work duties and unrealistic or unfair work evaluations (Björkqvist & Niemela, 1992). Further, women are more socially adept as adults than they were as teens, making them even more able to utilize those skills (Kaukiainen et al. 1999, cited in Chesler, 2009, p. 121). There are several theories that try to explain the use of indirect aggression in adult women. Griskevicius et al. (2009) hypothesizes that this type of aggression is an evolved strategy that is dependent on both status and mating contexts. In other words, as women have to compete with other women, including when they have to compete for a mate, the motivation for using indirect aggression increases. The problem with this theory is that indirect aggression by adult women does not only occur in the contexts of mating or competition. Sometimes the motivation may be something as simple as retaliation. For example, in a study by Hess & Hagen, college students read a scenario in which a peer lied about them. The students were then asked about preferred methods of reaction, including use of violence or threats of violence, indirect aggression, and so on. Compared to men, women had a much stronger wish to get even using indirect aggression (Hess & Hagen, 2006).

Indirect aggression by women appears to be pervasive, appearing in work and social arenas. As Björkqvist and Osterman (cited in Chesler, 2009, p. 130) found, women in the workplace may engage in such aggressive behaviours as spreading false rumours and giving the 'silent treatment' to peers, as well as forming alliances whose purpose is to exclude a peer (Benenson, Markovits, Thompson, & Wrangham, 2011). This appears to be what happened to Helen Green while employed at the Deutsche Bank. Green experienced several years of indirect aggression by several female peers, who engaged in such petty behaviours as intentionally withholding Green's mail, excluding her from meetings, removing her from the internal memo mailing list, stealing work from her desk if it was left unlocked and making claims that she had body odour. When she informed her employers that the extremity of these behaviours was interfering with her ability to do her job, Green was told that it was something that she would have to tolerate and was sent for 'assertiveness training', implying that it was her behaviour that should be altered rather than the behaviour of her aggressive peers. She sued, reporting both anxiety and depression due to the experience, and was awarded €12 million (Dodson & Iredale, 2006). A noteworthy component of the Green case is that none of the women who attacked Green was in direct competition with her; they were all in different departments or divisions. Therefore, the aggression lacked a functional purpose such as removing Green as an opponent. Instead, it apparently occurred with the sole purpose to demean Green, to make her suffer. Björkqvist notes that this form of workplace aggression is often motivated to bolster the perpetrator's self-esteem, to make her feel more powerful by humiliating the victim, rather than for some tangible gain (Björkqvist, 2001).

As in the Green case, power dynamics are an important factor in the modern workplace. Power in the workplace can come in various forms, including the power to coerce, to reward, the power from expertise, the power over one's admirers and the legitimate power based upon one's position (French & Raven, 1959). Workplace gossip is closely tied with power dynamics, with those who listen to negative gossip aware of the implied threat that they too could become victims of the gossiper (Kurland & Pelled, 2000). This places them in the power of the gossiper due to the fear of also becoming a victim. The gossiper further demonstrates a form of expert power, as she casts herself as possessing information about the victim (e.g., 'I heard she slept her way to the top').

The case at the Iowa Civil Rights Commission shows that the pursuit of this power via indirect aggression can occur in unlikely places. Civil rights investigators Tiffanie Drayton, Michele Howard and Wendy Buenge were sacked over the derogatory emails about co-workers the three exchanged on their work computers. The sheer volume of these communications is notable; in just over two months, one woman sent out over 1,600 emails. The emails included using derogatory names for peers: 'I have nicknames for all my co-workers. Let's see, there is, Teen Wolf, Monster, Roid Rage, Tupac, Psycho, Eliza Doolittle, Ready for the World, Foster Brooks, Mr Bentley, Homeless McGee, Red Foxx, and Rainman', and gossiping about co-workers' behaviours or appearance: 'Psycho is flirting with the new stoned intern'; 'Sarg is dressed in all black with dark lipstick – like a Night Ranger or something'. The irony of this indirect aggression occurring in a state agency for civil rights was not lost on the judge James Timberlane, who stated 'While employed by an agency whose purpose is to confront, remedy and eliminate discrimination, Ms Howard engaged in a remarkably broad, persistent campaign of discrimination and otherwise offensive conduct through her abuse of the employer's electronic communication system' (Gardner, 2011b).

The stress caused by workplace indirect aggression does not end at the end of the workday. Ferguson (2012) studied workers and their partners, finding that co-worker behaviour such as gossip and exclusion have a spillover effect, with the victim bringing negative reactions home after work. There is then a cross-over effect as well, with the victim's partner then carrying that stress into his/her own job. In other words, the indirect aggression by a peer in Company A can actually affect the work life of an employee in Company B, via a cross-over effect.

Indirect aggression and power dynamics by female peers does not only occur in the workplace. Friendships between women can involve cattiness, breaking of confidences and exclusionary behaviours, giving birth to the current colloquial term 'frenemy'. Research indicates that women who are anxious about their status in friendships will engage in indirect aggression with female friends, despite the likeliness that this will result in harming the relationship (Duncan & Owen-Smith, 2006). Because indirect aggression is sometimes subtle or denied by the perpetrator, victims may feel confused and unsure of whether or not to confront a peer.

Compared to domestic violence, infanticide and murder, women's indirect aggression remains under-studied, despite clear indications of the damage it causes and its connection to direct, physical violence. Further research is needed in this area, especially with the growth of social media as a possible site for engaging in this type of aggression. In the last few years, there appears to have been a growth in cyber indirect aggression, with cases such as Rosemary Port setting up an anonymous website called 'Skanks of NYC' in order to insult a fellow model (Samaniego, 2009). The anonymity of the internet may be a factor in the seeming increase in this problem but research is needed to ascertain the severity of the problem and its causes. Research should also focus more on adult, rather than adolescent and child, perpetration, although it is clear that naturalistic observation of this behaviour is more easily done with schoolchildren than with adults. Finally, research on indirect aggression by women should begin to focus on individual and systemic ways to counteract the problem; to date, there appears to be little research available to assist the victims, although workplace and school anti-bullying campaigns are a good beginning.

4

Child Abuse and Neglect by Women

Introduction

The abuse of children by women is a neglected topic. It is not neglected in terms of research; there is a plethora of data in this area. This is one of the most common forms of violence in the domestic arena and yet it does not seem to be subject to the same degree of public awareness campaigning as, for example, violence against women. There are few public service announcements on television or pamphlets at the local library, let alone fundraisers and walk-a-thons for this topic. This may be because child abuse and wife abuse were viewed for many years as a single topic, victims of abuse by men. However, children are not just at risk of being abused by men. Women can and do abuse children, at very high rates.

Society has constructed views of women that involve very specific behaviours. Nurturance is one of these behaviours. Women are often described as nurturing and caring for the needs of others. This prescribed role, by its very nature, excludes violence towards those in need. In western society, women are the ones who raise children, nurse the sick, and care for the elderly and infirm. However, given that this gender role is socially constructed rather than biologically determined, then there must be those who do not engage in the role behaviour at all, as well as those who engage in it only in terms of its external form without any subjective experience of nurturing. What if motherhood does not turn every woman into a nurturing, self-sacrificing angel of domesticity? The maternal relationship then can become an ideal site for exercising a woman's need for power and

Female Aggression, First Edition. Helen Gavin and Theresa Porter.
© 2015 John Wiley & Sons, Ltd. Published 2015 by John Wiley & Sons, Ltd.

control, for expressing her anger and resentment or for displaying her inability to regulate her own emotions and behaviour. The biological ability to conceive and bear a child does not automatically equate to the emotional desire and intellectual competence to raise that child. Motherhood is not the same as a maternal identity. Some women make a commitment to acquiring skills and maintaining a highly focused positive involvement in the care of children (Mercer, 2004). Others may view children as interfering, demanding, challenging or simply unwelcome; these are not invalid views but simply views that should discourage a woman from taking on the role of a mother. Worse, they may view their children as objects, as their identified property to do with as they please. Children's age defines their status, or lack thereof, in our society (Lawrence, 2004) and, generally speaking, humans with higher status aggress against those with lower status. While it can be argued whether or not women lack the social and legal status of men in postmodern society, it is clear that women's status remains greater than that of children.

Prevalence

Child physical abuse, for the purposes of this chapter, is defined as the intentional use of physical force against a child that results in or has the potential to result in physical injury, whereas neglect is the failure to meet the child's basic physical or medical needs and/or failure to provide adequate nutrition, hygiene or shelter, or the failure to ensure the child's safety (Gilbert et al., 2009). Included within this definition are cases of Munchausen's syndrome by proxy (MSBP), also known as factitious disorder by proxy, which involves the inducement of physical ailments upon a child as a way for the mother to gain attention for herself.

How common is child abuse by women? The answer depends upon which data set one reads. There are three types of studies conducted on child abuse and neglect: those that report official rates from child protective agencies (CPAs); those that use abusive parents' self-report; and those that use abused children's self-report (Gilbert et al., 2009). All of these have a degree of bias within them and there is a large disparity between the rates indicated by CPAs and those reported by victims. Everson et al. (2008) found that children were reporting four to six times more abuse episodes than the official CPA records included.

It appears that between 4% and 16% of children in western society are physically abused annually and another 10% are neglected (Gilbert et al., 2009; May-Chahal & Cawson, 2005). Many of these children are victimized by women. For example, Sedlack and Broadhurst (1996), using recent epidemiological data for the United States, found that 65% of maltreated children were victimized by women, and women perpetrated 87% of the child neglect. Further, they found that children living with a single parent had a significantly greater risk of being seriously injured by physical abuse than were children living with both parents; in western culture, if children are in single-parent families, they are more likely to live with a single mother than with a single father. In Canada, a similar epidemiological study found that biological mothers accounted for 41% of the child maltreatment perpetrators and stepmothers accounted for an additional 3% (Trocmé et al., 2001). There appears to be a trend towards more abuse and neglect of male children and for male children to receive the most serious injuries from mothers (Gilbert et al., 2009). This is also true in MSBP cases as well (Feldman & Brown, 2002). For MSBP-type of child abuse, Feldman and Brown (2002) found that mothers were the sole perpetrator in 86% of the international cases.

The argument has been made that women are abusing children frequently because women are the main providers of childcare (Kates, 2010). However, this argument is based upon a false premise. It implies that women are abusing children as a function of being around them more, as if increased contact with children increases everyone's likelihood of abusing them. It also ignores the likelihood that increased hours engaging in childcare may result in an increased ability to parent effectively and therefore less abuse could be expected from the more experienced caregivers (D. Blitz, personal communication, 21 October 2010).

Compared to children who experience unintentional injuries (i.e., car accidents), abused children are more likely to experience retinal haemorrhages, intracranial, thoracic and abdominal injuries and to be admitted to intensive care units (DiScala, Sege, Li, & Reece, 2000). In other words, abuse is more dangerous than childhood accidental injuries. Abuse can also include the malicious use of pharmaceuticals to sedate children. Yin (2010) conducted a retrospective study of pharmaceutical exposures involving young children that were reported to the US National Poison Data System from 2000 to 2008. Yin found an average of 160 cases annually of children less than two years old being given cold medicine, analgesics and street drugs for the purpose of sedation, generally by the mother.

Unintentional death due to child physical abuse and neglect is extraordinarily common. The World Health Organization estimates that there are 155,000 deaths of children annually due to abuse or neglect (Gilbert et al., 2009), with women playing a significant role in these events (Abel, 1986; Haapasalo, & Petaja, 1999; Karakus, Ince, Ince, Arican, & Sozen, 2003). The official figures for child death due to abuse and neglect are likely to be underestimations. Several studies have shown that these types of death are often miscoded, misidentified or simply underreported. For example, Crume, DiGuiseppi, Byers, Sirotnak and Garrett (2002) compared records for all children who died in Colorado, USA, between 1990 and 1998 and they found that only half of those who had died due to child abuse or maltreatment had accurate information regarding this cause of death on the official death certificate. Similarly, Ewigman, Kivlahan and Land (1993) found that approximately 50% of the child abuse and maltreatment deaths in Missouri, USA, between 1983 and 1986 were incorrectly coded on their vital records and less than 60% of the records were included in the Federal Bureau of Investigation (FBI) Uniform Crime Report database. Underreporting of child abuse and neglect death is not just a problem in the United States either. Tursz, Crost, Gerbouin-Rerolle and Cook (2010) reviewed 247 child-death cases with related official death coding in France over a four-year period and found that 75% of the cases had some form of inconsistency with 80 child abuse homicides being miscoded. This trend towards underreporting child abuse, especially a child-abuse death, suggests that officials may be avoiding designating such deaths as a homicide (Porter & Gavin, 2010).

A percentage of child deaths officially coded as sudden infant death syndrome (SIDS) or accidental death might be more appropriately labelled as a child abuse or neglect death had there been a more comprehensive investigation. McCurdy and Daro (1994) reviewed national data for the United States and found that a high percentage of children who are listed as having accidental death or SIDS were involved with their local Child Protection agency for abuse or neglect prior to their death, suggesting the possibility of child abuse or neglect playing a role in the child's death. Southall et al. (1997), using covert video recordings in hospitals, found that 33 out of 39 cases of life-threatening health problems in the study's children were caused by covert behaviour by the child's mother. The covert videos showed mothers suffocating infants, poisoning children and so on when hospital personnel were out of the room. Had the children not been in a hospital, they might have died and the cause of death been listed as accidental or SIDS. An important corollary to this study was that these 33 children had a total of 41 siblings, 11 of whom had allegedly died of SIDS. After being apprehended in the above video-recording cases, nine of the parents of the 11 'SIDS' cases admitted to either suffocating or poisoning these children.

The motivation to abuse or neglect a child is not easily apparent. Theorists have suggested multiple motivations and causes, including mental illness, social learning from one's own abused childhood, evolutionary pressures (such as step-parenting), anger management problems and antisocial abuse of power. While all of these show a degree of relevance in child abuse, none appear to fully explain it.

Mental Illness

One of the commonly reviewed motivations for child abuse is mental illness. Because of the way society constructs women's roles, it is easier to view an abusive mother as mentally disturbed, rather than view her as voluntarily cruel or sadistic.

There is evidence that a percentage of women who commit child physical abuse and neglect are mentally ill. Famularo, Kinscherff and Fenton (1992) and DeBellis et al. (2001) compared mothers who maltreated their children with those who did not and found that the abusive mothers had a greater incidence of mood, personality and substance disorders. Similarly, Kaplan, Sunday, Labruna, Pelcovitz and Salzinger's (2009) study of abused adolescents found that abusive mothers had a high rate of depressive disorder. The problem with these studies, besides their small sample sizes, is that mood and substance abuse disorders are not major mental illnesses. A major mental illness, such as schizophrenia, is one that is inherently debilitating and generally viewed as interfering with one's judgement and behaviour. Mood and substance symptoms lie on a very wide spectrum of severity, from inconvenient to debilitating, and studies reporting that a woman met the criteria for a 'mood disorder' in no way explicates the severity of her symptoms. Being depressed or abusing substances does not remove voluntary control of behaviour, including behaviour towards children. In Husain and Daniel's (1984) study of Canadian abuse cases, only 7.7 per cent of the mothers had a major mental illness of the type generally viewed as severely affecting behaviour. Margolin, in a study of fatal child neglect (1990), found no evidence that neglect could be blamed on the mother's severe mental illness. In Southall et al.'s (1997) study using covert video recordings of child abuse in an emergency setting, while many of the mothers were diagnosed with personality disorders, none were psychotic at the time of the abuse. Leung and Slep (2006) noted that, while depressive symptoms were associated with a mother's laxness in discipline, it was her anger that was predictive of overactive discipline or abuse. However, as our society is more comfortable viewing women as mentally ill, rather than as aggressive, women who abuse children are more likely to be referred for psychiatric treatment while men who abuse children are more likely to be subject to child protection measures (Wilczynski, 1997).

Social Learning and Own Abuse History

Another possible explanation for women's abuse and neglect of children comes from social learning theory. It has been suggested that a woman who was herself abused during childhood is more likely to become an abusive parent, having learned this behaviour. For example, in their study of US navy recruits, Merrill, Hervig and Milner (1996) found that exposure to parent–child physical violence during one's childhood was the single best predictor of future risk of child abuse perpetration. Similarly, in Milner et al.'s (2010) study of navy recruits and college students, the risk of perpetrating child abuse as an adult was largely related to experiences of past childhood abuse. Child physical abuse history remained a significant predictor of child abuse risk even after controlling for trauma symptoms, and the odds of being at risk for perpetuating child abuse as an adult were two to three times higher among those who had experienced abuse than among those who had not. One of the symptoms that was most strongly predictive of adult risk was defensive avoidance, that is, the avoidance of thinking about one's past abuse, resulting in a lack of resolution and therefore heightened risk towards one's own children.

While the above studies show a correlation, however, there is no direct causal relationship between past abuse and future perpetration. If such a causal relationship did exist, then every person, male or female, who was physically abused as a child would go on to abuse a child themselves and this is not the case (Alder & Baker, 1997; Azar, Nix & Makin-Byrd, 2005). Miller and Challas (in Korbin, 1986) found in a longitudinal study

that 45 per cent of people abused as children were not at risk for perpetrating child abuse, and a nearly equal percentage who were at risk for
abusing children had no history of being abused as children. Similarly,
Hunter, Kilstrom, Kraybill and Loda's 1978 prospective study of 282
infants found that, of the 49 parents who reported a history of childhood
victimization, only 18 per cent abused their infants. Simply stated, most
abused children do not grow up to be abusers themselves (Buchanan,
1996; Dixon, Hamilton-Giachritsis, & Browne, 2005; Gelles in Richards
2000; Wolfe, 1999).

Conditioning theory may also have a role in helping us understand child
abuse, especially child abuse displayed as Munchausen's syndrome by proxy.
Rand and Feldman (2001) found that people involved in MSBP behaviour
tend to experience intense anger and frustration yet lack the internal
inhibitions to manage these feelings appropriately. They theorize that
MSBP may develop habit strength after repeated use as a dysfunctional
coping method for angry, frustrated parents.

While it is clear that some women who engage in child abuse and neglect
are mentally ill, psychosis alone does not account for the high prevalence of
child abuse by women. Further, although there is some association between
one's own victimization and the perpetration of child abuse, most people
who experienced abuse do not go on to inflict abuse on their own children,
suggesting that the cause of abuse is more complex than intergenerational
transmission.

Antisocial Mothers

While some abusive behaviour may be connected to the women's own
abuse history, or mental illness, there is evidence that many other factors
play a role, including personality, age and empathy. The designation of
antisocial is more commonly used with men than women, yet antisocial
character clearly plays a role in some women's physical abuse and neglect
of children. Obviously women who have antisocial personalities can and
do become mothers, and, despite traditional beliefs to the contrary, there is
no evidence that maternity cures antisocial character. For example,
Giordano et al. (in Putallaz & Bierman, 2004) suggested that the continuing
force of gender socialization, including nurturing role obligations, could
cause antisocial young women to 'mature' out of their antisocial behaviours.

However, the majority of research shows that, rather than motherhood decreasing a woman's antisocial behaviour, motherhood can become a forum for it. For example, Bosquet and Egeland (2000) studied 141 pregnant women utilizing personality testing. The women and their children were studied at 13 and 24 months postpartum and it was found that mothers scoring high in antisocial traits had more hostile parenting styles than non-antisocial mothers.

Antisocial behaviour in mothers may be preceded by antisocial or conduct problems as girls. Conduct disorder is the term used for antisocial traits in minors and includes physical, verbal or sexual aggression, destruction of property and serious violations of rules. Block, Blokland, van der Werff, van Os and Nieuwbeerta (2010) conducted an original study of more than 400 career-criminal women, reviewing retrospective criminal histories back to age twelve and prospective data until the women's death or until 2003. They found that earlier onset of problem behaviour was highly related to its chronicity; in other words, girls who show antisocial problems early will continue to act in an antisocial manner for a long time. They also noted that the women continued their criminal careers throughout their childbearing and child-caring years, suggesting that the women's criminal behaviour could continue within the home with easily accessible potential victims – their children. This is supported by Serbin et al. (cited in Putallaz & Bierman, 2004) who reviewed longitudinal data for aggressive and violent young women and found their children had more annual emergency medical visits, hospitalizations and emergency surgeries than children of non-aggressive mothers, suggesting that the children of these young women were at higher risk for injuries. According to Zoccolillo, Paquette, Azar, Cote and Tremblay (2004), who reviewed both the Longitudinal Study of Child Development in Quebec and the Montreal Adolescent Mother Study, antisocial young women pose significant risk to their offspring when they become antisocial mothers. These antisocial women are much more likely to become irritated by their child's normal behaviours due to unrealistic expectations for their infant's developmental abilities and also due to viewing the infant's normative behaviour as intentional.

Even if a woman is not antisocial or hostile towards her child, she may simply lack empathy. Empathy is the feeling of warmth, compassion and concern that we have for others. It allows us to take another's perspective; dispositional empathy can be conceptualized as a stable character trait. Several studies (De Paul, Pérez-Albeniz, Guibert, Asla, & Ormaechea,

2008; Perez-Albeniz & de Paul, 2003) have found that women at risk for child maltreatment showed less dispositional empathy compared to women who were not at risk for child maltreatment. In addition, even if a mother is generally empathetic, she may choose to overrule that feeling when the child's needs conflict with her own. De Paul and Guibert (2008) suggest that if a mother does not think that behaving in an empathetic, compassionate manner towards her child will improve her own feelings and if she does not expect any negative reaction from her social network, she may choose to ignore any empathetic impetus towards her child.

Other Factors in Child Abuse

Western society has a stereotype of the 'evil stepmother' that is viewed with humour and disbelief. However, a review of child abuse literature shows that the stereotype is based on a degree of fact. In a study of more than 800 children, including those who lived with biological mothers and those who lived with stepmothers, Daly and Wilson (1985) found that, while 47 per cent of the children living with a biological mother were physically abused, 63 per cent of those living with a stepmother were abused. This finding was replicated by Creighton and Noyes (1989) who showed that rates of physical abuse by stepmothers and stepfathers, while similar to each other, were significantly higher than those of biological mothers and fathers. They also noted that adolescents are more likely to run away from a family with a stepmother than from one with a stepfather (Daly & Wilson, 2005). Evolutionary psychology theorists have suggested that non-biological caregivers are more likely to abuse children due to conflicts over limited resources (Daly & Wilson, 1988).

Maternal age has also been noted as relevant in research on child physical abuse and neglect. Connelly and Straus (1992) found that the mother's age at the time she gave birth to the child who she would later abuse was significant; the younger she was at the time she gave birth, the greater her risk for committing child abuse. Similarly, Lounds, Borkowski and Whitman's (2006) ten-year prospective study of one hundred adolescent mothers and their offspring found that young mothers who demonstrated maternal neglect early on were most likely to continue to demonstrate neglect as the child aged.

Single motherhood has also been implicated in research on physical abuse by mothers. In two separate national sample studies (Gelles, 1989; Wolfner & Gelles, 1993), researchers found that there was more physical abuse in homes with single mothers. Smaller studies have also shown the same high risk of child abuse among single mothers (Dubowitz, Hampton, Bithoney, & Newberger, 1987; Margolin, 1990; Schloesser, Pierpont, & Poertner, 1992). Relatedly, Guterman, Lee, Lee, Waldfogel and Rathouz (2009) recently found that single mothers reported greater parenting stress than married or cohabitating mothers and used more punitive behaviour and physical aggression.

Another factor related to maternal child abuse is the gender of the child victim. Wolfner and Gelles (1993), in their study of more than 3,000 households with minor children, found higher rates of violence in households with male children. Creighton (1985), in a study of more than 6,000 British children, found that male children were overrepresented in both abuse and neglect cases. Margolin (1990) also found that male children were much more likely to be neglect victims than female children. The reason for the targeting of male children by female perpetrators is unclear at this time, but this research is aligned with studies that show similarly higher rates of infanticide of male children in western cultures.

While research has implicated factors such as youth and lack of partner in child abuse and neglect, those factors are more likely to be correlational than causal. Having a child at a young age and single parenthood may both be associated with some other as yet unknown third factor such as impulsivity and trait aggression, or difficulty maintaining stable relationships, although this line of inquiry remains unstudied.

Failure to Protect

While not a direct form of child abuse or neglect, the issue of failure to protect against abuse by others is also relevant to any discussion of abusive women. In late 1980s' United States, no other case caused as much discussion as that of Hedda Nussbaum and her partner Joel Steinberg. Steinberg was charged with the beating to death of Elizabeth Lisa Launders, a child he and Nussbaum had illegally adopted. Nussbaum's supporters focused on her victimization by Steinberg as a defence for not safeguarding the child. However, as Brownmiller (1989) pointed out, Nussbaum's own victimization did not absolve her from her responsibilities. Nussbaum was an editor of an international publishing company, which gave her the financial ability to remove the child from danger. She was aware that the girl was illegally adopted and could simply have sent an anonymous report of this from her work phone to authorities. When the child was severely injured, Nussbaum could have called for an ambulance. Ultimately, Nussbaum did none of these, choosing her relationship with Steinberg over the child's safety. This passive tolerance of child abuse by one's partner is not uncommon. In 1998, her mother's boyfriend murdered eight-year-old Justina Morales after years of abuse, which Morales's mother, Denise Solero, ignored (*New York Times*, 1997). In 2005, his father beat three-year-old Ronnie Paris to death. The boy's mother, Nysheera Paris, was sentenced to five years in prison for culpable negligence for allowing the child to be repeatedly beaten (*Saint Petersburg Times*, 2006). In 2006, seven-year-old Nixzmary Brown was beaten to death by her stepfather while her mother, Nixzaliz Santiago, 'failed to act' (Shilling & Geller, 2008). Cases such as these are highlighted in the media with unfortunate regularity. In 2006, Rebecca Lewis was convicted of familial homicide for failing to prevent her boyfriend killing her 13-month-old son (BBC News, 2006). Familial homicide was then a new inclusion in the Domestic Violence, Crime and Victims Act (2004) covering England and Wales, and closed a legal loophole in which people jointly accused of murder could avoid prosecution by blaming each other.

In common law, a duty of care is said to exist if there is a 'special relationship' between two parties. In the past, courts have stated that there is a special relationship between parties such as innkeepers and their guests. If such a duty exists between strangers, then the duty between a parent and a child is obvious. Ultimately, a mother who acts in a way to maintain a relationship with a violent partner rather than in a way to maintain a child's safety is negligent. Non-abusing parents are often a child's only advocate and the child's right to safety must outweigh any other consideration (Liang & Macfarlane, 1999).

Abusive Mothers' Perspective on Their Children

If women do not abuse children due to mental illness, antisocial traits or other factors within the woman herself, then perhaps the abuse is due to some factor within the child. This appears to be the thought process of some researchers who have attempted to identify the behaviour characteristics that increase the likelihood that a child would be victimized by a 'vulnerable' adult (Mash, Johnston, & Kovitz, 1983). This theory, that abused children are 'more difficult' to manage than non-abused children and that the average person would become abusive if made to parent such difficult children, is highly problematic. It suggests that, in certain situations, child abuse would be a normal, expected behaviour. If we change the language to state that 'researchers are attempting to find the women's behaviour characteristics that increase the likelihood that a woman would be battered by a vulnerable spouse', we see how fallacious this argument is. Further, as Zoccolillo et al. (in Putallaz & Bierman, 2004) point out, any research that tries to take into account so-called 'child effects' will likely overestimate those effects because by the time the child becomes 'difficult', any problematic parenting has had its effect on the child. One simply cannot take a child at eighteen months and assume one is seeing inherent child effects without any maternal impact since birth.

However, the 'difficult' child concept may still be useful in understanding child abuse. What if the problem is not that abused children are more difficult to parent but that abusive parents perceive their children as unusually difficult and challenging, regardless of the child's true behaviour? Several studies (Dopke, Lundahl, Dunsterville, & Lovejoy, 2003; Graham, Weiner, Cobb, & Henderson, 2001; Lorber & Slep, 2005; Mash, Johnston, & Kovitz, 1983; Oldershaw, Walters, & Hall, 1989) have compared physically abusive mothers and their children to control mothers and their children. They found that physically abusive mothers were not simply more hostile towards their children, but they also perceived their children's behaviour more negatively, even when their children behaved in a manner similar to the control children. In other words, it was not that their children were observably more difficult, but that the abusive mothers perceived the children to be more difficult. This is called a negative appraisal bias (Lorber, O'Leary, & Kendziora, 2003). These mothers were also more controlling of their children's play, directing or intervening in the children's behaviour unnecessarily. The abusive mothers in these studies further reported higher levels of stress than the control mothers, a finding replicated in several other studies (Dietrich, Berkowitz, Kadushin, & McGloin, 1990; Graham et al., 2001). This suggests that the abusive mothers may have high internal distress and react externally by abusing the child rather than regulating their own behaviours in relation to their child's actual compliant behaviour.

One problem in child abuse cases appears to be the parent's lack of knowledge of developmental norms. Korbin (1987) found that the mothers who had fatally abused their children had unrealistic expectations of the child's developmentally normal behaviour. As Mugavin (2008) notes, competent parenting requires the ability to accurately perceive and monitor a child's developmental needs. If a parent expects a child to control her bowels or focus his attention at an age when this is developmentally impossible, then the child may be misperceived as 'difficult'.

Along with a distorted understanding of developmental norms and a negative appraisal bias, an abusive mother may also misattribute the child's behaviour. When we evaluate another's behaviour, we can attribute it to external, situational issues or to factors within that other person. Several researchers (Dix, Ruble, Grusec, & Nixon, 1986; Nix et al., 1999; Slep & O'Leary, 1998) found that abusive mothers are more likely to attribute a child's behaviour to the child's negative intent or a negative disposition, rather than to either normal developmental or situational issues. For example, instead of attributing a child's crying to distress, an abusive mother would attribute the crying to a desire by the child to annoy her (Seng & Prinz, 2008). Wilson, Gardner, Burton and Leung (2006) showed that mothers who attributed the cause of their child's behaviour to something internal in the child were more likely to use negative and reactive behaviours to control the child. In other words, an abusive mother may think that a crying infant is intentionally rejecting the mother, and react violently to this perception.

Milner (2003) suggested that abusive parents go through four steps of processing information about their child's behaviour, any or all of which can be distorted. A mother can focus only on her child's negative behaviour while ignoring compliant behaviour (selective attention and perception), can interpret the child's neutral or developmentally normative behaviour as negative (negative evaluation), can choose an aggressive response to the child and, finally, can abuse the child. However, Milner (2003) noted that these information-processing errors alone cannot explain child abuse. Along with these errors, the mother is likely to have deficits in her ability to inhibit aggression and to problem-solve.

If the mothers perceive their children as misbehaving, then how do they perceive themselves? Dietrich et al. (1990) found that most abusive mothers felt their actions were justified, given that their child had been defiant. In a study of mothers incarcerated for fatally abusing their children, Korbin (1987) found most of the mothers viewed their children as somehow having been rejecting towards the mother, again justifying the abuse. Korbin (1989) later suggested that for an abusive mother to admit that she is abusive to her child is too threatening to her self-concept as a good mother, and therefore she turns to justification of the abuse by blaming it on the child.

Recidivism

Unfortunately, it does not appear that child abuse is a one-off behaviour for most women who engage in it. Rather, it becomes a chronic manner in which some women behave. As noted above, when Southall et al. (1997) covertly video-recorded in-hospital child abuse, they found that one third of the abused children had siblings who had been fatally abused by their mothers by either suffocation or poisoning. Sheridan (2003) reviewed 451 MSBP cases and found that most of the victims had been abused for an average of 21 months, rather than just once, with 6 per cent dying and 7.3 per cent experiencing long-term or permanent injury. Further, a quarter of these child victims of MSBP had a deceased sibling, suggesting the possibility of serial abuse and homicide, as in the Southall study.

Effects of Abuse on Children

What effect does child abuse have on children? One of the more prevalent findings is that it is a likely cause of homelessness in youth. Four large studies, with samples ranging from 195 to 375 homeless youths, found that physical abuse, mostly perpetrated by the mother or stepmother, was what caused the young person to run away from home. Janus, Archambault, Brown and Welsh (1995) found that most of the Canadian runaways in their study reported chronic and extreme abuse from a young age. In the Powers, Eckenrode and Jaklitsch sample (1990), nearly a third of the abused youths reported that their abusive mothers were single mothers. Tyler and Cauce (2002) noted that, while 36 per cent of the youths reported their biological mother as the main perpetrator of their abuse, another 44 per cent reported being abused by another female, either a relative or an acquaintance. Finally, Mallett and Rosenthal (2009) noted that female youths were more likely to have been the target of their biological mother's violence but male youths were more likely to be targeted by a stepmother. As with the Janus study, most of the youths in Mallett and Rosenthal's study reported that the violence was a well-established part of their family's functioning rather than a rare event.

A less surprising outcome of maternal abuse and neglect involves infant attachment. Attachment theory is related to social learning theory. It suggests that infants learn through observing and imitating, forming cognitive models (either negative or positive) of relationships that have an impact on later interpersonal functioning (Milner et al., 2010). According to this theory, based on the quality and consistency of their experiences with their parents, infants develop a primary attachment strategy which allows them to seek and obtain safety from parents in the early months of development. Most children develop organized and secure attachment strategies and some will develop secondary strategies that either maximize or minimize security seeking in a way that adapts to their parents' behaviours but is still organized. However, attachment research has shown that there is a subset of children whose attachment behaviour is markedly disorganized, without a coherent way of securing parenting care or coping with disruption of care. These children demonstrate chaotic, non-adaptive responses. Not surprisingly, many of the mothers of disorganized, non-adaptive infants are abusive or neglectful. Adshead and Bluglass (2005) found that mothers who engage in MSBP behaviour were more likely to have children with disorganized attachments. In Carlson, Cicchetti, Barnett and Braunwald's (1989) study, only 14 per cent of the maltreated children had organized secure attachments. In Egeland and Sroufe's (1981) comparison of maltreated and well-treated infants, the maltreated infants were markedly less likely to have organized secure attachments. Baer and Daly Martinez's 2006 meta-analysis of eight attachment studies found that maltreated infants were significantly more likely to have insecure/disorganized attachment than control infants. They theorized that infants cannot develop organized cognitive models in adaptation to their mothers' behaviours because the mothers themselves do not demonstrate organized behaviour with the infants. George (1996) found that the mothers of these infants tend to feel helpless and stressed and to perceive their children as out of control, prompting them towards inappropriately harsh and inconsistent behaviours, which becomes the model for the child.

Conclusion

The research to date has demonstrated that women in western society abuse and neglect children, often to death, in frighteningly high numbers. Rather than being due solely to mental illness, past abuse or the child's own behaviour, child abuse by women is often a function of the woman's own hostile, aggressive tendencies and lack of knowledge regarding developmentally normative behaviours in children. In addition, the agencies tasked with safeguarding these children may not be suitably trained to intervene appropriately in these cases.

In 2010, a multi-site review of American child protective service investigations found that there was no difference between high-risk families investigated for child maltreatment and high-risk families who were not investigated. Fewer than 40 per cent of the abused children received any services after the investigation and up to 62 per cent of the children were referred back to protective services for new concerns for abuse (Campbell, Cook, LaFleur, & Keenan, 2010).

One possible way to decrease child abuse and neglect by women in the future would be for child protection services to mandate the use of evidence-based treatments (EBT). Chafinn and Friedrich (2004) investigated multiple treatments for abusive parents and suggested several that have significant positive effects. Abuse-focused cognitive behaviour therapy (Kolko, 1996) utilizes both individual and family therapy in order to teach offending parents new ways to think about, perceive and act towards their children. Another treatment that shows promise is parent/child interaction therapy. This uses a form of coaching to increase positive interactions between parent and child and increase nurturing behaviours. Several studies have suggested that this treatment is effective in abusive families (Querido, Bearss, & Eyberg, 2002; Timmer, Urquiza, Zebell, & McGrath, 2005).

Mothers who abuse their children due to misattribution and misperception can learn new ways to think about their children. A cognitive retraining programme for abusive mothers in the United States found that prevalence of abuse by mothers who had cognitive retraining was 4 per cent, compared to 23 per cent for mothers who only had supportive home visits (Bugental et al., 2010).

As with the issue of spousal abuse, child abuse and neglect would also profit from better public information campaigns. If women's magazines, newspapers and other forms of media increased their coverage of the issue of child abuse and neglect by women, if there were coloured rubber wristbands or coloured ribbons raising awareness of child abuse by women as there are for breast cancer and AIDS, if the issue of abusive mothers was covered on talk shows, perhaps it would stop being just a topic for researchers and public health officials.

5

Intimate Partner Violence by Women

Introduction

Growing up in the United States, many schoolchildren saw a 1958 film that taught that lemmings, small arctic rodents, committed mass suicide by running off cliffs into the ocean. For years, the concept of 'lemming suicide' existed in the minds of those who saw this film and became a metaphor for the danger of going along with something without thinking about it. However, it turns out that this was an intentionally constructed fiction. Lemmings do not, as a rule, commit mass suicide. The animals in the film had been launched off a cliff using a turntable and filmed using multiple camera angles to make their deaths appear volitional.

The lemming suicide fiction is instructional in showing that myths can be constructed easily, especially if repeated often within an educational setting. In some ways, the issue of intimate partner violence (IPV) has similar myths. Everyone 'knows' that IPV is perpetrated by men against women and women only engage in IPV for self-defence. How do we 'know' this? Because that is the oversimplified factoid that the mass media has reported for many years, despite the reality that IPV is a highly nuanced area of research. In western society, we have constructed the image of an IPV perpetrator as male, with the passive female as his polar opposite. This construction not only ignores that women are responsible and rational agents capable of choosing their behaviour, it also ignore that sometimes women choose to be violent.

Female Aggression, First Edition. Helen Gavin and Theresa Porter.
© 2015 John Wiley & Sons, Ltd. Published 2015 by John Wiley & Sons, Ltd.

For many years, there has been a battle within academia over the existence of women's domestic violence and how to discuss it. On one side were researchers who studied IPV by both sexes, which obtained reliable research findings, but also resulted with women's violence continually being compared and contrasted to that of men as if women's violence was not a relevant topic in its own right. On the other side were those who claimed that the above research was somehow misogynistic and theorized that all IPV was a result of a patriarchal society and then generated data to support this theory. Unfortunately, some of these researchers have put more emphasis on the agenda of promoting their background theory rather than on objectively reporting all results. An example of this includes suppression of evidence of women's IPV, such as when the Kentucky Commission on the Status of Women obtained IPV perpetration data for both males and females but then only published the data on male perpetration, implying that women were only victims and never perpetrators (Schulman, cited in Straus, 2007). It was much later that Hornung, McCullough and Sugimoto (1981) published the finding that 38 per cent of the attacks by women in this study were on men whom the women characterized as non-violent; in other words, the IPV by women in that study was not in self-defence. Another example of a specific agenda impeding accuracy was in 1995 when the Canadian Violence Against Women Survey took a well-researched IPV questionnaire tool and omitted all questions about perpetration by women from the questionnaires used during their survey (Straus, 2007). The worst example, however, was attempts to intimidate researchers involved in studying women's perpetration of IPV. The most famous victim of this is Suzanne Steinmetz, who published 'The Battered Husband Syndrome' in 1977 and later had to deal with bomb threats and threats against her children. These events suggest that some of those involved in research or policy making on the issue of IPV are over-invested in a specific perspective rather than in promoting objective findings.

Some in the field have argued that women's use of IPV can only be understood within a contextualized, gendered discourse and to conduct research in any other way would be inappropriate (Renzetti, 1999). This is correct; women's violence occurs within a society with a significant double standard about violence. In our current culture, women's violence is seen as funny or of little consequence or simply not seen at all (Bowen, 2008). For example, in 2006, the American television show *Primetime* secretly filmed a staged scenario where a man was publicly abused and assaulted by a woman, watching to see if anyone intervened. Over two days, 163 witnesses passed by, but only one group of four adults intervened. When asked afterwards why they did not intervene, many witnesses denigrated the victim and stated their assumptions that he was deserving of the 'punishment' he was receiving or stated that they felt the assault by a woman wasn't 'harmful' (Taylor, 2006). That is the gendered context within which research on women's IPV occurs. In postmodern western culture, women's IPV is still viewed as circumstantial and due to something beyond women's control and agency (Kierski, 2002). Only men's violence is relevant, serious and voluntary.

In the past, the discourse on women's use of IPV has often employed techniques of neutralization, which served to remove agency from women via practices such as denial of responsibility, denial of injury to victim, transformation of the victim into someone deserving punishment and shifting focus of attention off the women perpetrators (Sykes & Matza, 1957). Researchers on women's IPV have been accused of being part of a 'backlash' against women's rights, a useful technique for shifting the spotlight away from women's aggression (Malloy, McCloskey, Grigsby, & Gardner, 2003). These neutralization techniques do not withstand a review of the literature. The majority of men, despite living within western patriarchal society, do not engage in intimate partner violence against women, which strongly suggests that patriarchy is not having a pervasive causal effect (George, 2003). Other neutralization techniques used in the dominant discourse about women's use of IPV included denial of injury to the victims and transformation of the victim into someone deserving of punishment. In that construction, women only use IPV in 'self-defence' against violent men, who are not viewed as severely injured. Again, these neutralization techniques do not stand up to scrutiny; studies suggesting that women only use IPV in self-defence tend to come from self-report data, which is open to criticisms of lack of reliability (Ford, Tappin, Schluter, & Wild, 1997; Huizinga & Elliott, 1986; Weinhardt, Forsyth, Carey, Jaworski, & Durant, 1998). Further, researchers cannot rely solely on victim self-reports for one gender but not the other, although this is done in much of the research; women's self-report is taken as credible but men's self-report is viewed as self-serving (Graham-Kevan, 2009). In reality, both genders are capable of minimization and denial (Henning & Feder, 2004) and the use of language in the discussion of IPV should also be applied more uniformly. Discussions of male perpetrators of IPV tend to describe them as 'violent men', while studies of female perpetrators of IPV use language to distance the women from the violence, by utilizing expressions such as 'women's use of aggression' (Archer, 2006; Babcock, Miller, & Siard, 2003; Hughes, Stuart, Gordon, & Moore, 2007) rather than 'aggressive women'. In other words, men *are* violent, and women are not violent but do sometimes *use* violence.

It is time for a shift in our discourse on IPV by women away from simple comparisons with men and for it to be seen as worthy of study as its own independent topic. In the second decade of the twenty-first century, we must not simply recognize women as possible agents of aggression, but also ask how we can intervene effectively with them, rather than simply asking 'how are these women different from men?'

Prevalence of Women's Violence Against Heterosexual Partners

As noted above, much of the research on women's use of IPV has been done within the context of massive community studies of IPV in general, with comparisons to IPV by men. While this chapter will focus on women's IPV without repeatedly comparing it to that of men, it should be noted here that the vast majority of research to date has shown that women's perpetration of IPV is equal to that of men and that the majority of violent relationships are mutually violent (Straus & Gelles, 1985; Stets & Straus, 1990).

What does research show about domestic violence perpetrated by women in English-speaking countries? Based on multiple large-scale IPV studies, we know that women engage in high rates of IPV, often use weapons, often injure their victims and engage in IPV in both cohabitating/ married relationships and dating relationships. For example, McLeod's 1984 study of over 6,200 spousal assaults in Detroit, USA, showed that most victims were male, most of the serious injuries were experienced by males and mostly due to weapon use by women, using either a cutting object (55%), a gun (18.1%) or a club (12.1%). This weapon use by women was substantiated with Mechem, Shofer, Reinhard, Hornig and Datner's (1999) study of male victims in emergency rooms; 37% of the male victims of IPV reported having a weapon used against them. Additionally, the American National Violence Against Women Survey (2000) studied 16,000 men and women, and found that women committed approximately a third of domestic assaults overall and an even higher rate (39%) when the data is broken down into past-year rates (Straus, 2004, cited in Richardson et al., 2005). A meta-analysis (Archer, 2002) of 82 studies of IPV found that, when specific acts of violence are measured, women are significantly more likely to have engaged in physical violence towards a partner.

Similar results have been found in large-scale surveys in Britain (Carrado, George, Loxam, Jones, & Templar, 1996). George (1999) surveyed 1,455 British adults and found that 50% of all men who reported a history of being assaulted had been assaulted by a woman partner or ex-partner. In Canada, Laroche (2005) surveyed over 25,000 Canadians and extrapolated the results. Larouche found that 17 men per 1,000 were victims of their current partners' violence within the last twelve months, and 40 men per 1,000 were victims of severe violent acts by their female partner in the last five years; this extrapolates to 319,000 Canadian men who were victimized by their female partners. Comparable findings were made by Brinkerhoff and Lupri (1988), Bland and Orn (1986) and Fergusson, Horwood, and Ridder (2005).

Women in the military have also been shown to engage in high rates of IPV. Newby et al. (2003), using a random sample of 1,185 female US army soldiers, found high levels of IPV, with more violence aimed at unemployed spouses than employed spouses. Merrill et al. (1998) and Heyman and Neidig (1999) had similar findings with related populations.

In the United States, arrest rates for women who commit IPV have increased in recent years. Generally, arrest rates have not been viewed as a strong measure of women's use of IPV, due to policy-based and culturally based biases; male victims may be ignored by police and may also be reluctant to report their victimization. However, DeLeon, Wells, & Binsbacher (2006) found that California had a 500% increase in arrests of women for IPV between 1987 and 1997.

Although one may expect greater levels of domestic violence by women in the United States compared to other countries, due to the overall higher rate of violence in the United States, studies carried out in other nations have shown that IPV by women is an international problem. For example, 21.6% of Jordanian students surveyed in 2001 had witnessed wife-perpetrated IPV (Araji & Carlson, 2001), 36% of victims of IPV in a Karachi, Pakistan study were victims of female-perpetrated IPV (Niaz, Hassan, & Tariq, 2002) and 25% of men in an Indian study had been victimized at least once within the last year by a female partner

(Sarlar, Dsouza, Dasgupta, & Fiebert, 2008). Further north, both Ukrainian and Russian women engage in problematic levels of IPV (Lysova & Douglas, 2008; O'Leary, Tintle, Bromet, & Gluzman 2008). Finally, an International Dating Violence study in 2004 surveyed 8,000 couples in 16 countries and found the same pattern of equal or higher rates of violence by women as found in the United States and the United Kingdom (Straus, 2004).

Intimate partner violence is not only a problem for adults. College age and even adolescent girls engage in high rates of IPV (Billingham & Sack, 1986). The National Longitudinal Study of Adolescent Health surveyed more than 14,000 young adults, and found that 71% of the instigators of sole, non-reciprocal violence were girls (Arehart-Treichel, 2007). Young women admit to both engaging in IPV (Burke, Stets & Pirog-Good, 1988; Schwartz, O'Leary, & Kendziora, 1997) and causing serious physical injury (Hines & Malley-Morrison, 2001). In the United States, the most common victims of female-perpetrated IPV are young black males. For example, Holt and Espelage (2005) found that 53% of black male middle-school and high-school students reported having been violently victimized by their girlfriends, and West (2008) found that black males were the more likely than white or Latino males to be victims of dating violence. Intimate partner violence also occurs at a high rate among British and Canadian young women (Archer & Ray, 1989; Dutton, Nicholls, & Spidel, 2006). The Dunedin Multidisciplinary Health and Development study in New Zealand, which followed youths for more than 20 years, has provided some of the best information about young women's use of IPV: 35.8% of the young women in the study reported engaging in minor physical violence and 18.6% admitted to engaging in severe physical violence such as hitting, choking, using a knife and so on (Magdol, Moffitt, Caspi, Newman, Fagan, & Silva, 1997). In non-English speaking countries, the Global School-based Health Survey conducted by the WHO with 13–15-year-olds found that 18% of Zambian girls and 15% of Jordanian girls admitted perpetrating IPV against a male partner within the last year (Straus, 2008). However, more research is needed on IPV by young women in more countries.

Women do not appear to 'age out' of engaging in IPV. Just as IPV by women is a problem among youth, it is also a problem among the elderly, although rates of IPV among the elderly are difficult to discover, as they are often subsumed under elder abuse data. However, Pillemer and Finkelhor (1988), in their sample of 2,000 men and women over the age of 65, found that 58% of the perpetrators of so-called 'elder abuse' were intimate partners, and 36% of those were women (Reeves, Desmarais, Nicholls, & Douglas, 2007).

Prevalence of Women's Violence Against Homosexual Partners

While IPV by women in heterosexual relationships has been consistently documented, there is less research on women's IPV within homosexual relationships. This may in part be due to the general lack of research on homosexual relationships until recently. One of the first such studies was conducted by Brand and Kidd (1986), comparing heterosexual and homosexual women; these groups showed comparable rates of IPV. Two later studies (Lie & Gentlewarrier, 1991; Lie Schilit, Bush, Montagne, & Reyes, 1991), surveying large samples of homosexual women, found the majority admitted to engaging in IPV against a female partner, as well as having been victimized in the past by a female partner. These and the few other available studies (Waldner-Haugrud, Gratch, & Magruder, 1997) demonstrate that IPV by women is not confined to only male victims or only self-defence against men.

Severity and Injury

Because past discussions regarding women's use of IPV have generally been made within a comparison with male use of IPV, several studies have tried to operationalize which gender causes more damage, with the theory being that men probably hurt women more than women hurt men. Ultimately, this is not a highly relevant argument as no one should be subjected to violence, especially within an intimate relationship and no child should grow up watching one parent batter another. Even one domestic violence victim is one too many, regardless of the genders involved (Kelly, 2002). If a male attempts to punch a woman but misses and hits the wall, she still experiences a traumatic event, regardless of whether or not she was injured.

The same is true when the genders are reversed. If the victims of female IPV suffer fewer injuries overall than victims of male IPV, the victims were injured nonetheless.

Victims of IPV committed by women may be burned (Duminy & Hudson, 1993; Krob, Johnson, & Jordan, 1986), have their genitals attacked (Balakrishnan, Imel, Bandy, & Prasad, 1995), or suffer broken bones and teeth (Cascardi, Langhinrichsen, & Vivian, 1992). Women often use weapons against their victims as a way of minimizing the size/strength differences with male victims (McLeod, 1984) and are more likely to throw objects and threaten a partner with a weapon (McDonald, Jouriles, Ramisetty-Mikler, Caetano, & Green, 2006).

Recidivism

Based on the available recidivism research, it appears that women who perpetrate IPV tend to do so with some regularity. Straus's family violence survey (1986) findings showed that IPV perpetrators have a two-out-of-three chance of reoffending (Dutton, 2006) and Menard, Anderson and Godboldt (2009) found that substance abuse and relationship termination also predict violent recidivism by women (Menard et al., 2009).

Current tools to evaluate the risk of recidivism of IPI have only been validated on males, however, and cannot be used to predict recidivism in women perpetrators. Professionals working with female perpetrators of IPV would do better to use general violence risk assessment tools that take into account relevant factors such as antisocial attitudes (Henning, Martinsson, & Holdford, 2009). Another option would be the revised version of the danger assessment tool (DA-R), which has been found to be useful in predicting future danger in homosexual female relationships (Glass, Perrin, Hanson, Blood, Gardner, & Campbell, 2008).

Women's Intimate Partner Violence and Stalking

It has long been known that IPV and stalking often go together, so much so that some theorists have suggested that stalking can be viewed as a specific form of domestic violence (Logan, Leukefeld, & Walker, 2000; Walker & Meloy, 1998). Although most stalking research has been conducted on male stalkers, the association between IPV and stalking has also been recognized for women perpetrators. Women account for between 12% (Purcell, Pathé, & Mullen, 2001) and 43% (Palarea et al., 1999, in West & Friedman, 2008) of all stalkers. Of these, 48% had threatened their victims and 30% had followed up those threats with violence. If there was a previous sexual relationship between the stalker and her victim, then the risk of the woman stalker engaging in violence exceeded 50% (Meloy & Boyd, 2003).

Intimate Partner Violence by Women Resulting in Homicide

Like stalking, homicide is a possible result of IPV (Geberth, 1998). Some homicides between intimate partners may be the result of careful planning, and other homicides are the impulsive result of IPV in its most extreme form. In 1987 and 1988, Goetting published a set of studies on women arrested for homicide in Detroit. In both studies, the majority of the homicidal women were black, in their thirties, and had been residing with the partners they murdered. In both studies, the murder was the result of a final violent argument that was the culmination of a long history of IPV within the relationship. These women shot (55.4%), stabbed (41.1%) or bludgeoned their partners to death. These studies were followed by Mann's (1988) seminal work on women's domestic murders, which also showed that the majority (53.3%) of the cases involved a degree of premeditation and 41.1% were not listed as self-defence; 29.5% of the victims were incapacitated in some way at the time of the homicide (e.g., sleeping, intoxicated or bound/tied). The homicides may have been the final point on a trajectory many of these women were following, with significant histories of violence and prior arrests (Mann, 1988; McClain, 1982). It is noteworthy that 49.6% of the women in the Mann-Richey study were never sentenced and fewer than 40% were given any prison time. This low rate of retributive justice was corroborated by the 1994 Bureau of Justice Statistics 'Violence Between Intimates' report, which noted that the average sentence for a woman convicted of murdering her husband was 6.2 years, compared to the 17.5 years the average male receives for murdering his wife (in Gelles, 2007).

Intimate Partner Violence Initiation vs Self-Defence

The past discourse on IPV by women has been from the perspective of self-defence; she struck back at the person who struck her first (Saunders, 1986; Hamberger, 1997). However, multiple studies have shown that this perspective is inaccurate. Women initiate IPV and they do so for reasons other than self-defence (Makepeace, 1986). The rates of women's initiation of IPV range from 29% (Fiebert & Gonzalez, 1997) to 73.4% (Bland & Orn, 1986), depending on the study population. There is also research that demonstrates that women engage in IPV as the sole aggressor in non-reciprocally violent relationships. Graham-Kevan (2009) reviewed seven studies which indicated that, in unilaterally violent heterosexual relationships, the sole perpetrator was more likely to be the woman. Women's self-report has also demonstrated the use of non-defensive violence. Swan and Snow (2006) noted that 45% of the women in their sample had used IPV in revenge rather than in self-defence and 38% had threatened violence in order to force or coerce a partner to do something.

Some theorists have suggested that women may initiate violence as a defensive reaction to pending violence by the partner. However, there is evidence that women may falsely claim the need for a pre-emptive strike as a form of self-defence without there actually being any real danger to them. For example, Sarantakos (2004) questioned a sample of IPV-perpetrating women, their male victims, the women's mothers and the couples' children in order to assess for the accuracy of the women's self-reported reasons for their violence. This landmark study found that the violent women's self-reports were dubious, based on witness reports of their mothers and children. The majority of the female perpetrators' mothers indicated that the male victims were not violent and the women were not acting in self-defence.

Moffitt, Krueger, Caspi and Fagan (2000) point out that, if women only engaged in IPV for defensive reasons, these women would be qualitatively different than men who engage in IPV (presuming men do not engage in IPV for self-defence). In other words, the personality traits that predict IPV in men should not predict them in women if women are only using violence in self-defence. Moffit et al. tested this theory using data from the Dunedin Multidisciplinary Health and Development Study and found no significant gender difference in personality factors such as approval of the use of aggression, which correlates with both general and partner violence. If women approve of the use of aggression, it is unlikely that they will use it only in self-defence.

Anger, Communication and Control

Rather than just self-defence, multiple motivations have been shown to be related to women's perpetration of IPV. Olson and Lloyd (2005) indicated that explanations for women's IPV are comprised of six themes: self-defence; anger; retaliation; establishing control; resisting male control; and attention/communication. The idea that violence can be a dysfunctional form of communication or attention-seeking was confirmed by Walley-Jean and Swan (2009) and several other researchers have confirmed that women perpetrate IPV to feel powerful, to force a partner to agree with something, when jealous or as retribution for a perceived wrongdoing by a partner (Stuart, Moore, Gordeon, Ramsey, & Kahler, 2006; Swan & Snow, 2003). Multiple studies have shown that one of the most common motivations given by women who engage in IPV was anger (Hettrich & O'Leary, 2007; Follingstad, Wright, Lloyd, & Sebastian, 1991). For example, Munoz-Rivas, Graña, O'Leary and González (2007) evaluated more than two thousand young adults and found that women cited anger as their primary motivation for IPV.

These findings shouldn't be surprising; anger and violence are commonly understood to be related. However, our culture maintains a stereotyped image of anger as a male purview only (Archer, 2004) or considers women's anger and its related violence not important or serious. For example, in one Finnish study the violent women felt their IPV was not important because they were 'only expressing their anger' (Flinck & Paavilainen, 2010, p. 311), as if expressive violence was less painful or relevant than instrumental violence.

Control, as well as anger, is a strong motivator for domestically violent women. Follingstad et al. (1991) found that more women than men in their study reported engaging in IPV as a way to gain control over a partner or feel powerful. Similarly, women responders to the National Violence Against Women Survey were as motivated as men to control their partners (Felson & Outlaw, 2007). Dasgupta (2002) established that both genders use violence to control a partner, with women focusing more on immediate situations. When Graham-Kevan and Archer (2005) investigated explanations of women's IPV violence, they found a strong positive association between both control and retaliation and the use of physical violence.

Finally, women's IPV may not be due to single motivations but, rather, to multiple, complex motivations. Olson and Lloyd (2005) demonstrated that women in their study gave on average three reasons for an act of violence. Humans experience multiple motivations for any given behaviour, suggesting that the dichotomy of violence (by either gender) as either instrumental or expressive is artificial (Bushman & Anderson, 2001).

Social Learning and Intimate Partner Violence
by Women

Besides anger, control and retaliation, another possible explanation for women's IPV is social learning. This is the theory that children learn behaviour by witnessing models of the behaviour. In the case of aggression, a child exposed to violence learns to behave violently and see violence as an acceptable behaviour (White & Widom, 2003). If children are exposed to parent-to-parent violence, it increases the likelihood that these children will display violence to a partner upon adulthood (Capaldi & Clark, 1998; Kaura & Allen, 2004). The home environment models both the physical expressions of anger and the acceptance of violence as a normal way of dealing with relational conflict. Jankowski, Leitenberg, Henning and Coffey (1999) corroborated this model, finding that witnessing a same-gender parent engage in inter-parental violence increased the child's risk of later perpetrating violence within a dating relationship. In other words, girls who watched their mothers attack their fathers were more likely to become women who attacked their partners and to believe that such behaviour is acceptable.

This learning can generalize into general violent behaviour. Babcock et al. (2003) compared partner-only violent women to women who were generally violent and found that the generally violent women were more likely to report having witnessed inter-parental violence perpetrated by their mothers. Generally violent women also were more likely to report being violent as a means of controlling their partners and to report more trauma symptoms than partner-violent women, although they did not report more traumatic experiences. This may be because the generally violent women had less resilience to their traumatic experiences and had fewer alternatives to violence in their repertoire of coping behaviours (Bonanno, 2004).

Personality and Intimate Partner Violence by Women

A further possible explanation for women's IPV involves personality traits. As noted above, violence is related to certain personality traits. Some women who perpetrate IPV have personality disorders or character dysfunctions such as borderline personality or antisocial personality. Several studies have demonstrated that the presence of borderline personality disorder or borderline traits was positively associated with engaging in IPV by women (Dutton et al., 2006; Hines, 2008; Hughes, Stuart, Gordon, & Moore, 2007). This makes sense as emptiness and rage are the common emotions experienced by people with borderline personalities. Other studies have shown that antisocial personality traits correlated with women's domestic violence. Stuart et al. (2006) found a high rate of antisocial personality disorders in their group of women referred for treatment for IPV. In another study of domestically violent women, 33 per cent of the women met the criteria for at least one personality disorder, antisocial personality being one of the most common (Spidel, Nicholls, Kendrick, Klein, & Kropp, 2004, cited in Dutton et al., 2006). Bland and Orn (1986) found a strong association between antisocial personality, partner violence and weapon use by women. These women were often exploitative, minimizing of their own responsibilities and viewed violence as a normal part of a relationship (Flinck & Paavilainen, 2010; Simmons, Lehmann, Cobb, & Fowler, 2005). This antisocial style shows itself in other areas of these domestically violent women's lives. For example, Goetting (1987) found that the majority of the women who committed domestic homicide in one study had criminal records, and Conradi, Geffner, Kevin Hamberger and Lawson (2009) found that the domestically violent women in their sample were violent across multiple relationships and situations.

Antisocial personality traits can arise early in a girl's development. In the Dunedin study mentioned above, personality disturbances and behavioural features in 15-year-old girls predicted their use of violence in relationships at age 21, independent of violence by their male partners (Moffitt, Caspi, Rutter, & Silva, 2001). The researchers noted that approval of violence, negative emotionality and poor behavioural control predicted these women's perpetration of IPV. Other studies have shown similar connections between adolescent conduct problems or juvenile delinquency and later domestic violence by women (Giordano, Millhollin, Cernkovich, Pugh, & Rudolph, 1999). Bardone et al.'s study (1996) of 15-year-old girls found that conduct disorder exclusively predicted later partner physical abuse at age 21. What seems to distinguish women who perpetrate IPV from those who don't is a history of adolescent conduct problems and adult antisocial personality (Ehrensaft, Moffitt, & Caspi, 2004).

Moffit et al. (2001) found that other risk factors for IPV by women include impulsivity, low intelligence, negative emotionality and a general lack of empathy towards others, traits which begin early in life and remain generally stable. According to Lewis (2010), girls with conduct problems were more likely to go on to commit violence as adults than girls without conduct problems. These girls also tend to leave home at an earlier age, engage in childbearing at an earlier age and, through the process of assortative partnering, find equally antisocial boys to cohabitate and mate with (Capaldi, Kim, & Shortt, 2004). In other words, rather than suddenly becoming violent or aggressive within the context of a relationship, these women had always had behavioural problems, secondary to personality deficits, and these manifest within the context of relationships but also pre-date them.

Typologies

Researchers have devised multiple typologies for male batterers but typologies of women who engage in IPV are relatively new. Holtzworth-Munroe and Stuart's (1994) typology for men showed that most batterers could be divided into one of three types: the family-only abuser (least violent and violence generally confined to intimate partners), the dysphoric/borderline abuser (moderately violent within the home with occasional general violence outside of home) and the generally violent/antisocial abuser (most violent and violent in multiple situations outside of domestic sphere). It appears that this typology also could be used to classify women who engage in IPV. For example, 50 per cent of Babcock, Miller and Siard's (2003) sample met the criteria for generally violent/antisocial type. In Simmons et al.'s 2005 study, domestically violent women were much more likely to have previous arrests, a history of weapon use and attitudes that condoned violence, suggesting these women met the generally violent/ antisocial typology.

Several researchers have examined the role of attachment typologies in IPV. Attachment theory posits that the experiences within the infant and caregiver relationship become organized into an 'internal working model' or internalized representations within the infant. These representations go on to function as unconscious information processors regarding relationships in the child's later life (Moretti, Penney, Obsuth, & Odgers, 2007). The nature of the attachment can be secure, insecure or disorganized. Children who witness inter-parental violence have a higher risk of insecure attachments (Moretti et al., 2007). Insecure and disorganized attachment in adults is linked with emotional dysregulation and impaired ability for self-reflection. Theoretically, a child with an insecure or disorganized attachment will bring that representation of others as unresponsive and hostile into her adult relationships. Babcock, Jacobson, Gottman and Yerington (2000) found that adults with insecure attachment were more aggressive when a partner withdrew during argument and were more likely to use violence as a way of forcing a partner to comply. These theories suggest that some women who perpetrate IPV may in part be reacting to their partners based on early childhood experiences, rather than simply reacting to actual behaviours by their partners.

Reporting Issues by Victims

There are large discrepancies between crime statistics, which tend to show low rates of IPV by women, and violence surveys, which show high rates of IPV by women, because crime statistics are subject to reporting biases. For example, in order for a woman's partner to be counted in the crime statistics, he or she would first need to contact the police and admit to being victimized by a woman. For a male victim to do this means he must overcome his socialization that men are not victims, as well as risk public stigma and gender bias by the police and courts (Stanko & Hobdell, 1993). Several researchers have noted that male victims are particularly reluctant to report domestic victimization to the authorities for these reasons (Felson & Paré, 2005; White & Kowalski, 1994). In lesbian relationships, for a victim to come forward, she must be willing to 'out' herself in a community that may be homophobic. Further, victims of female- perpetrated IPV may also see no point in contacting the authorities, due to a sense of hopelessness (Follingstad, Wright, Lloyd, & Sebastian, 1991; Simonelli & Ingram, 1998). There are few services available to male victims, such as shelters or hotlines. One study of a new hotline specifically designed for male victims of domestic abuse found that 17.9% were disabled and unable to work and 3.2% were stay-at-home fathers, leaving both groups financially dependent on their violent wives and without the resources to leave without assistance (Hines, Brown, & Dunning, 2007). In Tilbrook, Allan and Dear's (2010) study, 72% of the men reported financial abuse at the hands of their wives including seizure of assets and income. If the only services to assist victims of IPV are for female victims of male abuse, as can be observed in many places, then other victims may view contacting the authorities as an act of futility.

Witnessing Inter-Parental Violence

Intimate partner violence often occurs within plain sight of children. As noted above, it has long been understood that children learn violence in part by witnessing violence (Gelles, 1972) and multiple international studies have shown that witnessing one's same-sex parent use IPV can increase one's own risk of using IPV in later dating situations (Jankowski et al., 1999; Kaura & Allen, 2004; Moretti, Obsuth, Odgers, & Reebye, 2006). Findings from a 20-year prospective study on the intergenerational transmission of IPV found that exposure to parent-to-parent aggression triples the likelihood of one being violent to one's partner in adulthood (Ehrensaft et al., 2003).

Not only is a girl at risk of later perpetration of IPV if she witnesses her mother domestically assault her father, she is also at risk of being abused by her mother. Child abuse and domestic abuse are highly correlated (Herrenkohl, Sousa, Tajima, Herrenkohl, & Moylan, 2008; Merrill, Hervig, & Milner, 1996). For example, Merrill Crouch, Thomsen and Guimond (2004) reported that those who were at risk for one form of abuse were twice as likely to be at risk for the other form and women were more at risk for IPV (Merrill et al., 2004). Child abuse then can become another form of social learning that violence is an acceptable form of behaviour. White and Widom's (2003) prospective study of children with documented histories of prepubescent abuse and/or neglect showed that, compared with a control group, abused/neglected girls grow up to have significantly higher rates of perpetrating IPV. They suggest that these girls have developed a hostile schema of the world, misreading neutral or positive social cues as dangerous ones and reacting with aggression.

Treatment

If a woman engages in IPV with her partner, where can she go to receive treatment, learn new conflict and anger management skills and possibly avoid committing new acts of violence? Unfortunately, many violent women find their communities lack resources to help them, as the focus has been solely on male perpetrators for so many years. Kernsmith and Kernsmith (2009a) looked at state standards for IPV interventions in the United States and discovered that most standards were designed for male perpetrators of IPV; 55% of standards stated that IPV was primarily a male problem and others standards implied this by using male pronouns for the perpetrators. The state of Minnesota, USA, has guidelines for male batterer programmes, without any mention of possible programmes to assist women. Illinois has a programme for female perpetrators of 'heterosexual partner abuse', implying that lesbians will not need these services (Kernsmith & Kernsmith, 2009a). Further, many IPV intervention programmes use the 'Duluth model' which is based on the outdated theory that males engage in IPV due to the inherent patriarchy of society, thereby denying the existence of any female perpetrators who may seek assistance (Hines & Douglas, 2009) or any other possible reasons for relationship aggression such as substance abuse, mental illness, social learning and so on.

Often, domestically violent individuals can only obtain services through court referrals, and women are less likely to be referred or mandated to domestic violence treatment. For example, in 2002, the California Department of Justice noted that, while women make up 16% of IPV arrests in Contra Costa County (a suburb of San Francisco), they only make up 4% of offenders mandated to IPV treatment in that area (Hamel, 2005). Further, if a woman enrols in a treatment programme without being mandated, she may not follow through. Several studies have demonstrated that women who are not mandated to IPV treatment have drop-out rates as high as 55% (Carney & Buttell, 2004; Dowd, Leisring, & Rosenbaum,

2005). Why the high drop-out rate? A 2005 study by Loy, Machen, Beaulieu and Greif gives some ideas. They discovered that the domestically violent women in treatment were resistant to doing work in a group, tried to control the group and generally were unused to looking at their own behaviours (Loy, Machen, Beaulieu, & Greif, 2005). This may be connected to the findings noted above that people with insecure attachments find self-reflection difficult. It also may be related to the societal construction that women are not violent or aggressive, and so discussing one's IPV in public involved a degree of cognitive dissonance.

If there are services for women available and if a woman can get referred to them and if she sticks with it rather than dropping out, what are her treatment needs in order to stop assaulting her partner? Treatment suggestions include teaching healthy communication, assertiveness, empathy, problem solving, stress management, emotional regulation (Bowen, 2008), parenting and substance abuse treatment (Dowd & Leisring, 2008). Does treatment for domestically violent women work? Because of the near-exclusive focus for many years on male IVP, there is little research on treatment outcomes for domestically violent women. Carney and Buttell, in a tiny study of only 26 women who graduated from a programme for women batterers, found that only one woman was arrested within twelve months post-treatment (Carney & Buttell, 2004). It is hard to generalize from one small study but it does suggest a road to follow in the future for more research.

Conclusion

Coney and Mackey (1997) studied the occurrence of domestic violence imagery in the public press and discovered that articles showing women as recipients and men as perpetrators were published at least ten times more often than the reverse, despite the fact that epidemiological studies show women engage in domestic abuse at very high rates. While there was some politically motivated debate in the past, we have reached the point where we can say there is enough research to show relational violence by women is a social and health problem that must be addressed. Much of the research in the past has focused on incidence but, in the future, we need to address prevention and treatment issues. For example, what can be done to interrupt the progression from conduct problems to antisocial personality in girls? What treatment interventions with domestically violent women work to prevent recidivism? Would longer jail times serve as a warning function for women batterers? At what age can we intervene with girls who have witnessed inter-parental violence in order to prevent them from becoming batterers? Langhinrichsen-Rohling, Turner and McGowan (2007) showed that providing both parenting and partnering skills to adolescent mothers decreased the teens' use of aggression towards both children and adult partners. More research of this type is needed if we hope to make any progress on the problem of intimate partner violence.

6

Rape, Sexual Assault and Molestation by Women

Introduction

The public awareness and acknowledgement of sexually abusive behaviour by women is very new. In the 1970s and 1980s, due to multiple factors, including the growth of the women's movement, western culture began to look at issues involving sexual assault of adult women and of minor children seriously. Literature on topics such as father–daughter incest were published and survivor groups came into being, focusing on male perpetration and female victimization. Laws were passed and policies were written using highly dichotomous language in which rapists were male and victims were female. Researchers began studying male sex offenders, designing treatments to better understand the offenders and therefore prevent recidivism. However, because the definition of sex offenders was gendered, there was little acknowledgement of female sex offenders until relatively recently. Research in this area has been difficult, due in part to the mentality that 'women don't do that' and in part to the stigma against victims of women, making it less likely that they will come forward to tell their stories.

Rape, Sexual Assaults and Coercion: Beyond the Male Perpetrator–Female Victim Paradigm

Traditionally, rape had been viewed as an act of penis–vagina intercourse, which ignored other forms of sexual harm that could be perpetrated by males, including oral or anal penetration or penetration by objects other

Female Aggression, First Edition. Helen Gavin and Theresa Porter.
© 2015 John Wiley & Sons, Ltd. Published 2015 by John Wiley & Sons, Ltd.

than a penis. Once modern society began to acknowledge the existence of these forms of sexual assault, it was also forced to acknowledge that the assaults could be performed by a woman as well as a man. Women can and do sexually assault other women as well as men, utilizing a variety of methods (Sarrel & Masters, 1982). As Bourke, in her landmark history of rape states, 'Female sex offenders serve as a reminder that not only the female body but the male body as well is violable, penetrable' (2008). As a consequence of acknowledging this, many countries have updated their rape laws to be gender neutral (Rumney, 2007).

Besides the physical brutality of sexual assault, women also engage in coercive sexual practices. Struckman-Johnson et al. wrote that sexual coercion is 'the act of using pressure, alcohol or drugs, or force to have sexual contact with someone against his or her will; ... tactics of post-refusal sexual persistence [used are] defined as persistent attempts to have sexual contact with someone who has already refused' (Struckman-Johnson, Struckman-Johnson, & Anderson, 2003, p. 76). In other words, women may threaten, use a date-rape drug, get a victim drunk, use emotional pressure to intimidate and bully someone into having unwanted sex or simply sexually humiliate someone. One of the best examples of the latter is former US army reservist Lynndie England, who was court-martialled in 2005 for the torture and abuse of prisoners of war. Photos released at that time show her smiling while forcing hooded prisoners to masturbate publicly, holding a leash on a naked inmate lying on the floor and standing by a 'pyramid' of naked male prisoners. This case was a visually striking reminder that women in power may abuse that power in a sexual manner.

The Prevalence of Female Sexual Assaults Based on Perpetrator Self-Report

In the 1990s, US researchers began asking women about their sexual aggression histories, with rates from 18%–32% of admitted coercive sexual practices. Straus et al. (1996), for example, using the Revised Conflict Tactics Scale, found that 18% of the women in his study engaged in sexually coercive behaviours. Anderson (1998) asked college age women in the American east and south about their lifetime sexual behaviours and found that 54.2% admitted to sexually coercive behaviours, 28.4% reported behaviours that were sexually abusive and 8.7% reported engaging in forced sexual behaviours. This is not a problem restricted to the United States. In Australia, 6% of the surveyed female medical students admitted a history of engaging in intercourse against a partner's will (McConaghy et al., 1993). In Canada, 14.3% of the young women interviewed admitted to using sexual coercion in heterosexual relationships (Poitras & Levoie, 1995). In Poland, 40% of the college women surveyed had engaged in sexual coercion, with 6% engaging in behaviours that met the Polish legal standard for rape (Doroszewicz & Forbes, 2008).

Victim prevalence reports

When victims are asked about their history of being involved with sexually aggressive or coercive women, the prevalence rate increases compared to the rate given by perpetrators. Multiple studies conducted with college-age males have shown that high numbers of young men experience coercive or aggressive sexual behaviours by their female partners (see Table 6.1.) For example, a multinational study of university students conducted in 2007 found that of more than 2,000 males surveyed, 22% had experienced sexual coercion by a female partner and 2.8% reported having been forced into sex by a female partner (Hines, 2007).

Studies of non-college populations have shown similar results (see Table 6.2).

Two prisons studies found that male inmates, who cannot give consent for sex due to their legal status, reported high rates of sexual activity with female staff in positions of power (Beck & Harrison, 2008; Struckman-

Table 6.1 Studies of college males reporting coercive sexual experiences by women.

Author	Date	% of males reporting victimization
Sigelman et al.	1984	20.9
Aizenman & Kelley	1988	14
Murphy	1988	12
Sandberg et al.	1987	25
Stets & Pirog-Good	1989	22
Lottes &Weinberg	1997	45
Straus et al.	1996	38
Struckman-Johnson	1998	16
Struckman-Johnson	1998	43

Table 6.2   Studies of males reporting coercive sexual experiences by women.

Author	Date	Nationality	% of males reporting victimization
Struckman-Johnson	1991	USA	16
Muehlenhard & Cook	1988	USA	62.7
Lottes & Weinberg	1997	USA & Sweden	22–50
McConaghy & Zamire	1993	New Zealand	30

Johnson & Struckman-Johnson, 1998). A 2012 study by the US Bureau of Justice Statistics found that 42.2% of male former inmates reported experiencing involuntary sex with female staff while they were in prison (Beck & Johnson, 2012).

Women victims also report high rates of sexual victimization by other women, although there has been far less research on this population. Waterman, Dawson and Bologna (1989) found that 31% of the lesbian women surveyed had a history of forced sex by a past female partner. Sloan and Edmonds's 1996 study found that 23% of the lesbian women reported a history of sexual assaults by a past female partner. Other studies of lesbians report a history of sexual victimization by other women as high as 50% (Waldner-Haugrud & Gratch, in Girshick, 2002a). In the above study of the US prison system, 2.8% of the female former inmates reported involuntary sex with female staff while they were in prison and an additional 13.7% reported sexual victimization by other female inmates (Beck & Johnson, 2012). Girschick found that the majority of women who experienced sexual aggression by other women did not go to the police or a sexual assault agency, feeling that both services did not focus on victims of women. This experience was echoed in Gilroy and Carroll's 2009 article, in which victims of woman-to-woman sexual assault were traumatized by so-called 'survivor support' groups that were unable to conceptualize women as perpetrators and therefore left their victims feeling invisible.

Theories Regarding Sexual Assault by Women

If one reviews the available literature regarding the aetiology of sexual aggression in males, one sees multiple theories. According to available research, a man is sexually aggressive because of:

- anger;
- a desire to humiliate his victims;
- feelings of entitlement;
- misogyny (assuming the victim is female);
- need to compensate for feelings of inadequacy.

One of the most promising areas of research in male sexual aggression involves implicit theories. Based on studies of heterosexual male rapists, researchers have found that many hold distorted beliefs about themselves, their victims and the world in general, including ideas that women are unknowable but are also sexual objects, that male sex drive is uncontrollable and that they personally are entitled to sexual satisfaction and fulfilment (Polaschek & Ward, 2002). While this research has focused on male heterosexual rapists, it does give us some clues to understanding sexually aggressive women. What if women also viewed themselves as entitled to sex, with little consideration for a partner's rights? What if women viewed others as sexual objects? What if women viewed male sex drive as, if not uncontrollable, at least readily available and theirs to exploit? What if women have sex and power fantasies that that they live out via sexual aggression (Bourke, 2008)? If a woman were to believe any of these underlying theories of the world and themselves, that woman could be at risk for sexually aggressive behaviour against others. Several studies of sexually coercive women suggest that these implicit beliefs may be operating for some women. Several studies (Clements-Schreiber, Rempel, & Desmarais, 1998; O'Dougherty-Wright, Norton, & Matusek, 2010) found that sexually coercive heterosexual women viewed men as always sexually available and viewed any refusal of sex to be a personal insult rather than a lack of interest on the male's behalf. The implicit theories model is not the only theory of male sexual aggression that appears to apply to women. Sexually aggressive women believe that 'no' can mean 'maybe' (Krahe, Waizenhöfer, & Möller, 2003) and may feel the need to regain power and status through sexual aggression (Hines, 2007; O'Dougherty-Wright et al., 2010), especially after a perceived rejection. Notably, Hines (2007) found that women's higher levels of hostility towards men were associated with higher levels of physical force and verbal coercion against men. In other words, like their male counterparts, some women show their dislike of men through sexual and physical aggression.

Women Who Sexually Offend Against Children

The idea that a woman would sexually assault another adult has been difficult for society to grasp. The concept that a woman would molest a child may be harder to understand, given our dual view that women are the protectors of children and that child molesters are men. This recognition barrier assists female sex offenders (FSOs) to minimize apprehension by others as well as to deceive herself that her actions are not abusive since they don't match the stereotypes she sees in media portrayals of male sex offenders (MSOs). However, the research concerning FSOs has been growing over time and demonstrates that child sexual abuse by women is a widespread problem.

Prevalence

As in the case of women who sexually assault adults, the prevalence rate of women child molesters varies, depending upon the data one reviews. Official arrest rates for FSOs tend to be low for a number of reasons, including the victims' fear of reporting the abuse. In 1994, Finkelhor estimated that 10% of sexual abuse is carried out by women. A decade later, Boroughs (2004) estimated that 25% of all child sexual abuse was carried out by women. It also appears that, rather than committing a single act of molestation against a single victim, FSOs are likely to have multiple victims. Several studies have indicated that women child molesters averaged three to four victims each (Faller, 1995; Wiegel, 2009).

Deering and Mellor (2010) found that different populations report different victimization prevalence, with university studies reporting up to 16% and children receiving medical or psychiatric treatment reporting up to 28%. Victim rates also depend upon how the questions are phrased. Males appear more comfortable responding to questions such as 'Have you ever had sex with a woman who was at least 20 years old when you were less than 13 years old?', rather than responding to a question such as 'Were you ever sexually molested by a woman?' (Frieden, 2003). When the stigma is removed from the question, male victims appear more able to disclose their abuse.

Similarities and differences compared with male sex offenders (MSOs)

In many ways, child molesters appear very similar, regardless of gender. Both MSOs and FSOs have limited empathy for their victims, deny causing harm and feel guiltless (Grier, Clark, & Stoner, 1993; Johannson-Love & Fremouw, 2009). Both genders use grooming to prepare their victims and use their authority to exploit children within their care (Moulden, Firestone & Wexler, 2007). Male and female child molesters may use force (Hendriks & Bijleveld, 2006) and their abuse is equally severe (Rudin, Zalewski, & Bodmer-Turner, 1995). Like MSOs, FSOs have distinct pathways to offending, some being more explicit and others more disorganized and impulsive (Gannon, Rose & Ward, 2010). As with their male counterparts, FSOs tend to hold distorted ideas that increase their risk, including the idea that children initiate sexual activities with adults. Both populations tend to use deviant sex and deviant sexual fantasies as stress-coping mechanisms (Elliott & Ashfield, 2011). There are important differences, however. FSOs may be less likely to admit their guilt than their male counterparts (Allen, 1991). FSOs are more likely to use a foreign object to perpetrate the sexual abuse of a child (Kaufman, Wallace, Johnson, & Reeder, 1995), are less likely to have an arrest record and are more likely to commit incest or offend against a relative (Elliott, Eldridge, Ashfield, & Beech, 2010; Kalders, Inkster, & Britt, 1997).

There are two other areas in which MSOs and FSOs appear to differ. One is in their use of a partner or co-offender. For many MSOs, child molesting appears to be a solitary event, but for many FSOs it appears to be a shared or social experience (Vandiver, 2006). Numerous early studies of FSOs noted that women tended to co-offend with others, particularly men, leading to the misinterpretation that women *only* molest when coerced by a male partner. Later research has demonstrated the existence of solo FSOs, as well as showing that co-offending women may partner with another woman, a man or even a group of people (Muskens, Bogaerts, van Casteren, & Labrijn, 2011; Wijkman, Bijleveld, & Hendriks, 2011). Co-offending does not in itself imply that the FSO was coerced rather than initiating the sexual offending (Nathan & Ward, 2002). For example, a study of female sex offenders in Holland found that 45% of the perpetrators were not dating or romantically involved with their co-offenders; the co-offender was collaborator, not a lover whose abandonment the woman was trying to forestall. These were child-molesting teams (Wijkman et al., 2011). Simons, Heil, Burton and Gursky (2008) reviewed FSOs' responses to polygraph and found that the women in this study not only admitted to more offences than had been officially recorded, but also were more likely to admit to solo offending despite previous claims of having been coerced.

Women are more likely to co-offend rather than solo-offend for non-sexual crimes as well, suggesting that co-offending is a normative form of offending for women (van Mastrigt & Farrington, 2009). Solo FSOs and co-offending FSOs do appear to have some important differences. Solo-offending women appear to target male victims and non-relatives, while co-offending women are more likely to target relatives of both genders (Muskens et al., 2011; Vandiver, 2006).

The other important area of difference between MSOs and FSOs is that of motivational schemas. These are the underlying beliefs we have about the world, and these beliefs influence our behaviours. When researchers first began to look at the differences in the underlying beliefs of MSOs and FSOs, they found that both genders saw the world as largely dangerous and uncontrollable and both groups saw children as sex objects who were not harmed by the sexual abuse by adults. Where men and women appeared to differ was in the area of entitlement. An early study suggested that men felt entitled to have their sexual needs met by children, but women did not appear to believe this. However, a later study found an interesting corollary to the entitlement belief. Women sex offenders who have male co-offenders viewed their partners as entitled to sexual fulfilment via a child (Beech, Parrett, Ward, & Fisher, 2009; Elliot et al., 2010), therefore the women accommodated the partner's entitlement at the cost of the children's safety in order to maintain that relationship. In other words, while the MSOs felt entitled to sex with children, FSOs felt entitled to use children to maintain a relationship with a male partner.

Typologies

To date, multiple typologies of FSOs have been formulated, many based on small sample sizes:

Sarrel and Masters (1982):

- Forced assault
- Babysitter
- Incestuous
- Dominant woman abuser

McCarty (1986):

- Independent
- Co-offender
- Accomplice

Faller (1987):

- Poly-incestuous
- Single parent
- Psychotic
- Adolescent
- Non-custodial

Matthews, Matthews and Speltz (1991):

- Teacher/lover
- Intergenerationally predisposed
- Male coerced
- Caregiver-babysitter
- Incestuous
- Experimenter/exploiter
- Psychologically disturbed

Mayer (1992):

- Rapist harasser
- Mother/molester
- Homosexual
- Team member

Vandiver and Kercher (2004):

- Heterosexual nurturer
- Non-criminal homosexual
- Female sexual predator
- Young-adult child exploiter
- Homosexual criminal
- Aggressive homosexual offender

Sandler and Freeman (2007):

- Criminally limited hebephiles
- Criminally prone hebephiles

- Young adult child molesters
- High-risk chronic offenders
- Older non-habitual offenders
- Homosexual child molesters

Warren and Hislop (2001):

- Facilitators
- Reluctant partners
- Initiating female partner
- Seducers/lovers
- Paedophiles
- Psychotic

At this point, none of the available typologies appear to be significantly useful in designing treatment or prevention strategies (Gannon & Rose, 2008), and they seem to position the responsibility for offending behaviour outside of the woman. The current typologies also don't assist in our understanding the wide heterogeneity in FSOs. For example, there are significant differences in the motivations and action of Mary Kay Letourneau (who molested a 14-year-old male student, eventually becoming pregnant by him and later marrying him), Carol Clarke (who spent 20 years molesting children in public toilets) and Melissa Huckaby (who kidnapped an eight-year-old girl, raped her with a kitchen utensil and then murdered her). A more functional way to look at FSOs may be to differentiate between those who offend against prepubescent victims and those who offend against postpubescent victims, whether the FSO is a solo offender, a partner-coerced offender or a team offender.

The incestuous mother or female relative is a subpopulation of FSOs whose existence is important to highlight. It is notable that Freud hardly mentioned Jocasta, the mother who married her son, instead focusing on Oedipus to develop the concept of Oedipal conflict. The issue of father–daughter incest came into public discourse more than twenty years ago, but we are still reluctant to focus attention on the issue of mother–child incest (Banning, 1989), despite clear indications that this form of incest is at least as damaging as that done by men (Marvesti, 1986; Peter, 2008). For example, Kelly, Wood, Gonzalez, MacDonald, & Waterman (2002) found that males who were sexually abused by their mothers reported more trauma symptoms than men who had experienced other forms of sexual violence. The survivors of mother–daughter incest reported to Krug (1989) that they used self-destructive coping behaviours such as self-mutilation and substance abuse. This avoidance of the issue of mother–child incest may in part be due to our tendency to view women and mothers as powerless, forgetting that mothers are in a position of power over dependent children (Peter, 2006). It may also be related to the widespread view of the maternal figure as asexual (Kramer, 2010).

Several studies have found up to 45% of reported child molestation is incest by a mother (Boroughs, 2004; NSPCC, 2009). Some researchers have found that incest is more likely to be perpetrated by women raising children in a single-parent home (Finkelhor, Hotaling, Lewis, & Smith, 1990; Solomon, 1992). This becomes particularly important when we realize that, in the United States., approximately 27% of children are raised in such homes (US Department of Commerce 1997). Rather than incestuous single parenthood being an accident of circumstances (i.e., developing an incestuous relationship with a young son, coincidental to the lack of an adult male partner), it may be that some women prefer the position of power over young, dependent males and choose this family type by design. Gannon and Rose found that some female child molesters misinterpret ambiguous stimuli about men as threatening and view men as dangerous and powerful (2009). While one might expect these beliefs to occur in a woman who is coerced into molestation by a powerful male partner, Gannon and Rose found that these beliefs tend to occur more often in women who molest alone, suggesting that these women prefer young, non-threatening boys rather than potentially 'dangerous' adult men.

Deviant arousal and mental illness

A review of the early literature on FSOs leaves one with the belief that these women have no sexual interest in children, as the issue of deviant sexual arousal is largely missing from those studies. Sexual deviancy appeared to be viewed as a problem occurring only in males, despite evidence that the full range of paraphilias, including autoerotic asphyxiation, bestiality, voyeurism and exhibitionism, occur in women (Behrendt, Buhl, & Seidl, 2002; Byard, Hucker, & Hazelwood, 1993; Cooper, Swaminath, Baxter, & Poulin, 1990; Federoff, Fishell, & Fedoroff, 1999). Some women find children sexually desirable; a study of young adult women who had histories of sexually molesting children found that these women reported sexual interest in the children, rather than engaging in the behaviour for non-sexual reasons (Fromuth & Conn, 1997). An analysis of postings on an internet website devoted to female paedophilia found that the users showed clear sexual interest in children and viewed that desire as acceptable (Lambert & O'Halloran, 2008). Similarly, a review of more than a thousand women evaluated for problem sexual behaviour found that not only did women who molested prepubescent children show deviant sexual interests in that age group, but so did many of the women who molested postpubescent teens (Wiegel, 2009).

Much of the early research on FSOs explored the behaviour from the perspective of mental illness. However, this model has not demonstrated strong evidence. For example, a Swedish study compared all known Swedish FSOs with other Swedish women violent offenders, as well as with Swedish women in general. This study found that there was no significant difference in psychosis or substance-abuse rates between the two groups of women offenders (Fazel, Sjöstedt, Grann, & Långström, 2010), indicating that the FSOs were not motivated by a psychotic illness any more than were non-sexual offenders. Further, some studies that looked at the occurrence of mental illness in FSOs had methodological problems that made their findings of limited use. Many of the early studies on FSOs were specifically focused on mentally ill sex offenders rather than sex offenders generally, possibly due to our preference to view FSOs as mentally ill instead of sexually deviant. If studies on FSOs obtain their subjects from psychiatric facilities, it isn't a surprise that they found high rates of mental illness. Further, many of the early studies utilized self-report of mental illness, which means that a percentage of the subjects may have been over-reporting symptoms in an attempt to garner sympathy or minimize their responsibility for their actions (Rousseau & Cortoni, 2010).

Past victimization

Another area that has been closely reviewed for its role in female child molesting is past victimization. Multiple surveys have shown that many women who engage in child sexual assault have a history of being victimized. However, women's self-reported rate of victimization is relatively high in general and the majority of women who were physically or sexually abused do not go on to become perpetrators. At this point, a history of past victimization does not provide useful causal information on female sex-offending behaviour. However, one area of promising research on FSOs and victimization involves feelings of power and powerlessness. A small study comparing female-abuse survivors with women who had not abuse history in terms of their feelings of powerlessness and the related compensatory need for power. Those women with victimization histories had higher power needs than women who lacked a history of victimization (Liem, O'Toole, & James, 1992). This drive to feel powerful may play an important role in women's molesting behaviour; women who have this need may sexually exploit their position as a powerful authority figure over dependent children.

Child Pornography and the Internet

Finkelhor et al.'s research on online victimization of children estimated that one third of all online solicitations for sex from minors are perpetrated by women (2000). As noted above, there are internet websites that cater to paedophilic women rather than paedophilic men. These sites validate FSOs' deviant interests and their distorted views of children as sexual objects (Lambert & O'Halloran, 2008). FSOs who use the internet to find victims may have social deficits which make the impersonal online world seem appealing and safe or they may find the anonymity of the internet to be disinhibiting (Elliot & Ashfield, 2011). Further, as most child pornography is produced by the victim's own family (Sheehan & Sullivan, 2010), and as children are more likely to be raised by women than men in our society, it is likely that far more FSOs are involved in making and distributing child pornography than previously thought (Kernsmith & Kernsmith, 2009b). Some women may produce it for their own deviant interests while others may trade it as a way of maintaining a relationship with peers who have similar interests (Elliot & Ashfield, 2011). As with contact offending, an FSO may view a male partner to be entitled to sexual images of her children and feel herself equally entitled to produce and distribute those images in order to maintain the illusion of a relationship with him.

One of the most infamous cases of internet child pornography is the 2009 case in Plymouth, England. Vanessa George, Angela Allen and Colin Blanchard were all involved in producing child pornography and then exchanging the images with each other. Some of the child victims were enrolled in the nursery/day-care centre where Vanessa George worked. It appears that none of the three perpetrators ever met in person and all inter-actions were via social media on the internet. Part of the computer mes-sages recovered for the case included discussions of abducting a child (de Bruxelles, 2009). This case highlights two factors salient to FSOs: deviant sexual interest in minors and sex offending as a social rather than a solitary behaviour.

Victim Effects

The women who use the paedophilia websites mentioned above view their behaviour as less damaging to children than similar offending by males, reit-erating the stereotype of women as gentle, nurturing and less dangerous than males. They do not see themselves as harming children but instead view sexual activity with minors as an acceptable form of showing 'love' or affection. However, victims of FSOs report long-term negative effects of the sexual abuse, including suicidal ideation, depression and relationship problems (Fromuth & Burkhart, 1989; Ray, 1996; Roys & Timms, 1995). For some victims, the abuse causes traumatic sexualization with either aversion to or overvaluing of sex and a tendency to confuse sex with nur-turing (Saradjian, 2010).

Further, there appears to be a correlation for some males between being victimized by a woman and future perpetration of sex crimes. According to Glasser et al.'s study (2001), sexual victimization by a female perpetrator is more likely to contribute to the male victim later becoming an abuser than does similar victimization by a male perpetrator. Similarly, Salter et al.'s (2003) longitudinal study of male victims found that sexual abuse by a woman was a risk factor for future sex offending by male victims. A retro-spective study by Briggs and Hawkins (1996) found that sexual abuse by women was 'common' among males convicted of sex crimes but not among non-criminal males. Other studies (Belanger 2007; Burgess, Hartman, & McCormack, 1987; Petrovich & Templer, 1984) have also shown a high rate of sexual victimization by women in the histories of men who are convicted of later sex crimes. For example, Groth and Burgess reported a signifi-cant discrepancy between the official crime statistics of female-perpetrated sexual crimes and the experiences reported by male subjects who had a history of committing their own sexual crimes (Groth & Burgess, 1979).

Condy, Templer, Brown and Veaco (1987) noted that the male inmates in their study reported more childhood sexual abuse by women than did male college students, including intercourse. In 2010, a Bureau of Justice special report found that the majority of the sexual abuse of youths in juvenile facilities was perpetrated by women (Bureau of Justice Statistics, 2010) While these studies are all correlational rather than causational, they suggest that there may be a special stigma for victims of FSOs that may increase the more general detrimental effects of the abuse. To be sexually abused by a woman in a society that denies the existence of FSOs or minimizes the effects of the abuse can cause shame, guilt, powerlessness and related func-tioning problems (Saradjian, 2010) and those emotions may be among the multiple factors involved in sexual offending behaviours by males.

Awareness, Gender Bias and the Social Construction of Women

Despite the growing body of research on the topic of FSOs, society seems to resist recognizing the problem. This may be due to the widespread view that women lack responsibility for their behaviours, including their sexual behaviour. Mental health professionals and child advocacy groups appear to be particularly slow to comprehend the risk posed by some women. In 1998, researchers surveyed child protection agencies regarding their views on FSOs versus MSOs, and discovered that FSOs were viewed as gentler and less serious an issue than MSOs (Hetherton & Beardsall, 1998). Similarly, Bunting found that most child protection staff lack training on this issue and have an institutionalized assumption that abuse is male-initiated (2005). Since then, a number of other studies have found similar dismissive attitudes not only among child protection professionals but also among law enforce-ment and mental health professionals.

Awareness may not be any better in the mental health field. Several studies have indicated that mental health professionals viewed sexual molestation by women as benign (Denov, 2001; Kramer & Bowman, 2011; Mellor & Deering, 2010) and so the professionals were less likely to make appropriate referrals when the perpetrator was female. These findings fit with the reported experiences of victims of sexual abuse by women, who indicate that their disclosures were often met with minimization and disbelief by pro-fessionals who should have been validating and supportive (Denov, 2003).

The general public also lacks awareness of the seriousness of child moles-tation by women. When asked to read vignettes about alleged child sexual abuse by either men or women, the general public sees male-perpetrated abuse as more problematic than female-perpetrated abuse (Fanetti, Kobayashi, & Mitchell, 2008; Fromuth & Holt, 2008). In a world where sex offenders are presumed to be male, how can a teenage boy feel safe to report molestation by an older woman? He may rightly fear being charged with rape himself, be told that he somehow caused the abuse because he responded to it (Saradjian, 2010).

Legal Issues

Lack of awareness and gender bias regarding child sexual abuse also shows itself in the legal arena. For example, in 2006, an American judge made national news when, as an explanation for giving a FSO probation rather than prison time, he stated 'I really don't see the harm that was done here …' (Kupelian, 2006).

Criminal justice professionals in Europe and Australia perceive female child molesters differently than male child molesters and that perceived difference influences the type of action taken against the perpetrator (Gakhal & Brown, 2011; Higgins & Ireland, 2009; Kite & Tyson, 2004). If law enforcement personnel do not view child molestation by women as harmful, then they are less likely to arrest the perpetrator or refer the victim to a child protection agency, who in turn may not view the problem as serious. Women who commit incest or who molest young children, per-haps because they are viewed as benign, are less likely than MSOs to be referred to the criminal justice system and more likely than MSOs to end up in the child protection system instead (Bader, Scalora, Casady, & Black, 2008). Possibly the best example of bias against viewing women as sexual offenders is the case of Karla Homolka. Homolka and her husband were accused of kidnapping, raping and murdering schoolgirls in Canada, including Homolka's younger sister. Homolka asked for immunity in exchange for testifying against her husband and was granted a plea bargain as the Crown's case against her husband depended heavily on her testi-mony. She was only charged with two counts of manslaughter but no sexual charges, while her husband was charged with two counts each of kidnapping, aggravated sexual assault and first-degree murder, as well as one of dismemberment. After this plea bargain agreement was made, video evidence came to light showing Homolka raping the female victims. The evidence was clear that she and her partner were a rape/murder team, rather than her being another victim. The Canadian criminal justice system was humiliated for having made a 'deal with the devil', which was the result of their presumption that a woman would not voluntarily engage in sex-offending behaviours.

This lack of awareness of FSOs and gender bias is also seen in juror decision-making in sexual abuse cases; male perpetrators are viewed as more responsible and more culpable for their acts than female perpetrators, and the effects of child sexual abuse is viewed as more severe when committed by a male (Duke & Desforges, 2007; Pozzulo, Dempsey, Maeder, & Allen, 2010; Quas, Bottoms, Haegerich, & Nysse-Carris, 2002). The bias in favour of FSOs becomes even stronger when the victim is a boy. In those cases, rather than viewing sexual molestation as a violation, the male child is viewed as somehow benefiting from sex with an adult female, either as 'instruction' or by having 'bragging rights' among his peers (Howell, Egan, Giuliano, & Ackley, 2011). Since judges and juries minimize the damage done by FSOs, it is no surprise that these women serve less prison time than their male counterparts (Deering & Mellor, 2009). For example, a comparison of MSOs and FSOs in New York State from 1986 to 2005 showed FSOs had a significantly reduced likelihood of incarceration compared to male perpetrators (Sandler & Freeman, 2011). Deering and Mellor suggest this is due to a form of paternalism termed 'chivalric justice'; the criminal justice system would rather view women as sexually non-responsible or non-dangerous (2009). Chivalric justice may explain why there are only 140 women in custody or under community supervision in Britain for sexual molestation of children, despite estimates that 20 per cent of British paedophiles are women (Townsend & Syal, 2009).

Assessment, Treatment and Recidivism

The field of assessment and treatment of FSOs is in its infancy. If one wishes to assess an MSO in order to predict his risk for future offending, there are multiple tools available, utilizing either actuarial or dynamic measures. These include the Sex Offender Need Assessment Rating (SONAR), the

Sexual Violence Risk-20 (SVR20), the Risk for Sexual Violence Protocol (RSVP), the Screening Scale for Paedophilic Interests (SSPI), the Sex Offender Risk Appraisal Guide (SORAG), the Risk Matrix 2000 (RM2000), the Minnesota Sex Offender Screening Tool-Revised (MnSOST–R) and the Static 99R and Static 2002R. These instruments, however, are not currently validated for use on FSOs, although tools for assessing FSOs are currently under development. Many factors that demonstrate increased risk of recidivism in males, such as youth or past criminal records, do not necessarily apply to FSOs, who appear more likely to offend at a later age than males and are less likely to have criminal records (Sandler & Freeman, 2009). To date, it remains unclear why women offend at an older age than do males; this may be an artefact of the age of arrest and future research may show that women are offending at a younger age but are not apprehended as young as males.

MSOs' deviant interests in children can be assessed using penile plethysmography or phallometry, which involves the use of a strain gauge to measure tumescence in response to stimuli depicting children. The instrument is relatively able to distinguish between men with sexual paedophilic interests and men without paedophilic interests. This appears to be due to men having categorical sexual arousal; men who are heterosexual tend to be aroused by heterosexual stimuli and not to be aroused by homosexual stimuli and vice versa. Women, however, appear to have more dimensional or indiscriminate arousal patterns with little category specificity. Several studies with women using a vaginal photoplethysmograph to measure arousal via vasoengorgement have shown that women will demonstrate arousal to stimuli outside their avowed category of interests; heterosexual women demonstrate arousal to lesbian stimuli and vice versa. Rather than being aroused by stimuli within a specific category, women demonstrated arousal or not based on the intensity of the sexual stimuli used, regardless of the category (Chivers, Rieger, Latty, & Bailey, 2004; Chivers & Bailey, 2005; Chivers, Seto, & Blanchard, 2007). This means that plethysmography cannot be utilized to assess paedophilic sexual interests in women.

One instrument that does appear to hold promise as a tool for use with FSOs is a measure of visual reaction time. With this tool, an offender views 160 slides of adults and children of different ages and genders (all clothed), moving from one slide to the next by pressing a computer key. She also rates her arousal to each image on a seven-point scale. The computer measures the viewing time for each image, with longer viewing time indicating more interest and less viewing time indicating less interest. Visual reaction time has been shown to be a measurement of sexual preference for women (Brown, 1979; Israel & Strassberg, 2009; Quinsey, Ketsetzis, Earls, & Karamanoukian, 1996; Wright & Adams, 1994), although, as with the studies of plethysmography, intensity or explicitness was also an important factor for women. Abel and Wiegel (2009) assessed 81 women who admitted to sexually abusing at least one child and 94 women who admitted to molesting at least one adolescent as part of a larger sample of more than 400 women who were evaluated for problematic sexual behaviour (i.e., exhibitionism, etc.) and found that the women who had molested children had significantly longer viewing reaction times than the other women in the study, suggesting that this tool may be of use in assessing women for paedophilic interests

Besides utilizing a visual reaction time tool, FSOs should also be assessed regarding what are termed dynamic needs. These include assessing for deviant sexual interests and denial or minimizing of the offence, which the women may do for legal reasons or because of their distorted thinking about sexuality and children. If one views children as valid sexual objects, then molestation will be viewed as benign. The FSOs should also be assessed for their emotional identification with children. Statements regarding past victims, such as 'He may have been 14 years old but he was very mature', suggests that the woman herself is markedly immature and therefore viewed the victim as similar to herself. Intimate relationship styles and dependency issues should be evaluated, especially in women who co-offend; if a woman views her male partner as entitled to have sex with her children, she remains at higher risk. Unhealthy coping styles and use of sex as a coping mechanism should be assessed along with antisocial, sadistic or psychopathic traits as some women molest with goals such as revenge or humiliation of the victim (Gannon, Rose, & Ward, 2008) rather than just sexual fulfilment.

Research on MSO recidivism has been very useful in designing actuarial measures to discriminate between those more likely to reoffend and those less likely to. As noted above, to date there are no such validated measures for use on FSOs. Just assessing recidivism rates for FSOs has proved difficult. Female non-sexual offenders have a lower recidivism rate than male non-sexual offenders, and when a base rate is very low, its predictive value is decreased. Further, studies on FSO recidivism have relatively small sample sizes compared to similar research with males and use rates for observed recidivists, those women who were officially re-arrested. It is possible that, due to issues such as the gender bias discussed above, women who sexually reoffend are not formally charged and therefore not included in the rates of observed recidivism. For example, Bader, Welsh and Scalora (2010) found that, while 17.5% of the 57 FSOs in their sample were formally charged with subsequent sex crimes, a total of 28% actually were involved in further sexually inappropriate behaviours but were diverted to social services and not formally charged. In comparison, Cortoni's (2010) meta-analysis of 10 studies with nearly 2,500 offenders found an observed sexual recidivism rate of less than 3%. This meta-analysis has the strength of a larger sample but only used formal re-arrests and may have missed women who reoffended but were diverted to non-criminal justice services despite their reoffending. Another problem measuring the recidivism rate of FSOs involves classification. A study of nearly 1,500 females convicted of sex crimes in New York State included women convicted of child pornography. An observed recidivism rate would therefore include both contact and non-contact offenders and is of decreased utility in predicting recidivism correlates for contact offenders. Relatedly, Vess (2011) notes that recidivism data for prediction of future offending is used in civil commitment cases to justify detaining high-risk offenders but may be difficult to apply to high-risk FSOs. To date, only five US women have been civilly committed under community protection laws, compared to more than 4,500 males (Vess, 2011). For example, after she completed 11 years of incarceration for sex offending, Charlotte Mae Thrailkill became the first woman in California to be labelled a sexually violent predator (SVP) after the 1996 SVP law was enacted. Thrailkill initially claimed to have been coerced but later admitted to solo offending against five children.

To date, treatment and management of FSOs has been haphazard. Not every country has a system dedicated to assessing and treating FSOs. England, for example, following several infamous FSO cases, began planning to accredit treatment programmes for their FSOs. This was a significant change after previous claims by the British Ministry of Justice that FSOs are rare and better treated individually (Smith, 2010).

Initially, treatment for FSOs seems to have been formatted in one of two ways; either gender-focused, which tended to minimize the offending behaviour, or gender-blind, which seemed to assume that MSOs and FSOs had identical needs and issues. More recently, the treatment has become more gender-informed and based upon empirical data. One area that has been valuable for this is using the risk/needs/responsivity principle, which originated in research on general offenders. Treatment of FSOs should focus on each offender's specific risk of reoffending and the factors involved. For example, women with antisocial traits have a different risk from those with dependent traits. Treatment should also focus on the individualized needs of each offender, such as coping-skill development or substance-abuse relapse prevention. Finally, treatment should be tailored for each offender's ability and motivation, with intellectually disabled offenders receiving treatment at their level of understanding (Poels, 2007). Treatment for FSOs should target issues around sexual deviancy and coping deficits (Cortoni, 2010). The treatment must focus on distorted beliefs involving children (i.e., children are sexual objects), sexuality (i.e., sex as the sole coping skill), and their crime (i.e., no harm was done). Because many FSOs engage in child physical abuse as well as sexual abuse, parenting classes and anger management skills should also be included in the treatment (Grayston & De Luca, 1999). Victimization histories, while not a cause of perpetration in female offenders, should be reviewed with FSOs in order to teach coping skills.

A Brief Note on Juvenile Female Sex Offenders

If the research into adult FSOs is in its early stages, then that of sex-offending adolescent girls is in its infancy. Based on current research, rates of sexually coercive and sexually violent behaviour by teenage girls range from 0.8% in a Scandinavian study to 12% in a 10-year British study (Chadwick & Top, 1993; Kjellgren, Priebe, Svedin, Mossige, & Långström, 2011; McCartan, Law, Murphy, & Bailey, 2011; Schmidt, 2008). Like the early research on adult FSOs, much of the research to date has compared juvenile FSOs to their male counterparts. For example, juvenile FSOs are more likely than juvenile MSOs to abuse victims they know, including incest of siblings (Slotboom, Hendriks, & Verbruggen, 2011), are less likely to be formally processed by law enforcement and are more likely to have a co-offender including triads and large groups (Vandiver, 2010). Juvenile FSOs are also more likely to have more than one victim and to have younger victims than their male counterparts (Hunter, Lexier, Goodwin, & Dennis, 1993; Vandiver, 2010). Juvenile FSOs often gain victim access through babysitting (Fehrenbach & Monastersky, 1988; Schmidt & Pierce, 2004), a position of relative power in the world of children. Compared to their delinquent female peers who don't engage in sex offences, teen FSOs are less likely to abuse drugs and alcohol (Kubik, Hecker, & Righthand, 2003). Like adult FSOs, these juvenile FSOs use violence, engage in forced penetration (Schmidt, 2008; Vandiver, 2010) and hold distorted beliefs around their offending (Kubik & Hecker, 2005). They are also motivated by deviant sexual interests. For example, Hunter et al. (1993) found that the juvenile FSOs in their study reported having fantasized about the offending prior to acting it out.

Conclusion

Current research data clearly indicate that women are engaging in sexual crimes against both adults and children at a significant rate, despite some cultural resistance to recognizing the problem. As western society becomes more educated on this topic, attitudes may change. However, it is also possible that the prevailing gendered construction of the topic may simply mutate to one that maintains the status quo by incorporating the existence of FSOs into its collective psyche without making alterations to existing gender stereotypes, leaving the view that FSOs are guilty of both the crime against their victim and a crime against their gender. The FSOs will then become the ultimate Other, something that MSOs do not experience. Somehow MSOs are more masculine by virtue of their offence, are almost caricatures of the male stereotype of aggression and sexual drive. FSOs are seen as less feminine because they have co-opted the male prerogative of sex and aggression. This can make it even harder for FSOs to face their behaviours and begin to make changes because admission of guilt would mean loss of identity as a woman. We seem to be mired in a view that men have irresistible sexual urges and women have equally irresistible maternal drives. Such a view is not only erroneous, but it is dangerous, especially when we turn to the question of women who kill. The next few chapters will explore these issues in detail.

7

Filicide by Women

Introduction

Media reports of the killing of unwanted children often focus on countries such as China or India, where the killing of unwanted infant girls is allegedly common. What is not often discussed is the killing of unwanted newborns, infants or children by women in western countries. The killing of infants and children is one of the most common types of murder that women commit. In the late twentieth and early twenty-first centuries, while rates of death due to childhood illnesses have decreased, there has been an increase in the rate of murder of children (Finkelhor, 1997) and the main murderers of children are women. This gender difference in filicide is rarely discussed however, possibly due to western society's difficulty in viewing women/mothers as murderers. The discourse on child killing by women is muted, due to our tendency to dichotomize the ideas of motherhood and violence (Alder & Baker, 1997). Instead of recognizing filicide as a public health issue, we continue to view it as a rare tragedy without examining our unrealistic beliefs regarding the nature of maternity and motherhood (Montaldo, 2011). Women can and do become mothers without having a superseding interest in parenting a child.

Female Aggression, First Edition. Helen Gavin and Theresa Porter.
© 2015 John Wiley & Sons, Ltd. Published 2015 by John Wiley & Sons, Ltd.

Neonaticide

Neonaticide is the murder of a newborn within the first 24 hours of life. Children are at most risk of being murdered by a woman during the first 24 hours of life and the most common perpetrator of neonaticide is the mother of the victim. The term 'neonaticide' was coined by Resnick in 1970, to distinguish the murder of a newborn under 24 hours old from the murder of an older infant. His review of neonaticides from 1751 to 1968 was one of the first of its kind and showed the difference between women who kill newborns and those who kill older infants (Resnick, 1970). Numerous other studies (Beyer et al., 2008; Brookman & Nolan, 2001; d'Orbán, 1979; Haapasalo & Petaja, 1999; Mendlowicz et al., 1998; Shelton, Muirhead, & Canning, 2010; Silverman & Kennedy, 1988; Spinelli, 2003; Taguchi, 2007) have substantiated Resnick's findings that, unlike women who kill older infants and toddlers, the majority of women who murder newborns are:

- relatively young, often under age 25;
- unmarried and often no longer involved with the baby's father;
- unemployed and possibly still in school;
- living with their parents or other relatives.

The main motivation for most of the neonaticidal mothers appears to be to remove the responsibility of caring for an unwanted child. Despite this, in the majority of the cases, the woman made no attempt to terminate the pregnancy at an early stage (Resnick, 1970). In a small number of cases, the woman had assistance in either committing the neonaticide or covering it up (Beyer et al., 2008; Shelton et al., 2010). The majority of neonaticides occur in the perpetrator's home, as the majority of the perpetrators of infanticide do not go to a hospital as they begin labour. From 1989 to 1991, 71 per cent of all homicides on the first day of life involved infants born at a place of residence (Overpeck, Brenner, Trumble, Trifiletti, & Berendes 1998; Paulozzi and Sells, 2002). There have, however, been recorded episodes of neonaticides at maternity wards (Mendlowicz et al., 2000, cited in Friedman, Resnick, & Rosenthal, 2009). The majority of the victims' bodies are discovered within 24 hours of the crime.

It is very difficult to accurately ascertain the rates of neonaticide as this is the type of child murder most easily hidden (Meyer & Oberman, 2001) and all rates are expected to be underestimates. Only known victims with both a birth and death certificate can be counted in government statistics. This means that any death without an officially recognized birth may not be counted and infants whose birth was hidden would not have a birth certificate.

A review of records in the US state of North Carolina from 1985 to 2000 showed a neonaticide rate of 2.1 cases annually (Herman-Giddens, Smith, Mittal, Carlson, & Butts, 2003). D'Orban estimates that 45 per cent of all child murders in the United States are neonaticides, while Meyer and Oberman estimate that between 150 and 300 cases of neonaticide occur annually in the United States (2001). McKee found that, in 1999 in Texas, more than fifty infants were abandoned in skips (2006). Internationally, the rates are equally difficult to ascertain. Girla (2005) found 11 cases of neonaticide in Moldova between 1996 and 2004. In Finland, from 1980 to 2000, there were 44 suspected cases of neonaticide (Putkonen, Collander, Weizmann-Henelius, & Eronen, 2007). In the Austrian province of Tyrol, which averages 7,000 births annually, between 1996 and 2004 there were four neonaticide cases (Danner, Pacher, Ambach, & Brezinka, 2005).

Neonaticides do not appear to be well planned in advance. The perpetrators are immature women who avoid thinking about or dealing with their situation in a mindful way. The weapons used in neonaticide reflect this, often involving a weapon of opportunity, such as drowning in a toilet, strangling with clothing or suffocating in a rubbish bag (Adshead, Brooke, Samuels, Jenner, & Southall, 2000; Bennett et al., 2006; Herman-Giddens et al., 2003; Mulryan, Gibbons, & O'Conner, 2002), although starving, defenestration and gross assault are also used (Dalley, 2000 [1997]; Rougé-Maillart, Jousset, Gaudin, Bouju, & Penneau, 2005; Stanton, Simpson, & Wouldes, 2000).

Pregnancy Concealment, Denial and Negation

A common legal defence by women who are accused of neonaticide is that they were ignorant of the fact of their pregnancy. The theory is that the perpetrator did not know she was pregnant and therefore was unprepared for and confused by the birthing process. However, research suggests that, while possible, it is unlikely. In Beyer, Mack and Shelton's (2008) study of neonaticides in 16 US states, nearly half of the perpetrators had been pregnant previously, which gave the women a past reference for the experience of pregnancy. In Shelton et al.'s study, more than 25 per cent of the women who committed neonaticide had previously given birth (2010). Carrying a pregnancy from gestation to birth over nine months involves multiple physiological changes, such as foetal movements, amenorrhea and weight gain, experiences which are not likely to be forgotten to a degree that a woman would not be aware of a second pregnancy for the full nine months and during the birthing process itself.

A series of three studies by Wessel and colleagues gives the best information on the possibility of being unaware of a pregnancy for an entire gestation period, up to and including labour. They looked at nearly 30,000 pregnancies and found that only 62 of the women did not realize they were pregnant until the fifth month. They estimated that one in 2,400 women could theoretically reach labour without having known she was pregnant, indicating that this was an extremely rare event (Wessel & Buscher, 2002; Wessel, Endrika, & Buscher, 2002; Wessel, Gauruder-Burmester, & Gerlinger 2007).

Being unaware of one's pregnancy is different from denying the fact of one's pregnancy to oneself. One can consciously choose to deny the existence of a medical fact, such as 'No, I don't really have cancer'. This is not in itself a sign of mental illness (Meyer & Oberman, 2001). Dulit (2000) found that there are several types of denial thought processes, including 'I hope this isn't really true', 'I know it's true but I need to make sure no one else knows' and 'I won't think about this now'. Denial of one's pregnant status is an active event as one must first admit the possibility of the fact, then refuse to focus on it or allow an emotional connection to the foetus, as well as avoiding engagement in behaviours that would highlight the pregnancy such as wearing clothing that would show one's distended womb (Drescher-Burke, Krall, & Penick, 2004; Lee, Li, Kwong and So, 2006; Miller, 1990). In other words, the refusal to acknowledge the pregnancy implies that one was aware of the pregnancy and then actively worked against thinking about it (Beier, Wille, & Wessel, 2006; Kohm and Liverman, 2002; Spinelli, 2001). When reviewing forensic and non-forensic pregnancy concealment/denial cases, Beier et al. (2006) found the cases were identical and they use the term 'pregnancy negation' to categorize women who choose to avoid contemplating their pregnant status.

There are perpetrators of neonaticide who claim to have dissociated during and immediately after labour, leaving them without memory of the murder and therefore without any culpability for their actions (Spinelli, 2001). Dissociation is not an event that can be measured objectively, however, and is easily malingered (Mendlowicz, Rappaport, Fontenelle, Jean-Louis, & De Moraes, 2002; Resnick & Hatters-Friedman, 2003). Further, neonaticidal women in the past did not claim dissociation; this is a relatively new phenomena. A review of records from 1900 to 1995 by Mendlowicz et al. (2002) showed that claims of 'amnesia' or dissociation during neonaticide only became common after 1940, although if it were a common event one would expect documentation of it dating further back.

While some women consciously deny their pregnancy to themselves, others simply conceal the pregnancy from those around them. In a study of 81 women who went without prenatal care and presented for medical care at labour or immediately following, the women were divided between 'Concealers' and 'Deniers'. The majority of the 'Concealers' had been aware of the pregnancy for at least 1 month and a substantial percentage of the 'Deniers' admitted the same (Friedman, Heneghan, & Rosenthal, 2007). As Resnick and others have noted, the majority of women who commit neonaticide are emotionally immature and do not wish to have their lives altered by parenthood, suggesting a strong motivation for consciously denying the pregnancy to themselves.

Ultimately, the issue of pregnancy awareness during gestation and labour is moot. What matters is the woman's reaction upon being presented with a newborn, regardless of her understanding of the context. If one were to come upon an unconscious person lying in the street, the expected reaction would be to try to provide assistance or to get help. If the person is dead, the expected behaviour is to contact the authorities, not to hide the body or throw it in the rubbish. If a woman gives birth and is confused as to how this event has occurred as she did not know she was pregnant, the expected behaviour is to obtain care for the newborn and, if she mistakenly believes the baby is stillborn, the expected behaviour still involves seeking help, not hiding the newborn's body.

Several sites in the European Union and the United States have implemented baby drops or safe havens, which would allow a mother of a newborn to safely leave the child without questions. The hope is that mothers of unwanted newborns would rather not kill them and would prefer to give them up, yet wish to do so secretly. While this would seem logical, the effects remain unclear to date. One of the problems is that the type of women who are most likely to engage in neonaticide may not be the type to utilize a safe haven. As noted above, most women who commit neonaticide are young, immature and view the pregnancy as an unwanted responsibility. When finally faced with a live birth, are these young women likely to engage in active problem-solving when, for the last nine months, they have shoved the pregnancy and all it symbolizes out of their minds? Further, in order to use a safe haven or baby drop, one must view the newborn as needing and deserving of care, rather than as an unwanted objected for disposal. It is not clear that most neonaticidal women view their victims as deserving of care.

Infanticide

Infanticide is the murder of an infant older than 24 hours and younger than one year. As with neonaticide, infanticides are generally motivated by the desire to remove an unwanted child. Compared to women who commit neonaticide, women who commit infanticide are slightly older (Drescher-Burke, Krall, & Penick, 2004). They are usually over 25 years old and often married, but, like neonaticidal women, did not engage in prenatal care and give birth outside hospital (Kauppi, Kumpulainen, Vanamo, Merikanto, & Karkola, 2008). As with neonaticides, infanticides by women tend to involve smothering, strangling, suffocation or drowning, although other methods such as blunt-force trauma and stabbing, are also used (Fujiwara, Barber, Schaechter, & Hemenway, 2009; Gillenwater, Quan, & Feldman, 1996; Porter & Gavin, 2010). The motivation for infanticide is generally the same as that in cases of neonaticide – a lack of desire to engage in parenthood, although revenge against others is also sometimes reported (Mugavin, 2008).

In the United States, homicide is the fifteenth leading cause of death during the first year of life, with the highest risk during the first four months (Paulozzi & Sells, 2002). In the United States, infanticide rates rose in the 1980s (Cummings, Theis, Mueller, & Rivara, 1994), with approximately 8.5 infants per 100,000 murdered annually by a parent (Overpeck et al., 1998). In Washington DC, specifically, the annual rate of infant homicide is 21.9 per 100,000 infants (Large, Nielssen, Lackersteen, & Smith, 2010). Infants most at risk are those who are the second child of a mother under the age of 19 years who had no prenatal care (Overpeck et al., 1998). As with neonaticides, infanticide is most commonly committed by women (Kohm & Liverman, 2002; Kunz & Bahr, 1996; Paulozzi & Sells, 2002).

Infanticide occurs internationally. Large et al. (2010) investigated the rate of infanticide in 48 countries in addition to the United States and found the annual rate varied considerably. Italy, Greece, Spain, Ireland and Denmark have rates of fewer than one infanticide per 100,000 population annually. The annual rate of infanticide was 1.8 per 100,000 population in the United Kingdom, 2.3 in France, 2.9 in Germany, 3.7 in Poland and Japan, 4.7 in New Zealand, 4.9 in Australia, 5.5 in the Russian Federation, 5.7 in Mexico and 8.7 in Hungary, with these rates assumed to be underestimations. Marks and Kumar (1993) found that the infanticide rate was 4.3 for the United Kingdom but Brookman and Nolan (2006) found it was 6.3. In the United Kingdom, infants are four times more likely to be murdered than any other age group (Marks & Kumar, 1993).

Infanticide rates may be underestimated for a variety of reasons. As with neonaticides, infant bodies are easily concealed and so infanticides may go unreported and unsuspected. Further, only victims with both a birth and death certificate are counted in official statistics. Overpeck et al. (1998) used linked birth and death certificates for a nine-year period and found that birth certificates were missing for reported deaths for more than 2 per cent of all deaths during that time period, with deceased infants less than one month old most likely to be missing birth certificates.

Jason, Carpenter and Tyler (1983) found that the rates of infant homicide in the United States have been under-reported since the late 1960s, due to classification changes to the standardized US death certificate. There were similar changes made to the International Classification of Diseases (ICD) which allowed for deaths to be categorized as 'undetermined'. Jason et al. noted that, since these changes to the classification systems, there has been a decrease in reported infant homicides, which may be due to officials avoiding labelling an infant death as a homicide when given the opportunity to use 'undetermined' instead.

Sudden Infant Death Syndrome and Infanticide

Another reason the statistics on infanticide are underestimated is due to false attribution of death to sudden infant death syndrome (SIDS). Estimates are that up to 10 per cent of all alleged SIDS cases are in fact homicides (Levene & Bacon, 2004). Part of the confusion stems from poor early research on SIDS that resulted in overestimations of the risk of recurrence within families (Bacon, Hall, Stephenson, & Campbell, 2008). While it was once thought that SIDS occurred in family clusters, there is little evidence of this and researchers now suggest that more than one unexplained infant death in one family suggests either an inherited condition or homicide (Craft & Hall, 2004). Cases that once were viewed as family tragedies are now more likely to be investigated and reviews of older alleged SIDS cases sometimes are re-investigated, resulting in homicide charges. For example, a German woman whose three infant daughters died in nine years, allegedly from SIDS, later confessed to murder (Bohnert, Grosse Perdekamp, & Pollak, 2003). A study of 300 SIDS cases from 1998 to 2001 found 12 cases of homicide (Bajanowski et al., 2005). A British study that used covert video recordings of parents–child interactions in the hospital, initially designed to detect child abuse, inadvertently uncovered several homicides as well. Of the 33 cases where a parent was covertly seen abusing the child in the hospital, one third involved families where a child had supposedly died of SIDS. Upon investigation, four parents confessed to eight of the eleven children's murders and to alleging the deaths were due to SIDS (Southall et al., 1997).

Stanton and Simpson (2001) interviewed a woman convicted of three murders (two of which were initially misdiagnosed as SIDS), as well as two attempted murders of children she was babysitting. Her descriptions of the murders focus on her own needs and comforts, her resentment of the children whom she did not want. She realized that, having one murder misdiagnosed as SIDS, she could utilize the same methods with the later deaths.

Child Homicide by Women

There are more motives for child homicide than generally seen in either neonaticide or infanticide. While all three involve the removal of an undesired child, child homicide cases may also involve issues such as revenge against the child's father or frustration due to caring for a handicapped child (Bötje, Schlöfke, Nedopil, & Hossler, 2011). As with infanticide and neonaticide, child homicide is a crime by parents, most often by mothers who are older than 25 years (Kauppi, Kumpulainen, Karkola, Vanamo, & Merikanto, 2010; Putkonen et al., 2009). Despite myths of 'stranger danger', child homicide by a stranger is not as common as child homicide by a family member or guardian (Crittenden & Craig, 1990).

Unlike neonaticide, child homicide rates are more easily attained. The National Violent Death Reporting System in the United States noted that the homicide rate for children in 2004 was 2.5 per 100,000 (Bennett et al., 2006), while, in Finland, the filicide rate is 5.09 per 100,000 (Kauppi et al., 2010). In the United States, homicide is the fourth leading cause of death in children between the ages of 5 and 14 years, and the second leading cause of death of those between 14 and 18 years (National Center for Health Statistics, 2007), with one out of 23 child deaths in the United States due to homicide (Finkelhor & Ormrod, 2001). Hodgkins and Dube found an annual average rate of 11.7 Canadian children murdered by their parents (1995). A Canadian review of child homicides found that mothers and stepmothers kill more children than do fathers or stepfathers (Dalley, 2000). In some countries, such as the United States and Japan, the annual filicide rate appears to be increasing (Finkelhor & Ormrod, 2001; Yasumi & Kageyama, 2009).

The most common methods of murdering a young child include suffocation, blunt-force trauma, fire and poisoning (Rogde, Hougen, & Poulsen, 2001; Shepherd & Ferslew, 2009). Older children, who can resist, are more likely to be shot or stabbed to death than are younger children (Dalley, 2000; Schmidt, Graff, & Madea, 1996; Toro, Feher, Farkas, & Dunay, 2010).Women who murder children older than one year tend to be older than neonaticidal or infanticidal women, no longer dependent on their parents and many cases involve a degree of premeditation.

Stepchildren may be especially at risk of being killed by a stepmother. In one study, children under the age of five years are approximately three times more likely to be murdered by a stepmother than by a biological mother (Weekes-Shackelford & Shackelford, 2004). Evolutionary psychological theories suggest that parents only invest time and energy in their own biological offspring and attempt to remove any competitors to their children, including stepchildren (Daly & Wilson, 1988). A review of data from 1976 to 1994 indicated that, in per annum homicide rates per million, the stepmothers' homicide rate was 20.6 deaths, compared with the 8.6 rate of biological mothers, with significantly more deaths due to blunt-force trauma by the stepmothers compared to biological mothers (Weekes-Shackelford, & Shackelford, 2004). The difference in homicide methods used by genetic parents versus step-parents may be related to the animosity or resentment the step-parent holds for the stepchild (Daly & Wilson, 1994). Several other forms of murder are quicker and less painful than death by blunt-force trauma so to choose that method speaks to the desire to cause more suffering in the victim.

Messing and Heeren (2004) examined the murders of 69 children by 26 women between 1993 and 2000 in order to ascertain the motivation behind the murders and found many of the murders were precipitated by the woman's perceived loss of status, such as during divorce or loss of custody (or shared custody). In other child homicides, the motivation was similar to that in infanticide and neonaticide, the desire for more autonomy than parenthood would allow. The authors observed that, while the motivations for most child murders by mothers could be divided into the two situations noted above, other issues, such as social inequality against women, poverty and stress, were often voiced as causal during the trial of these women. However, those problems are also common in the lives of mothers and stepmothers who do not commit child homicide. Most parents report child care to be demanding yet most parents do not abuse or murder a child. Clearly, poverty, stress and patriarchy do not fully explain child homicide by women when the majority of women do not engage in the behaviour (Diem & Pizarro, 2010).

So why resort to violence to manage a stressful personal situation when other options were not explored? In what they term as the matriarchal corollary to patriarchal ideology, Messing and Heeren observe that the women who commit child homicide 'believe that they had some unassailable propriety rights to their children's lives'. In other words, since she endured pregnancy and labour, she owns the child and may treat or dispose of the unwanted child as she wishes.

Language, Filicide and Objectification

We utilize language to communicate many things, including how we view others and how we view our own actions. Filicidal women show a marked tendency to use language in a way which distances them from blame and deflects agency. For example, a woman who killed an infant may say 'when my baby died', although the accurate statement would be 'when I killed my baby' (Stanton et al., 2000). Filicidal women, especially neonaticidal women, attempt to distance themselves not simply from the murders but also from their victims. One woman who was convicted of murdering three children repeatedly used the term 'it' when she spoke of one of the children, further distancing herself from the humanity of her victim (Stanton & Simpson, 2001). The way filicidal women dispose of their victims also shows attempts to distance themselves from their victims. As one study of abandoned newborn corpses noted, the majority of neonaticide victims were not clothed at the time of their disposal, which suggests that they are viewed as objects rather than people (Gheorghe, Banner, Hansen, Stolborg, & Lynnerup, 2011). Corpses are clothed in western society as a sign of the respect due the person who died. If one doesn't view a newborn as a person with its own rights, if one views the infant as an object, then one doesn't view the act as murder and there is no need to dress the child's corpse after the murder (Crimmins et al., 1997).

Filicidal mothers are not the only ones who use language to gain distance from such murders. Similar language patterns can be seen in some literature about women who kill their children. For example, an article may solely use the words 'mother' without ever using the word 'murderer' and the word 'victim' without ever using the word 'infant'. This emphasizes that a woman who murders her child continues to be conceptualized as a mother first, and a murderer second (Porter & Gavin, 2010), despite the more normal pairing of murderer/victim and infant/mother. Other writers use words in substitution of the term 'murder', as in 'she lost her children' (Stanton & Simpson, 2001), again showing a tendency to separate the concepts of mothers and murder.

Finally, this distancing via language is also seen in the way a woman is charged after she kills a child. Charges such as 'concealing a body', 'disposing of a body' and 'abuse of a corpse' all remove personhood from the deceased child, rendering the child an 'object' that was mishandled rather than a person who was harmed.

Gender and Filicide

There appears to be a significant gender difference in infanticide victim selection between eastern and western societies. Eastern societies such as India and China have a higher female infanticide rate (Porter & Gavin, 2010) but at least ten studies show a higher male infanticide rate in industrialized western countries (Beyer, Mack, & Shelton, 2008; Brookman & Nolan, 2006; Crimmins et al., 1997; Kunz & Bahr, 1996; Loomis, 1986; Marks & Kumar, 1993, 1996; Overpeck et al., 1998; Rougé-Maillart,

Jousset, Gaudin, Bouju, & Penneau, 2005; Schmidt, Grass, & Madea, 1996; Vanamo, Kauppi, Karkola, Merkanto, & Rasanen, 2001) . There are several theories for this, including the theory that males have a higher murder rate generally (Lester, 1991). However, this theory does not seem to apply to the higher infanticide rate as the majority of murders of adult males are done by other males and not by females (Fox & Zawitz, 2007). Another theory is that the higher male infanticide rate is an artefact, due to the higher male infant live birth rate (Marleau, Dube, & Leveillee, 2004). The problem with this theory is that there are only 1–2 per cent more males born than females, yet many of the large-scale studies show that 5–6 per cent more male infants are murdered than female infants (Porter & Gavin, 2010). It may be that the male infant is viewed as symbolizing other males in the woman's life towards whom she harbours animosity. It may be that the male infant is unwanted simply due to his gender, as appears to be the case with female infants in some eastern countries.

Typologies

Since the 1970s, multiple classifications have been devised to explain women who kill infants and children (Bourget & Gagné, 2005; d'Orban, 1979; Guileyardo, Prahlow, & Barnard, 1999; McKee, 2006; Resnick, 1970; Scott, 1973; Stanton et al., 2000), with most of the typologies including some version of the following categories:

- mentally ill mother
- mercy or altruistic killing (often described as using 'non-violent' methods)
- non-intentional killing due to blunt-force trauma
- killing of unwanted infant or child
- killing of children as retaliation against a third party
- neonaticide (killing of unwanted newborn)

One of the problems with these typologies involve the subjectivity of the language used, as some of the typologies list smothering or drowning as 'non-violent' methods of murder, a questionable assertion at best (Stanton et al., 2000). The idea of 'altruism' in filicide is also questionable, and may be related more to our view of mothers as nurturing rather than to any objective indication that a child was killed to end overwhelming suffering (Porter & Gavin 2010). Finally, many infanticidal cases do not seem to fit a single type, making the current typologies less applicable.

Mental Illness and Filicide

A small but notable subset of filicides are perpetrated by women who have a severe mental illness that impairs their functioning to such an extreme degree that the women are unable to be aware of the wrongfulness of their actions (Logan in Dalley, 2000; Friedman, Resnick, & Rosenthal, 2009). Compared to other types of child murders, filicides secondary to mental illness are rare and are associated with the death of older children rather than neonaticide (Dobson & Sales, 2000; d'Orbán, 1979; Resnick, 1970), with older mothers and with wanted rather than unwanted children (Holden, Burland, & Lemmen, 1996). Neonaticides rarely involve severely mentally ill mothers.

There appears to be a great degree of confusion regarding the true effects of gestation and labour on the mind of a new mother, including the degree to which there are significant hormonal changes. This confusion may in part be due to western media misrepresenting the postpartum or postnatal state as a time of dangerous hormonal changes and by misusing terms such as postpartum depression when describing psychosis or mania. In reality, there are no definitive studies that show that hormone changes following labour cause severe and persistent mood changes in women (Porter & Gavin, 2010). The research on postnatal hormone changes does not show that these changes have a significant impact on the woman's mental health. Repeated studies of serum hormone levels have not shown that these hormone changes account for clinical levels of mood disturbances in women (Harris, 1994; Wisner & Stowe, 1997). A 2003 study attempted to prevent postpartum relapse of psychiatric symptoms in women with histories of mania or psychosis by giving the women various doses of oestrogen (Kumar et al., 2003); none of the oestrogen treatments reduced the rate of relapse for these women, strongly indicating that there were other mechanisms involved rather than maternal hormones.

While the terms 'postpartum depression', the 'baby blues' and 'postpartum psychosis' seem to merged in media reviews, the terms describe very different phenomenon. Psychosis following childbirth is extremely rare, occurring at a rate of less than one per thousand births (Dobson & Sales, 2000). Women who experience a psychotic episode will usually need to be hospitalized in order to stabilize the symptoms, which include auditory hallucinations and bizarre, often religious delusions (Friedman, Hrouda, Holden, Noffsinger & Resnick, 2005). Psychosis following childbirth will generally occur within two weeks to two months and are not due to childbirth or hormonal changes (Agrawal, Bhatia, & Malik, 1997; Sit, Rothschild, & Wisner, 2006).

Rather than being the result of hormonal changes or childbirth, the women who have a psychotic episode in the first 90 days postpartum are women who had an underlying predisposition to psychosis, mania or bipolar disorder (Hay, 2009). Many of the women who have a psychotic or manic episode during the postnatal phase have a history of prior psychiatric treatments, including hospitalization (Friedman et al., 2005). For example, a large-scale study in Great Britain reviewed over 54,000 births, following all psychiatric admissions by new mothers during the first 90 days postpartum. They found a postpartum psychosis rate of less than 1 per cent, and the women most at risk were those with a history of mania (Kendell, Chalmers & Platz, 1987).

A 2001 study investigated women who came from families with significant histories of bipolar disorder. Women who had a first-degree relative with a history of postpartum psychosis had a significantly higher risk of having a postpartum psychotic episode themselves, but those women who did not come from families with a history of bipolar disorder have a lower risk of having a postpartum psychotic episode (Jones & Craddock, 2001). Other studies have found similar connections between a familial predisposition towards bipolar disorder and episodes of postpartum psychosis (Reich & Winokur, 1970; Whalley, Roberts, Wentzel, & Wright, 1982).

Several long-term studies have followed women with histories of postpartum psychosis and these show that the majority of the women go on to have further episodes, regardless of future childbirth (Robling, Paykel, Dunn, Abbott, & Katona, 2000). For example, a Danish study followed 50 women with episodes of postpartum psychosis for between 7 and 14 years and found that 60 per cent of the women had later episodes of psychosis and 40 per cent remained partially disabled due to mental illness, showing that cases of exclusive postpartum psychotic episodes are rare (Videbech & Gouliaev, 1995). These studies indicate that psychosis during the postpartum period is not a distinct form of mental illness (Tschinkel, Harris, Le Noury, & Healy, 2007). Rather, rapid onset of psychosis during the postpartum period appears to be due to an underlying familial predisposition towards mania and is likely to reoccur regardless of further childbearing (Porter & Gavin, 2010).

Filicides secondary to psychosis are significantly different from other types of filicides. Because the illness itself is rare, this type of filicide is infrequent (Friedman et al., 2005). A study compared filicides by psychotic and non-psychotic women and found that psychotic filicidal women tended to be older, more likely to have been married and to have killed wanted children in response to auditory hallucinations and/or paranoid delusions. The psychotic filicidal women were more likely to have a history of previous psychiatric hospitalizations and suicide attempts and to have killed multiple victims during the same incident. The psychotic filicidal women were also more likely to confess to the murders immediately without attempts to hide the victims' bodies (Lewis & Bunce, 2003).

Postpartum depression, while not as rare as postpartum psychosis, remains an uncommon illness. Clinical depression during the postnatal period affects between 7 per cent and 19 per cent of mothers and generally lasts up to a few months (Campbell & Cohn, 1991; Kumar & Robson, 1984).

Depression during the postnatal period does not appear to be a different form of depression than that which occurs in women (and men) generally (Dobson & Sales, 2000; Purely & Frank, 1996). Multiple large-scale comparisons of women ante- and postnatal and women in the general population did not show a significant difference in the rate of depression (Cooper, Campbell, Day, Kennerly & Bond, 1988; Troutman & Cutrona, 1990). The postpartum period therefore is not a time of increased risk of depression. Comparisons of childbearing and non-childbearing women found that depression in both groups was predicted by personal vulnerabilities (e.g., poor coping skills) and life stressors, rather than by childbirth (Cox, Murray, & Chapman, 1993; O'Hara, Schlechte, Lewis, & Varner, 1991; Troutman & Cutrona, 1990). Life stressors related to depression following childbirth may include ambivalence about parenthood or marital problems (Kumar & Robson, 1984). However, these stressors are not specific to women. A large-scale study in the United Kingdom found that new fathers also reported depression in the first year following a child's birth, with problems such as decreased sleep and increased responsibilities cited as stressors (Parker-Pope, 2010).

While psychosis or depression are neither common nor specific to the postnatal period, the 'baby blues' appear to be both. This period of tearfulness and irritability begins a few days after childbirth and ends within two weeks, affecting between 25 per cent and 85 per cent of new mothers (Dobson & Sales, 2000). It is not considered severe enough to be related to any form of filicide.

It should be noted that the majority of filicides do not involve a woman experiencing psychosis (Friedman et al., 2009; Silverman & Kennedy, 1988). Neonaticides occur within the first 24 hours of an infant's life but research indicates that psychosis following childbirth doesn't usually begin for one to two weeks, thereby making it unlikely that a newborn will be killed by a psychotic new mother. Further, most infanticides are done to rid the woman of an unwanted infant, whereas the victims of psychotic women were generally described as wanted. Rather than being mentally ill, filicidal women may be angry, impulsive or vengeful. McKee et al. found that women who murdered their children had similar personalities to women who murdered adults (McKee, Shea, Mogy, & Holden, 2001).

Serial Infanticide

If the idea of killing an infant is difficult to comprehend, then the idea of killing several infants over many years is unfathomable to many people. How could a woman repeatedly become pregnant, conceal the pregnancies and murder the newborns, often keeping the remains?

While serial infanticide is rare, it does occur. To date, there are at least nine known cases:

- Véronique Courjault, a French woman who has two living children, was found guilty of suffocating three infants after remains of two of the babies were found in the family freezer (Schpoliansky & Childs, 2009).
- Etta Alderen was found guilty of drowning four infants. Alderen's mother found one of the infant's remains in a plastic bag in the home where Alderen lived in Holland (Crumley, 2010).
- American Michele Kalina pleaded guilty to killing four infants and is thought to have murdered a fifth as well, keeping some of the skeletons in containers in a closet but disposing of at least one in a landfill. She had raised two children and given another up for adoption (Dale, 2010).

- Australian Kathleen Folbigg was found guilty of the death of four infants, ages ranging from 19 days to 19 months, over a period of nine years. Although the defence claimed the infants all died of SIDS, Folbigg reportedly documented the deaths in a diary (Glendinning, 2003).
- American Wanetta Hoyt was convicted of suffocating all five of her infant children, although she had initially claimed their deaths were all due to SIDS (Busch, 1997).
- Celine Lesage, a French woman who had a 14-year-old son, pleaded guilty to murdering six newborns over six years by strangulation or asphyxiation. She kept the remains in plastic bags in her basement (Allen, 2010).
- German Sabine Hilschenz was convicted of the death of eight newborns; the statute of limitations had expired for the ninth death. She kept the corpses in flowerpots and in a fish tank in her garden (BBC News, 2006).
- American Marie Noe was convicted of murdering eight of her ten infants when they were aged two weeks to 14 months. The children were initially thought to have died of SIDS (Fried, 1998; Laker, 2010).
- Frenchwoman Dominique Cottrezz raised two daughters but also killed eight newborns, hiding some of their bodies in her garden and others in a fuel storage tank in her garage (Allen, 2010).

Other cases exist where the murderer is known but has not become as infamous as the above. For example, Stanton and Simpson interviewed a woman who murdered three infants and attempted to murder two more (2001). American Shirley Winters pleaded guilty to the deaths of two infant sons but is thought to have killed two other children and three children of her friends during her career as a serial arsonist (Des Rosier, 2008). In 2003, a Polish woman named Jolenta K. admitted to killing her five newborns. The remains were found in a large plastic barrel by the woman's eight- and 12-year-old daughters (News 24, 2003). In 2010 alone, a Dutch woman listed only as Anita C. was investigated after the bodies of three infants were found in her garden (Dutch News, 2011), a second Dutch woman, Sietske H. was arrested after the police found the remains of four infants in suitcases in her attic (Global Post, 2011), and American Katie Stockton was arrested for murder after the remains of two infants were found in the boot of her car; her DNA also implicates her in the death of a third infant whose body was found in 2004 (Curry, 2009). There are cases that remain unsolved as well, including the case in Kiel, Germany, where infant corpses with matching DNA were found in the rubbish in 2006 and 2007. The mother remains unknown (Boyes, 2007).

The killing of several children simultaneously is not unknown. Some cases involve psychosis, such as the case of Andrea Yates, an American mother who drowned her five children while psychotic (Gardner, 2011a), but many others involve revenge during custody battles, where the mother seeks to prevent the father from 'winning the prize' by killing all the children involved. For example, Canadian Elaine Campione videotaped herself drowning her three- and nine-year-old daughters and then filmed herself telling the girls' father that she had done so in order to prevent him from having custody of 'her' children (Lodge, 2010). Similar cases include Americans Sandi Nieves, Susan Eubanks and Theresa Riggi, who all killed their children as revenge against the children's fathers (BBC, 2011; Liu, 2000; Lou, 2008). As disturbing as those cases are, they are quite different from recidivism, which involves the repetition of pregnancy, concealment, hidden childbirth, neonaticide or infanticide and, in many cases, long-term maintenance of the remains within easy access.

The serial nature of the neonaticides above begs the question whether they fit the criteria for serial killing. Serial killing typically involves two or more murders divided by an interim period (Egger, 1984). The above women all had at least one year between each of the infanticides. The keeping of the naked neonatal remains appears similar to the trophies kept by many serial killers (Herman, 2010). Serial killers are known to keep mementoes from their victims as a symbolic connection to the murder that can be viewed again and again as a way of experiencing the same feelings as those during the murder (see chapter 9). Did these women look at the flower boxes or freezers holding their victims remains and reminisce about the killing? What other reasons are there for murdering an infant and not disposing of the remains in a way that would prevent future discovery? Did the murders give the women a feeling of power over the victim, as happens in many serial killings, knowing they had the power to create and destroy life? Did these women feel powerful when they hid their pregnancies from their oblivious families? Did the women fantasize about killing the infants, as many serial killers report fantasizing about murder? In two separate studies, non-mentally ill mothers admitted to thinking about harming their children (Jennings, Ross, Popper, & Elmore, 1999; Levitzky & Cooper, 2000). For example, Levitzky and Cooper (2000) found that 70 per cent of the mothers in their study reported explicit fantasies of aggression towards their children.

If 'normal' mothers fantasize about harming their children, we must assume that the mothers who commit serial infanticide do so to a more severe extent. To date, however, we have more questions than answers in this area.

Legalities

In western law, the killing of an adult allows for multiple forms of prosecution and defence, each with its own degree of culpability: murder, self-defence, manslaughter, not guilty by reason of insanity. Only new mothers, however, have the option of claiming infanticide as a defence.

The Infanticide Act of 1938 is used in the United Kingdom, with similar laws in Sweden, Denmark, Brazil, Ireland, Australia, New Zealand and Canada. These laws have several factors in common:

- the defence can only be utilized by female defendants;
- time after childbirth is viewed as 'disturbing' to a woman's mental capacity;
- childbirth and/or lactation is blamed for this disturbance;
- there is a time limitation (generally up to a year following childbirth).

There are multiple problems with infanticide laws. The most obvious problem is the lack of scientific or medical data to substantiate the idea that a woman's mind is 'disturbed' due to childbirth, let alone due to lactation. As noted previously, the small subset of women who become psychotic during the postpartum period are women who have an underlying illness that is not caused by childbirth. Further, the postpartum period lasts approximately six weeks, not 12 months. For those few women who experience a psychotic episode during the postnatal period, an insanity defence would appear to suffice, rather than requiring a special infanticide defence. In the United States, for example, while the insanity defence is only successful in less than one case per thousand, it is successful in up to 65 per cent of maternal filicide cases where it is used (Stangle, 2008), strongly suggesting that there is no need for a separate form of defence. Finally, while the legal definition for insanity is well conceptualized in modern jurisprudence (generally regarding the ability to know right from wrong and to control one's behaviour), the vague term 'disturbed mind' is left without a concrete or measurable definition (Anand, 2010).

The infanticide defence may not be utilized often even where it does exist, due to the low percentage of infanticide cases ever reaching a court hearing. Several studies have shown that less than 50 per cent of neonaticides or infanticides by women ever involve court dispositions, although 90 per cent of male infanticide cases go to court (Putkonen et al., 2007; Wilczynski, 1997). Relatedly, infanticide cases involving women are more likely to be granted bail and to have treatment dispositions, while those involving men are less likely to be granted bail and more likely to have incarceration dispositions (Porter & Gavin, 2010).

This gendered way of handling infanticide cases may give insight into the reason that infanticide laws exist. The laws are a form of chivalric justice and date from a time when women had limited options for both pregnancy prevention and termination, a time when illegitimacy was stigmatized and children were a form of property (Anand, 2010; McLachlin, 1991). Society was reluctant to hold women accountable for infant deaths, not because the women were viewed as innocent but because they were viewed as having less status. One might expect that, by the twenty-first century, these outdated laws would be discarded as women's status and fertility options have changed. However, as recently as 2011, the Ontario Court of Appeals threw out an attempt to abolish the infanticide defence (Staples, 2006), despite support for the abolishment by the Canadian Children's Rights Council.

In the United States, there has been an attempt to introduce the concept of 'neonaticide syndrome' as a defence in cases where a woman murders her newborn. The theory is that a woman could be in a state of extreme denial while both giving birth then killing her newborn, and therefore should be viewed as not responsible for her action. In the United States, the use of a theoretical construct as a novel defence such as this must meet a standard of scientific admissibility, demonstrating that the construct is generally accepted by a meaningful segment of the associated scientific community and has been empirically tested, peer-reviewed and standardized; in the United States, these are referred to as the Frye Standard and the Daubert Standard. To date, 'neonaticide syndrome' has not passed either standard of admissibility (Bourget, Grace, & Whitehurst, 2006; *People vs Wernick*, 1996), and it is unlikely to. In order to establish its existence as this 'syndrome', one would have to show evidence that most women who commit neonaticide experience the same symptoms, yet international research for 30 years has shown that most neonaticides are perpetrated by non-psychiatrically impaired women who view their newborns as a threat to their current lifestyles (Friedman et al., 2009; Resnick & Hatters-Friedman, 2003). While some have suggested that neonaticidal women 'dissociate' during the murders, this is also an immeasurable construct that is easily malingered by individuals (Porter & Gavin, 2010).

Conclusion

Filicidal women populate western mythology. Consider Medea and Agave in Greek mythology, La Llorona in Mexican folktales, Aoife in Celtic mythology, Mother Kali in Bengali tradition, even Sethe in Morrison's *Beloved*. These stories symbolize our attempts at understanding the hostility, objectification and ownership with which children, especially infants, are treated by some women. While the statement 'I brought you into this world and I can take you out and make another one just like you' is used by most parents as a humorous warning, it also shows the ownership and interchangeability with which children are sometimes regarded.

Myth-making around filicidal women continues to occur, transported to the realm of laws which allow for a special defence based upon antiquated beliefs that lactation, hormones and labour can unhinge a woman's mind. Most women who kill children, especially infants, do so because they do not desire the responsibilities of parenthood and do not view the children as having the rights of an autonomous person. While we have made strides to improve the power and status of women, by comparison children have lower social status, no power and significant physical vulnerability (Lawrence, 2004). Society must address this discrepancy as well as our dichotomized view of women and violence, especially in light of the cases of serial infanticide. Rather than viewing each case of child homicide as an incomprehensible tragedy, we should begin to question the ideas that fertility and parenthood result in altruistic, non-violent behaviour.

8

Homicide and Women

On Monday, 29 January 1979, 17-year-old Brenda Spencer opened fire on the elementary school opposite her San Diego home with a gun her father had given her. She killed two teachers and injured a police officer and eight children. When asked why she did it, she said, 'I don't like Mondays'. The strange response ensured her notoriety, as it inspired a song by the Irish band the Boomtown Rats, making Spencer, or at least her listless excuse for shooting several people, world famous (Butler, 2010). It can be argued that the other element of this case that made it attention grabbing enough for both the world media and the Boomtown Rats is the simple fact that Spencer is female. To the world at large, women who kill and who do not have an abusive husband to blame for their outburst, or postpartum psychosis to explain their baby's death, are a strange and alien group.

What Is Homicide?

Homicide is the term used for the killing of one or more people by the action or omission of another person. Murderers can be spouses, children, parents, strangers or politicians; they can also be male or female. Female killers are not as numerous as their male counterparts; according to the US Bureau of Justice Statistics, men are ten times more likely than women to be murderers, and four times more likely to be murdered. This chapter will examine the forms of homicide recognized in law, the psychological

Female Aggression, First Edition. Helen Gavin and Theresa Porter.
© 2015 John Wiley & Sons, Ltd. Published 2015 by John Wiley & Sons, Ltd.

theories that attempt to explain why they occur and why female murderers are rare and seen as anomalous.

Types of Homicide

Genocide

The 1948 United Nations Convention on the Prevention and Punishment of the Crime of Genocide (CPPCG) defined genocide as crimes:

- committed with intent to destroy national, ethnic, racial or religious groups, including killing members of the group;
- causing serious bodily or mental harm to members of the group;
- deliberately inflicting on the group conditions of life calculated to bring about its physical destruction in whole or in part;
- imposing measures intended to prevent births within the group;
- forcibly transferring children of the group to another group.

These acts distinguish genocide from terrorism, which is not necessarily directed at only one national or ethnic group, but against an agency of the state (Post, 2007). Genocide is also distinguished from ethnic cleansing, although genocidal acts may happen during the forcible removal of an ethnic group (Winton & Unlu, 2008).

Various psychological explanations of genocide are available, but none of them seems able to encompass all of the issues. Waller (2002) demonstrates that identity and self-concept are central to the psychology of genocide. Card (2003) suggests that genocide leads to social death, a loss of identity for the victim group, and this distinguishes genocide from other mass murders, and encompasses the difference in the impact of genocide on men and on women. Prior to the twentieth century, women have not participated in genocide as perpetrators in any significant way but as victims. In addition, women are victimized in different ways to men, particularly in relation to rape and enslavement, and the consequences of this, such as incorporation into the perpetrator's community or ostracism of rape victims, are also almost exclusively female problems. Traditionally, this situation has been explained in terms of the reproductive capacity of women, together with physical weakness and the assumption of sexual property by men. But none of these things is necessarily explained by the action inherent in the treatment of women during genocide; a major element of genocide that is difficult to reconcile is that it is often accompanied by mass rape, the victims of which are then killed. The rape of female members of the victim population is well documented, even in the relatively recent conflicts in Nanking, Rwanda and Bosnia (Dutton, 2007). Theoretical and psychological explanations for single or serial rape do not seem pertinent to the mass rape and killing appearing in genocide incidents. Dutton suggests that this is not rape for sexual needs (although many argue that no rape is), but that it is an example of the extraordinary brutality accompanying genocidal killing, and is another example of behaviours such as torture, killing children in front of their parents and sexual humiliation of the living and the dead. Such behaviour, it is suggested, is similar to that found in the sexual sadism of some serial killers (Marshall & Kennedy, 2003).

Examples of genocide can be found throughout history, and, sadly, in more recent records. During one hundred days in 1994, an estimated 800,000 Tutsi Rwandans were killed by Hutu people, the ethnic group then in power; it is suggested that this was over 75 per cent of the Tutsi population at that time.

Rwanda houses three ethnic groups: the Tutsi, the Hutu and the marginalized Hwa, who are probably the aboriginal group and are classified as a pygmy race. The Tutsi were favoured when the country was colonized by Germany, then Belgium. The Tutsi have a more 'European' (taller, with paler skins) appearance than the other ethnic groups and the colonizers assumed they were the dominant ethnicity. They allowed only the Tutsi to be educated and placed them in government positions. This naturally caused tensions between the groups, and there have been many instances recorded of murderous acts committed by both sides of this ethnic divide. The racial tensions became particularly deadly after the colonists withdrew, culminating in a civil war (1990–4) and the final attempt to eliminate the Tutsi. Accounts record that the killing was not the only aim of the attack on the Tutsi people; the men were to be killed but the women were to be raped before their own deaths. The raping was as important as the killing, with the militia wielding rape and sexual humiliation, and subsequent sexual mutilation of bodies, as weapons (Human Rights Watch, 1999).

Many such atrocities have been reported to the International Criminal Tribunal for Rwanda (ICTR), which was established on 8 November 1994 by the United Nations Security Council. Even though the conflict was a civil war, it merits international concern. Many have been called to answer for their crimes, including three Catholic priests convicted of genocide and crimes against humanity, numerous military commanders and former politicians.

One perpetrator has attracted a huge amount of attention, however, much more than any other. Pauline Nyiramasuhuko was the minister of family and women's development in President Habyarimana's government. After the president's assassination in 1994, Nyiramasuhuko was sent to her home province of Butare to oversee the response to Tutsi resistance. It is alleged that she carried out her agenda mercilessly, inciting her militia to kill all the Tutsi men, to rape and then kill all the women (Sperling, 2005). A particularly horrific plan was to spread the news that the Red Cross had set up a safe haven at a local stadium where Tutsis could find food and security. Thousands of refugees flocked to the stadium, where soldiers quickly surrounded them. The women were removed from the crowd and taken to a forested area to be raped. The men were then massacred with machine guns, grenades and machetes. It is also alleged that Nyiramasuhuko used the possibility of rape as a reward for her soldiers, and that she ordered about seventy women to be burned to death, supplying the gasoline herself. At her trial, according to Sperling (2005), the world's press seemed to be focused on Nyiramasuhuko's gender rather than the crimes charged against her. This fascinated horror is coupled with the realization that Nyiramasuhuko's role, as minister for women and families, was to preserve, educate and empower women. The fact that she ordered and then supervised the rape and murder of thousands of women and their families seems more shocking somehow when she is a tubby, middle-aged woman and mother, rather than a male military commander. On 24 June 2011, Nyiramasuhuko was found guilty of seven charges, including genocide and incitement to rape, and sentenced to life imprisonment. She was 65. She was the first woman to be tried for crimes against humanity by an international criminal tribunal, but sadly not the only one to have faced charges of genocide and using rape as a weapon.

In Cambodia during 1975–9, approximately 1.7 million people (21 per cent of the country's population) were killed (Fawthrop & Jarvis, 2005). The Khmer Rouge regime headed by Pol Pot combined extremist ideology with ethnic animosity. The Khmer Rouge was a radical communist group whose seizure of power after a civil war (1970–5) was followed by a period of instability. The Khmer Rouge's wish to create a classless society meant that they attempted to eliminate all social classes apart from the poor. This sounds like a road to equality, but in fact it meant that people in all other classes, including intellectuals, professionals, and priests, were eliminated. Towns and cities were emptied, with those refusing to leave being killed, and everyone set to work as agricultural slave labourers in a federation of collective farms. So many people died in these forced movements, in the farms and in execution centres around the country, that the areas of Cambodia where they are all buried were dubbed the 'killing fields' (Kiernan, 2009). In July 2007, a mixed UN/Cambodian tribunal in Phnom Penh found evidence of crimes against humanity, genocide, torture and religious persecution. In 2009, the war crimes court charged the former social action minister, Ieng Thirith, with genocide. Ieng Thirith was the sister of Pol Pot's first wife Khieu Ponnary and married to Ieng Sary, the former minister of foreign affairs. Ieng Thirith was the most powerful woman amongst the Khmer Rouge. She had already been charged with crimes against humanity, as the murder of people within the same ethnic group as the perpetrator is not regarded as genocide. She is alleged to have instigated and ordered the commission of crimes against humanity, including directing and enforcing policy and practice characterized by murder, extermination, imprisonment, persecution on political grounds and other inhumane acts, such as forcible transfers of the population, enslavement and forced labour (ECCC, 2010). Ieng looks like a frail little old lady; indeed, she is. She was 76 when she was finally charged by the UN war crimes court. It is easy to forget that the killings took part in the 1970s when the Khmer Rouge was in power, and when Ieng was in her thirties.

Steans (1999) uses examples such as these to suggest that women are as capable as men of committing such atrocities; the small number of such, it is argued, is simply due to lack of opportunity, not capacity. This lack of opportunity is more a reflection of women's status and biological characteristics than their capacity for brutal murder. Women hold physical attributes, such as reproductive capacity and motherhood, and are generally weaker than men. As such, they are at the same time physically vulnerable and valuable. Assumptions of a patriarchal society include the assertions that women are weak and dependent, but this weakness leads to the male appropriation of female bodies and reproductive power. The status of women as male property therefore assumes that they will not behave in any other way than as subjugated, weak and vulnerable. This then extends to the perception of women as unable to behave in any other way.

The examples of Nyiramasuhuko and Ieng simply demonstrate that, given the opportunity, women will behave very much like men, but as Adler, Loyle and Globerman (2007) point out, we know little enough about male-perpetrated genocide and how to prevent it, and it is even more difficult to understand why women actively participate.

Genocide is an atrocity that the world condemns; at some point, it is always exposed to global scrutiny, due to its political and human consequences. The fact that women have been implicated in the widespread murder of their neighbours is simply another addition to the horror. Women will kill or order others to kill for reasons that are the same as men in those positions – the need for political or financial power, the assertion of ethnic superiority or plain, simple hatred. This then demonstrates the inclusion of women in the pantheon of the genocidal. Does it explain their inclusion in the homicidal?

Mass murder

Multiple murders committed on one occasion or very close together, and outside the arena of war or civil conflict, are termed mass murders (Aggrawal, 2005), with different motivation than the genocidal acts described above. Mass murders by individuals are also sometimes referred to as spree killings, although there are distinctions, such as spree killings taking place in different locations, and mass murder in one only. A common element of these events is the final act of suicide by the killer (Knoll, 2010) or the manipulation of the police into killing the perpetrator(s), known colloquially as 'suicide by cop' (Stincelli, 2004) or more technically as officer-assisted suicide or victim-precipitated homicide. This high number of suicides of the mass murderer is the major difficulty with the psychological examination of such occurrences. Knoll (2010) terms this the 'pseudocommando' phenomenon: an individual, or sometimes a pair of killers, acting publicly in daylight, and demonstrating planning and gathering of weaponry. Planning does not extend to escape; the pseudocommando is prepared to die in the execution of these acts. Such people have strong feelings of anger, persecution or mistreatment, and the 'spree' is often therefore an act of revenge.

Mass murderers are overwhelmingly, but not exclusively, male. Female mass murderers tend to be treated as oddities by the media, and hence are remembered by the public. The case of Brenda Spencer, for example, has notable differences when compared to male-perpetrated shootings, as

Spencer did not end her own life and is still in prison. However, some female mass murderers do exhibit the same elements of the pseudocommando, including suicide, but they are more likely to be identified as having had mental health problems prior to the spree than are male killers (Pearson, 1997).

On 30 January 2006, Jennifer San Marco shot and killed seven people, then herself. Six of her victims were employees at the mail-processing plant where she had previously worked, the other was a neighbour. It became clear during the ensuing investigation that San Marco had been subject to several paranoid delusions, and was clearly mentally ill for some time prior to her rampage. In fact, the odd behaviour she exhibited was the reason she was fired from her job at the plant. In retrospect, it is difficult to understand why she was not offered help if she was so clearly mentally ill, but it is a ready explanation for the shootings.

In addition to the likelihood of being regarded as mentally ill, female mass murderers are distinguished from their male counterparts in several ways. The first is their victims. Women kill children, quite often their own, as described in the chapter on infanticide. Other than these cases, victims are often known to the female mass murderer. These can include family members and relatives, friends and neighbours or, quite often, work colleagues. On 12 February 2010, a meeting was taking place in the biology department of the University of Alabama, when neuroscientist Professor Amy Bishop killed three colleagues and wounded three others when she opened fire on them. At 44 years old, Bishop had been denied tenure (a permanent contract); a reportedly arrogant and ambitious woman, this would have been a great blow to Bishop. However, there is speculation that this was only the trigger to her murderous behaviour, as she had killed her brother some years before in what was deemed to be a shooting accident. This verdict of accidental death is now being re-evaluated. This, together with other violent events in Bishop's past, meant that Bishop is being considered as a risk that was never identified. In 1993, for example, Dr Paul Rosenberg, Bishop's then lab supervisor, received a pipe bomb in the mail that, thankfully, failed to detonate. Rosenberg had previously stated that Bishop appeared to be mentally unstable and that co-workers feared she could become violent (BBC, 2010). When investigators tried to interview Bishop, they had to break into her house as she refused them access. They found items that could have been used to make the bomb, but could not establish a link. They did find that Bishop had been writing a novel about a woman who kills her brother. She and her husband were completely cleared of any link to the incident but, after the 2010 shooting, agencies are not quite as confident that she was not involved. She had a fierce temper, as evidenced when she assaulted a woman in 2002 over an argument about a high chair. She was sentenced to six months' probation and ordered to enrol in an anger management course. She never took the class. She moved to a tenure track post in Alabama, and things seemed to be looking up, but reactions to her work were mixed. She did not quite achieve the level of research output expected and, in March 2009, the university denied tenure, effectively terminating her employment. This was obviously stressful to someone of her age, already older than the age that most American academics achieve tenure, and she had a family to support as the main breadwinner. Whatever the cause, stress, mental instability or massive frustration at a system perceived to be unfair, Bishop erupted with fatal consequences.

Roy W. Miller, Bishop's lawyer, has described her as a paranoid schizophrenic, but retracted this later. James Anderson, Bishop's husband, describes her as a brilliant scientist whose work is undervalued, and that other people have taken the credit for it. Others are not as sympathetic, and there have been calls for the death penalty. Whether Amy Bishop is mentally ill or not is still unclear; there was clearly a catalogue of behaviours that was never labelled as such except by those very close to her at work, but which seen in retrospect seems indicative of intermittent explosive disorder. This is a behavioural disorder characterized by extreme expressions of uncontrollable anger disproportionate to the context, and categorized as an Axis I impulse control disorder (DSM V).

Male mass murderers more often than not kill themselves along with others, and this ends their murderous rampage. Although there are cases of the female suicidal mass murderer, such as San Marco, several female spree/mass killers have not ended their lives, Spencer and Bishop amongst them. This alone suggests that these two forms of murder are different, with the distinguishing characteristic being gender, not motive or operation.

Pearson (1997) suggests that, in western civilizations at least, women are viewed as non-aggressive not only because it is easier to envisage men committing violence due to their larger and more muscular build, but because violence is framed in masculine terms. She also speculates that the way that a society defines gender and violence determines how the issue of female aggression is studied. If a culture sees women as providing care not harm, then it is difficult to perceive women as capable of aggressive acts, as these are defined in specific ways that exclude the feminine expression. It is difficult therefore to actually see the aggression carried out by women. However, there is one very public, very violent act that is becoming more prevalent and appears to shock the world when women take part.

Mass murder for ideology

Wafa Idris was a pretty 28-year-old paramedic when she killed herself and an old man, and wounded 150 people in a Jerusalem street in 2002 when she set off a bomb in a backpack (Brunner, 2007). Many assumed that the bomb had gone off accidentally, but examination confirmed that Idris was the first female suicide bomber of the Israeli–Palestinian conflict.

Being prepared to die for a cause is something many find difficult to understand. Hence, it has a profound psychological effect (Patkin, 2004). Such an act is an ancient one, but its use in both physical and psychological warfare is still very effective (Hoffman, 2003). The majority of these 'martyrs' have been male, but the use of women has increased since the first recorded use in modern times in 1985. Women draw less suspicion than men in areas that are subject to military or security personnel scrutiny; in cultures where women are not allowed to disrobe, checkpoints are easier to pass. It is difficult to determine why a woman (or indeed anyone) would turn themselves into a human explosive device, and an examination of demographics does not help. They are young, with an average age of around 22, but some are unmarried, some are widows, some are mothers, some are pregnant. Some have recently experienced a bereavement. All are recruited, in the same way that male suicide bombers are, as a result of levels of innocence, personal distress and a thirst for revenge (Schweitzer, 2003). However, some intelligence agencies suggest that women who become suicide bombers are essentially victims of trafficking into the terrorist organization, who are subsequently drugged or brainwashed into killing themselves in this way or are raped and blackmailed if they do not participate (McDonald, 2003). Others believe the women (and men) are highly motivated, with high levels of patriotism and religious fervour (Zoroya, 2002), with religion offering a justification for murderous and/or suicidal behaviour. For example, devout Muslims believe that martyrs, male and female, are greeted in heaven by a number of *houri-al-ayn* (non-gendered inhabitants of heaven) who wipe away sins and provide the pleasures of paradise (Nydell, 2006). Hence, to enter heaven having killed and died for one's cause means to receive the desired rewards in the service of God. There is also evidence that suicide bombers may be offered reward in this life, too, in both financial gain and enhanced reputation (Bloom, 2007). Murder in the service of an ideology, then, is an act that the perpetrator thinks will return great reward.

Murder is of course carried out for many other reasons than political ideology, ethnic hatred or mental illness.

Murder

The legal definition of murder stretches back to the early part of the seventeenth century, when English jurist Edward Coke wrote a description of murder for law that is still relevant today:

> Murder is when a man of sound memory, and of the age of discretion, unlawfully killeth within any country of the realm any reasonable creature in *rerum natura* under the king's peace, with malice aforethought, either expressed by the party or implied by law, so as the party wounded, or hurt die of the wound or hurt within a year and a day after the same. (Coke,1997[c.1628])

In the seventeenth century, the year and a day rule was appropriate. Without this, a person who wounded someone would remain under threat of prosecution for his or her murder forever, and would be charged with such if the victim died of his or her injuries. This rule still applies in various jurisdictions across the world, and in some states of the United States, but was abolished in the United Kingdom as a result of the Law Reform (Year and a Day Rule) Act 1996. Given the advances in medicine and life support technology, the rule is almost universally thought to be outdated.

In some jurisdictions, particularly the United States, there are distinctions between different types of murder, depending on the intention to kill. First-degree murder is any murder that is wilful and premeditated, whereas second-degree murder is not premeditated or planned in advance. Voluntary manslaughter is an intentional killing that involved no prior intent to kill, and which was committed under such circumstances that would cause emotional or mental disturbance. Involuntary manslaughter is a death that occurs due to unintentional, but reckless or criminally negligent, behaviour.

There are similar distinctions, although sometimes using different terminologies, in several countries around the world.

Therefore, the second issue in the legal position of murder is intention. The question arises as to whether a suspect intended to act, knowing that it was probable these actions would kill or cause serious injury. This does not consider any extenuating circumstances surrounding the actions. Another amendment in UK law that allows the courts to take such circumstances into account was the Homicide Act 1957, introduced after the outcry against the hanging in 1955 of 28-year-old Ruth Ellis. Ellis killed her lover in a fit of jealous rage, and was charged without legal representation. She was hanged four months after she shot David Blakely outside a public house in Hampstead, London. Many prominent people were horrified at the death sentence, and the reform allowed someone to be convicted of manslaughter if provocation could be shown. This clearly has implications when considering women or girls who have murdered one person, as the potential for mitigation is clear when the death was caused by someone in the thrall of jealousy or rage. Women who kill their partners have been the subject of a great deal of debate, and there appear to be three reasons, with a few notable exceptions, for killing a partner: love, fear or greed.

Killing for love

Jean Harris was a respected teacher, headmistress of a girls' school, when she shot Dr. Herman Tarnower, a well-known cardiologist and author of the best-selling book *The Complete Scarsdale Medical Diet*. Harris met Tarnower in 1965 and they had a 14-year relationship. However, he was not content with one woman and paraded his other lovers in front of her, whilst also prescribing medications that disturbed her delicate emotions. On 10 March 1980, Harris was upset by events at the school, had had several arguments with Tarnower, including on the topic of a new woman in his life, and he had changed her medication. She drove to his house with a gun, later saying she had intended to commit suicide in front of him. When she got there, they had an argument in which Tarnower allegedly told her to leave him alone. She shot him four times at close range. She later claimed that he was trying to get the gun off her and it went off accidentally.

The case and trial attracted a great deal of attention, as Tarnower was famous and both of them inhabited what many saw as a privileged and elite world. Harris appeared unemotional throughout, and this is thought to have contributed to a lack of sympathy from the jury; she was convicted of second-degree murder. She had refused to offer a defence of extreme emotional disturbance, which might have led to a conviction for manslaughter.

Harris was consumed by her jealousy and feelings of abandonment. There is evidence to suggest that Tarnower behaved badly, but he was undoubtedly killed because his behaviour led to a fatal set of emotions in Jean Harris.

Women who kill because they develop a fatal jealousy either perceive their partners as desirable by others and/or they have feelings of inadequacy in their own value as a mate. Hence, the motive for murder is the infidelity, real or imagined, of a partner. This pathological jealousy is one that leads a person to seek conflict in contrast to a normal jealousy (White & Mullen, 1989). Some jealousy is normal, and there are concrete reasons for it, but pathological jealousy results from imagination of infidelity. A desire to hurt the partner follows from a need to express intense feelings of anger and humiliation in a person predisposed to behave aggressively. This seems to describe Jean Harris, but in fact her jealousy was triggered by real events, as Tarnower did not hide the fact that he was seeing other women. Jean Harris killed her lover because she was either jealous of his new sexual interest and she was afraid of losing him to a much younger woman, or because she was suicidal, unhappy and killed him by accident as she tried to end her own life. Whatever she was, she was not afraid of Tarnower. There is a set of women across the world sitting in prison because they feared their partners so much that they killed them.

Women who kill from fear

In chapter 4, the issue of intimate partner violence was discussed, and the question of its very existence within a gendered discourse was considered. There is little doubt now that women can and do act violently within relationships but that this is a very small proportion of all violence leading to physical injury between partners. Overwhelmingly, the larger proportion of violent partners is male, and women represent a small number of those who are violent within relationships. This does not in any way negate or belittle the experience of the partners of violent women, and the existence of the 'battered person syndrome' should be considered and examined. This chapter, however, concentrates on women who kill, and, clearly, some women kill their partners. There is no greater example of the disparity in the perpetration and consequences of male and female violence than in the killing of an abusive partner. Battered person syndrome refers to any person presenting with identified physical descriptors of adult physical abuse, classified under 'Injury and Poisoning' (ICD9 code 995.81, 2006). The DSM V does not list diagnostic categories for reactions to physical abuse but may place them under separate diagnoses of PTSD or depression. The syndrome has a legal status beyond the condemnation of the person who batters the victim. It has been used as the basis of the so-called 'battered woman defence' (Law Commission, 2004) to explain how a woman has killed a partner through self-defence when the killing appears to be premeditated, in other words, for anyone who has experienced constant and severe domestic violence, including physical and/or emotional abuse, and become unable to take independent action allowing escape from the abuse. Hence, the abused person is unable to seek assistance, fight the abuser or leave. There is an accepted body of research supporting this issue. Legally, courts have recognized that there are circumstances in which domestic violence may lead to a situation in which the abused will kill.

In 1989, Sara Thornton killed her husband Malcolm as he lay in a drunken stupor. She had endured several beatings during their relationship, and she had sought help in several ways, including the police, which led to him being charged with assault. She stabbed him to death before he appeared in court. In 1990, she was convicted of murder and given a life sentence, with the judge saying that she should have walked out, or left the room when he was beating her. An appeal on the basis of a long-term provocation lost. She was finally set free in 1996 after her conviction was reduced to manslaughter (Bennett, 1996).

Contrast this case with that of Joseph McGrail. His partner was alcoholic and swore at him. So, in 1991, he killed her by repeatedly kicking her in the stomach when she was drunk. At his trial he was given a two-year suspended sentence and walked free, the judge telling him that 'This lady would have tried the patience of a saint' (BBC, 2008). The disparity between the two cases has led to the examination of the concept of provocation, Mrs McGrail never attacked her husband physically, yet he was determined to have been provoked into murder. In Sara Thornton's case, there was a large body of evidence that her husband had beaten her, and that she felt that she and her daughter were in danger, yet she was convicted of murder. These cases led to the formation of the UK campaign group Justice for Women who point out that men who kill their female partners often justify their actions by claiming that they lost control. In court, judges expressed sympathy for this defence, suggesting men who were nagged or cheated on by female partners were justified in killing them. However, there is little sympathy for women who kill after experiencing domestic violence. The dominant emotions in women who are battered are fear and despair, not a sudden, explosive loss of self-control. Hence, the distinction between the acts appears to be an acceptance of male reactive aggression and a condemnation of acts that seem to be instrumental. A woman is unlikely to be in the position of killing her often physically larger and stronger husband in a physical altercation, and she must therefore leave the situation to get a weapon, thus making the act appear premeditated. Historically, women who killed husbands in this way were seen as mentally unbalanced and were committed to an asylum, if indeed they escaped the death sentence. Sara Thornton lives in the United Kingdom, but in the United States it is estimated that there are more than two thousand women in prison because they have murdered an intimate partner in self-defence (Messing & Heeren, 2009).

Battered person syndrome as a defence for killing is highly controversial. It evokes many emotions, some dependent on the sex of the observer. For those who do not live in fear every day, it is difficult to comprehend how such feelings can lead to killing another human being. Possibly a more understandable, but no less heinous, motive is sheer greed.

Women who kill for money

Murder for money is an age-old crime, and women are not innocent of it. There are two basic patterns amongst women who kill for money: the so-called black widow, and the manipulator.

The black widow is a spider, the females of which sometimes eat the male after mating. The term is also applied to a woman who kills her husband for the inheritance she can receive. The second type of female greed killer is the manipulator who gets another person to kill the inconvenient husband or parent. Historically, such women have not been the immediate suspect in a murder, but investigators are moving more to a position of including the wife, daughter, or sister in the pool of suspects.

In October 2004, on the outskirts of Phoenix, Arizona, human remains were found in a storage box. In the bottom of the box were some black bags and a single bullet casing. Forensic and DNA analysis showed the remains to be the partial torso of Jay Orbin, a 45-year-old art dealer reported missing by his wife a month previously. Since then, she had reportedly been behaving in a callous and suspicious manner. Jay was Marjorie's third husband, all of whom were rich. The problem with Jay was that he was a workaholic and the marriage was strained. When he went missing, Marjorie seemed unconcerned about his welfare. Police found she had been having an affair with a computer programmer called Larry Weisberg, who was found in the house when police called on her about the body of her husband. Jay's clothes also appeared to be missing from the home, along with several paintings, but there was a brand new piano in the living room. The garage had also been recently repainted. Police also discovered an envelope containing over US$3,000; Marjorie admitted to liquidating Jay's accounts containing US$100,000. Six weeks later, Marjorie was arrested and charged with her husband's murder. In 2009, she was found guilty of Jay's murder and sentenced to life in prison.

Black widows are more common than might be thought. In 1994, Julian Webb was killed by his wife Dena with poisoned curry. He was buried in a family plot in Hayling Island, Hampshire, United Kingdom, but his body was exhumed after Dena was cleared of trying to kill her third husband, Richard Thompson, in 2000. She attacked Thompson with a baseball bat and knife because she feared for her life during a bondage sex session. However, she was sentenced to three years and nine months in prison for conning Thompson and two former lovers out of £12,000. Webb's exhumation and examination showed a very high level of aspirin in his body.

The problem with women who kill for gain is that the money never seems to be enough, and they become serial killers if not detected early (Robbins, 2003).

Girls who kill

Children can and do kill. Children who kill are rare in comparison to adults, but homicides and the reasons for them fall into several categories. Children or adolescents most frequently kill within their own family, but there are cases of murder outside these confines.

Children who kill within their own family usually kill parents. According to Hart and Helms (2003), there are several reasons why this happens – the child is mentally ill, antisocial or abused. Mental illness in these cases tends to result in delusional states or hallucinations (Heide, 1992). They may have a history of treatment but lack understanding of their psychiatric state. As with adults who murder, mental illness may mean that a police case is not pursued against the child, but it is also possible that young people are found fit to plead despite an obvious disorder. Such children may be unaware of what they have done, or that they have done anything wrong.

West and Feldsher (2010) point out that there are gender distinctions in the killing of a parent. Sons who kill are more likely to be diagnosed as having a psychotic illness, usually schizophrenia, whereas daughters are less likely to be seen as psychotic, unless they kill overbearing mothers with excessive force. A different form of disorder leading to violence is conduct disorder. The DSM describes adolescents with conduct disorder as aggressive, destructive, deceitful and tending to violate the rights of others with little or no remorse. This is essentially a precursor to the adult antisocial personality disorder, with psychopathy its underlying problem. Juveniles with this issue may exhibit antisocial behaviour due to family problems, but may also have a mental disorder that is being masked by the behaviour (Ewing, 1997). It is also possible that this may be masking child abuse, too. The severely abused child is the most likely to kill her parents. Abuse throughout childhood is a clear indicator of someone who may kill; adolescents who kill abusive parents just reach that point sooner. There may be mitigation for a child who kills an abusive parent as there is little way of escaping the abuse; an adult who has been abused as a child has at least survived through it and can use alternative ways of coping with the parent, such as distancing (Gavin, 2011). A child suffering from abuse who then kills often raises the questions as to why she did not seek help or run away. These are the same questions that women are asked who use the battered wife defence in the murder of an abusive spouse. These issues are pertinent here in that the victim of abuse develops a sense of helplessness (Goodwin & Sachs, 1996). In addition to this, children become hyper-vigilant to any sign of the abuser's behaviour that signals abuse. In these circumstances, it would seem reasonable that self-defence would be a judicious defence to any charges of murder, but this is difficult to prove. The original definition of battered child syndrome was given by Kempe in 1962, but has been broadened, allowing more cases to be viewed as self-defence (Smarty, 2009). It is still difficult in many cases to reconcile the murder and the abusive state. There have also been some very infamous cases of defendants attempting to use the abused child defence in some very tenuous ways, such as the Menendez brothers who killed their parents in 1989.

There are very few cases of girls who kill, but evidence suggests that they are more likely to kill family members and to use accomplices, than boys (Roe-Sepowitz, 2009), the exception being the pregnant teenager who kills her baby (Porter & Gavin, 2010). Motives for family killings are as cited above – abuse, killing witnesses to other crimes – but coercion by boyfriends or gangs is one to add for female juvenile murderers. The research literature on girls who kill is sparse, and usually uses a direct comparison to boy killers. Young women or girls who kill are seen as particularly anomalous, as motivations, outside of abuse, are difficult to understand.

Holly Harvey was fifteen when she decided she had found her true love, 16-year-old Sandra (Sandy) Ketchum. The problem was that Holly had been living with her grandparents, the Colliers, Carl, 74 and Sarah, 73, for four months, and they were strict and disapproved of the relationship. Harvey decided she would not let them interfere any more and made a plan with Ketchum to kill them and run away together with the Colliers' valuables. Holly even wrote the plan in ink on her arm: 'Kill, keys, money and jewelry'. The Colliers were lured to Harvey's room by the smell of marijuana, and then Harvey stabbed her grandmother in the back. In the ensuing struggle, Ketchum went to Harvey's assistance, and Sarah Collier ended up with twenty stab wounds. Carl was stabbed repeatedly but managed to attempt a call to the police before succumbing to fifteen stab wounds. The girls ransacked the house, then fled in Carl's truck and went to a friend's house, telling her they had been mugged as an explanation for why they were covered in blood. They eventually told their friend what had happened and her parents called the police. Police officers reported that Harvey was cold and callous, laughing when arrested, but Ketchum did show remorse. Various explanations have been presented for this callous and extraordinary behaviour. Ketchum, it is reported, was abandoned by her mother, and a series of stepmothers had physically abused her. Abuse figures largely in the background of murderers. Harvey, on the other hand, was the daughter of the Colliers' adopted daughter who had always been wayward and unruly, unable to look after her daughter due to being imprisoned on a drugs conviction, which is why Holly was living with her grandparents. It is reported that Sarah Collier was cruel and had a hair-trigger temper. This may have been the source of a good deal of poor interactions between the two, exacerbated by Harvey's adolescent wild streak and Sarah Colliers's disgust at the relationship with Ketchum. Whether the two girls had any signs of psychopathy cannot be determined, but it is clear that they planned the murder and had well-defined reasons for doing it, namely money to set them free to be together. They are now incarcerated in different prisons, many miles apart.

Harvey and Ketchum's murder of Harvey's adopted grandparents was sensationalized by the media. The element of lesbianism, the youth of the two perpetrators and the very fact they were female made headlines around the world. Is such violent behaviour by young women so unusual? Heide and Solomon (2009) noted that arrests of girls between 1976 and 2005 averaged 8.1 per cent of all juvenile arrests for murder, but were of a different pattern to that of boys. The arrests of boys steadily increased over this period, but that of girls peaked in 1983 and then dropped. Additional differences were also revealed in Heide, Solomon, Sellers and Chan's (2011) analysis of data for the same period, in that girls are more likely to kill younger victims, female victims, family members, intimate partners and their offspring than are male juvenile homicide offenders. They were also more likely to use knives and to kill in conflict situations. Girls who kill alone or in pairs, like Harvey and Ketchum, are rare; girls in packs are more likely to kill than a lone female.

This raises a further question: the issue of street violence. This issue is much more visible in terms of policing and policies, as the concern about the rise in street violence perpetrated by gangs is seen as a major problem. A gang is a loosely organized group controlling a territory through violence. The perception is, and the research data perpetuates this, that street violence is perpetrated only by boys and young men in gangs, loosely organized groups controlling a territory through violence. According to Klein (2005) gang members spend most of their time outside their home and their identity includes involvement in illegal activity. Much of the research has been in the United States, where street gangs are seen as a growing menace by the police, and it is also where much of the global view of them originates, particularly through the media portrayal in news, social commentary and crime drama. Almost exclusively, modern gangs are portrayed as comprising predominantly young ethnic-minority men. In such representations, if women or girls are involved in the gangs, they are shown as the sexual property of the male members of the gangs, or as satellites of male groups. The media representation and the research appear to have trivialized female gangs (Campbell, 1991). There appears to be an overriding impression, both in law enforcement agencies and in the general public's perception, that girls are not violent in exclusion to male involvement. However, violent crime carried out by girls is on the increase, but so is that by boys (Chesney-Lind & Brown, 1999). Statistics on this trend are very difficult to find and even more difficult to interpret. Female arrests number less than a quarter of all arrests for under-eighteens, and violent crime constitutes a small percentage of that. Police data and research findings, such as that cited above, also suggest that the nature of girls' violent crime is different, in that knives rather than guns are involved, and that any assaults happen during conflict rather than in the commission of another crime (like rape or burglary), as with boys. However, even if the proportion of female arrests in comparison to male arrests is low, the actual numbers are not insignificant. It is clear that the number of arrests for violent crimes or weapon-carrying is rising overall, and the numbers of girls involved in such crime is therefore rising with the trend. Early research suggested that delinquency and gang activity were strictly male pursuits with girls as sexual associates of the gang members. However, this was not supported by the findings of Lagerspetz, Björkqvist and Peltonen (1988) who looked at 11–12 year olds and their social structures. They discovered that the social interactions of the girls were more ruthless and aggressive than previously suggested because this study found that indirect social aggression was the norm for girls, rather than physically violent behaviour. Lagerspetz et al. concluded that the girls were behaving as mini-adults, mimicking the social interactions of their parents, whereas boys were still using immature social strategies. However, the likelihood of girls in gangs that commit violent offences is still not inherent in a view of girls as using indirect forms of aggression. This is simply not a realistic view of what is happening at street level, according to police sources. Estimates of female involvement in gangs vary between 4 per cent and 30 per cent, depending on the agency carrying out the estimates and the way in which gang membership is viewed. Numbers then are meaningless here; what is clear is that young women are becoming more prevalent in violent crime and gang culture, and the question should be not 'how many' but 'why'. In her research into female gang culture, Ann Campbell (1984, 1991) explored the lives of several African-American and Latin-American girl gangs in New York. Campbell discovered acute hardship in the lives of the young women she talked to and followed in their activities. The gang, she concluded, served a social function and was a replacement familial connection: 'family' was where the women were abused, and 'gang' was where they were accepted. They participated in violence because it was a survival strategy and a way to provide status and protection for themselves and the other female gang members. Joining the gang is an adaptive solution to hardship, lack of educational or financial opportunity, social isolation and economic marginalization. She also discovered a rejection of the typical roles available to women, such as the 'good wife', and 'sex object', although the women's interpretation of these stereotypes is atypical. For example, Campbell suggests that the gang members define 'sex object' as procuring sex for male counterparts and seducing men in other gangs in order to accuse them of rape.

Returning to the overriding question here, is there evidence to suggest that girls in gangs are more likely to kill, given the issues Campbell exposed? Such questions remain as yet unanswered.

Manslaughter

Manslaughter is homicide without intent to kill, and it is distinguished from justifiable homicide (killing someone in self-defence or the defence of another person). There are also distinctions between voluntary, involuntary and reckless manslaughter, causing death by dangerous driving or whilst intoxicated. The main difference is that voluntary manslaughter requires intent to kill or cause serious bodily harm, but which is not premeditated, while involuntary manslaughter does not.

Voluntary manslaughter is an intentional killing that is accompanied by additional circumstances that mitigate, but do not excuse, the killing. Such mitigations might be provocation, as seen in several cases of wives who are the recipients of extreme domestic violence killing their husbands.

Involuntary manslaughter does not involve intent to kill or harm. Such deaths might occur as a result of negligence or a failure to act.

Suicide

Suicide is not strictly a form of homicide, but several categories of suicide do blur the line between the legal definitions. People take their own lives for many different reasons. In some cases, an individual may need assistance, such as in the circumstances of debilitating and degenerative illnesses. Whilst physician-assisted suicide is illegal in many countries, and any person who aids the suicide may have charges brought against him or her, it is also true that several nations do not currently have such restrictions. As Dees, Vernooij-Dassen, Dekkers and van Weel (2010) suggest, this is a controversial issue and the subject of heated debate.

Conclusion

There are several different forms of homicide that can be considered when trying to understand why someone would kill another human being. It is clear that the human race is still, even after thousands of years of 'civilization', a set of animals that will kill each other quite happily. Murder can range from the quiet poisoning of an inconvenient spouse to the rampaging extermination of a whole ethnic group. Men figure hugely in this group of people, but women and girls do kill. They are barely mentioned in the research literature, though; a search of academic databases or government agency databases suggests that the only female killers are those who kill abusive husbands when in the grip of fear or babies unwanted by unhinged women. Consideration of female killers in the media is a little less specific, but as Chesney-Lind and Eliason (2006) point out, gender stereotypes of femininity and masculinity are prevalent amongst press reports and popular crime-writing. They suggest this leads to demonization of women and girls who have been arrested for violent crimes, including murder, with any hint of non-conformity, such as lesbianism, leading to the depiction of women as violent predators, even if this is not merited. Hence, 'Women, particularly marginalized women, continue to be harshly judged for any departure from traditional feminine ideals' (Chesney-Lind & Eliason, 2006, p. 1).

However, it is clear that there are female murderers in addition to the battered wife and the pregnant teenager, and that women will kill for several other reasons – greed, love or the sheer pleasure derived from killing. This last is the most difficult to understand and is most easily studied when the variable of time is added. The murders discussed in this chapter, with the exception of genocide, all occur within one instance. The next chapter considers those that happen over several time periods and have added elements of sex, sexuality and lust. It is time to turn to the strangest creature of all: the female serial killer.

9

Serial Murder and Women

It is sixteenth-century Hungary, and young peasant girls are going missing. They have been offered well-paid work in the Castle Czejte, Transylvania, and then are never seen again. The king sends an army to the castle where they find one dead girl and one dying, several wounded and others locked up. There are witnesses aplenty to testify against the Countess Elizabeth Bathory (Branson-Trent, 2010). Historians agree that her story is one of the antecedents of the European legend of the vampire, the undead creature that stalks the night seeking human blood. The people in Elizabeth's village certainly thought she was a monster. Describing atrocities such as severe beatings, insertion of needles, burning or mutilation of hands, faces and genitalia, all of them over a twenty-five year period, it sounds like the peasants were happy to get their own back on a woman who history has determined was probably medically and legally insane. Elizabeth is inextricably linked to the vampire legend, stories about supernatural creatures of the night with monstrous habits and prodigious powers. Her depravities did not include the draining of blood from the young girls, drinking and bathing in it, as has been widely described (Grace, 2011), but certainly something odd was going on in that castle. If Elizabeth did kill indeed numbers of young women in a novel approach to servant discipline, then she is a member of a very rare class, one of history's least understood but perpetually fascinating creatures: a female serial killer.

Female Aggression, First Edition. Helen Gavin and Theresa Porter.
© 2015 John Wiley & Sons, Ltd. Published 2015 by John Wiley & Sons, Ltd.

What Is Serial Murder?

Serial murder is different from other forms of murder and mass or spree murder in several ways, notably the timescale of the killings, the motives for them and the mass murderer's final act of suicide, which is usually missing in serial murder. One of the most influential definitions of serial murder is that given by Egger (1984). Serial murder is defined as several (three or more) killings, separated by time and location and carried out by the same person(s). The murders may be motivated by compulsive fantasies, and the victims may hold some sort of symbolic meaning for the killer. In addition, the selection of the victim appears to be random at first; the connection between them is made by deduction, not other similarities such as familial relationship.

It is tempting to suppose that serial killers are a modern phenomenon because the first time this term was used was in the 1930s. Ernst Gennat, a German police officer who worked on several infamous cases used the term *Serienmörder* to describe the men (sic) who killed many people, often using gruesome methods. The first English use of the term is attributed to Robert Ressler of the FBI in the 1970s (Ressler & Shachtman, 1992). However, simply because they were not named as such does not mean that serial murderers have not been with us for some time; they may have just not been subject to the same scientific attention as now. Widespread literacy did not happen until relatively recently, but the descriptions of murder and mayhem found in folk tales, passed on orally, still appear to be stories about serial killers, albeit supernatural in nature (Gavin & Bent, 2012). Werewolves and vampires delight in multiple murders, but they probably represent creatures that are all too human in nature (Tatar, 1998), just like Countess Bathory. In addition, many folk tales include women as the central evil character, the murderer. For example, Hansel and Gretel encounter a witch who wishes to eat them, and it is unlikely they are the first of her potential victims. Baba Yagar, she of the walking house and flying mortar, is also a serial kidnapper and cannibal. Real-life serial killers choose victims weaker than themselves, often members of vulnerable populations, such as prostitutes, runaways and young people. As such, this vulnerability of the victim, reflected to a certain degree in folk tales, the danger, and how he or she overcomes it, is a recurring theme in both fiction and reality.

Morton and Hilts (2005) officially categorized a serial killer as a murderer with a minimum of three victims, with killings separated by a clear time period, termed a cooling-off period, as originally identified by Egger (1984). Victims are usually strangers, appearing to be random choices until links are identified, and the motive is rarely for profit. Victims are often in vulnerable groups, too, such as prostitutes or runaways; this is linked to their accessibility and the low risk associated with abducting and killing them. There usually appears to a sadistic element in the killings, with the possibility of the victims holding some sort of symbolic value.

Scientific writing about serial killers is almost as prolific as their fictional depiction. Early attempts at a systematic examination reflect a movement away from the ideas of magical influence or demonic possession being the cause of violent and sadistic behaviour, but were themselves flawed. Phrenology and physiognomy are now discredited, but are interesting in their historic value on the path to a more scientific approach. Modern approaches seek explanations in the psychology, upbringing and environment of serial killers.

Explanations for Serial Murder

The majority of research and media focus is on male serial killers. When there is a spotlight on a female serial killer, she is represented as if she were the only one, as in the case of Aileen Wuornos. Wuornos was convicted of the murder of seven men and is regularly referred to as America's first and only serial killer (CNN, 2009). This gives the impression that men are the only sex that repeatedly kills, and women serial killers are rare to the point of almost non-existence. This is not the case, but it is difficult to find explanations in the literature surrounding serial killing without reference to men. Therefore, it may be fruitful to consider those explanations and the application of them to the panoply of male murderers, and consider whether these can be applied to the much smaller group of women and girls who kill, then kill again and again.

Childhood

A large proportion of serial killers claim to have suffered high levels of physical, sexual, or emotional abuse during their childhood. Only some of these stories have been corroborated by witnesses, and it is generally accepted that most are exaggerations (Aggarwal, Bhullar, & Sharma, 2010).

The majority of children abused in childhood do not then go on to become serial killers, and many of those abused are girls, and there are very small numbers of serial killers who are female. This suggests that the abuse is a major factor in the development of a serial killer, but not the only one, and certainly not the only feature of upbringing that may contribute to the murderous behaviour of the adult; there are other contributions that the adult parent makes to the development of a potential serial killer.

Whilst not classified as abuse, various extreme forms of child rearing may contribute to the fledgling serial killer's cultivation. This does seem to fit much more the male serial murderer, however, the female or the feminine being the catalyst and/or target. Mother dominance in particular, seems to influence the early years of several male cases, such as Henry Lee Lucas, whose first victim was his sexually abusive mother (Petersen & Farrington, 2007). Serial Killer Ed Gein's mother was fanatically religious (Joshi, 2007) and convinced him that women were the vessels of sin and disease. When police searched Gein's farm, looking for a missing shopkeeper, they found that he had indeed made vessels out of women, using their skulls for bowls and other domestic objects. Gein's body may have escaped from sexual disease, but his mind was clearly contaminated.

The morals of the mother seem to be a recurring theme in serial killer background. In contrast to the religious fanaticism of Gein, mothers of other killers have exposed their children to inappropriate sexual behaviour, either as prostitutes or participants in casual sex (Joshi, 2007). However, whilst the mother's behaviour appears frequently as a source of blame, the father, either in his absence or his terrifying presence, also contributes. John Wayne Gacy, who raped and killed at least 33 young men and boys during 1972–8, had a sadistically disciplinarian father, a violent alcoholic, who, according to Hensen and Olson (2010), beat his wife and shot the pet dog to punish John.

Such parental abuse is not always present, or perhaps simply not observable. Jeffrey Dahmer's childhood appears to have been enviably serene. The cracks in this facade became apparent, however, when his father, Lionel, published a book about his infamous son. In this book, Lionel cites his wife's hysteria and psychosomatic illnesses during pregnancy as reasons for Jeffrey's later murdering. He also seems to be seeking answers beyond that, but never recognizes that perhaps his own emotional distance may have contributed in some way.

It is clear that abuse figures largely in the childhoods of male serial killers. But what about female serial killers? There does appear to be a high level of evidence that women who kill, and go on to kill more than one victim, are themselves victims of childhood abuse of one form or another. Aileen Wuornos, for example, claimed that each of her seven male victims had raped, or attempted to rape, her. As a plea of self-defence, this statement did not work, but examination of her upbringing goes some way to explaining her actions and the view she may have had of men. Wuornos's mother, Diane, was pregnant at fifteen and abandoned her children when Aileen was nine months old. Diane's parents adopted Aileen and her brother, bringing them up to believe that they were her parents, not grandparents. There has been speculation that Laurie, her grandfather, sexually abused Aileen, but there is no corroborating evidence for this. However, it is clear that the household was not ideal for young children, with alcohol abuse and violence a daily occurrence (Myers, Gooch, & Meloy, 2005). Aileen's grandfather beat her on a regular basis for even the smallest of mistakes. Aileen had few friends, due to the chaotic nature of the home and because she had a violent and unpredictable temper. It is also clear that the teenage Aileen learnt very quickly that having sex with neighbourhood boys would bring her rewards in the shape of cigarettes, alcohol and other drugs. Almost inevitably, she became pregnant at fourteen, her son taken away from her before she could see him. In retrospect, we can see this was a tragic start to life, and a tragedy waiting to unfold.

In Wuornos's case, it is difficult to determine whether her behaviour was due to any genetic predispositions to alcoholism and violence she inherited from her absent father, or the exposure to violence, cruelty and incestuous and promiscuous behaviour in her upbringing. What is clear is that she blamed the behaviour of the men she killed, claiming multiple violent rapes at the hands of those she offered sex for pay. Biopsychological theories would suggest that having an adolescent mother, being exposed to violence and addictive behaviours predisposed Wuornos to violence as an adolescent and adult. A further issue was that Wuornos, when assessed by clinicians whilst in prison, showed below average IQ, high impulsivity, low attention span and high psychopathy. Such anomalies taken together suggest a cortical dysfunction, possibly a result of drug and alcohol use by her mother whilst pregnant, and also Wuornos's own drug use. This cannot be separated from Wuornos's lack of engagement in school, and lack of any social support, together with her own tendency to fail to accept responsibility and the distorted belief, reported by Myers, Gooch and Meloy, 2005, that she was saving her victims' families from violence at the hands of the men. It also easy to see Wuornos as a victim, which she certainly was in many ways, but the chaos of her childhood does not mitigate against the fact that she was a serial killer.

Even within the most normal appearing and loving families, some childhood events are identified as problematic, possibly contributing to developmental difficulties. Adoption, or the discovery that one is adopted, can be distressing in the most stable of personalities. It is well established that the sense of identity developing during adolescence can be negatively impacted by the feelings of abandonment an adopted child encounters (Brinich, 1980). Furthermore, Gair (2008) identified a higher level of mental health problems within the adoptee population. Whether this reflects issues within the genetic pool of the birth parents or the experience of adoption is difficult to ascertain, but perhaps both of these items contribute to difficulties in later life. There is a set of psychological difficulties referred to as 'adopted child syndrome' (Kirschner, 1990) which is similar to DSM diagnostic criteria for an undifferentiated conduct disorder. However, not all adoptees ever display this form of behaviour difficulty, and fewer still will become serial killers. Examining the incidence of adoption amongst serial killers would seem to suggest that it is high (Carangelo, 2002), but in fact there are no official statistics on such occurrences. Some of the most notorious male serial killers have been adoptees, for example Kenneth Bianchi, Ted Bundy and David Berkowitz. The list of women is a little shorter, but they number some of the more infamous cases too. Aileen Wuornos, described above, is a case in point. Not only was she adopted, but her adopted family reportedly brutalized her. Another case is one of the few female murderers to claim to have received sexual gratification from killing, Jane Toppan. Her mother died when Jane (then named Honora, or Nora, Kelly) was an infant. Her childhood appears to have been normal and reasonably happy, but she had mental health problems that resulted in an unsuccessful suicide attempt as a young woman. As an adult, Jane worked as a nurse and poisoned at least thirty patients, but claimed to want to kill more.

Adoption does appear in the life histories of many of the serial killers we might examine, but again there are so few female examples that it is not possible to determine what effect it has. Other childhood experiences may have more of a bearing on possible explanations for serial killing.

A common claim by murderers, particularly those who are sadistic and/ or sexual in their manner of killing, is that they were exposed to violent events in childhood. Several male killers have pointed to watching farm animals being slaughtered or being told frightening childhood stories. However, not every child brought up on a farm becomes a killer, and stories do not seem to be a fruitful source of training for serial murder, despite the inherent violence they contain. Many children have been brought up in close contact with violence, children in war zones for example, but they do not turn into sadistic adults preying on others. In addition, it is difficult to find a female killer who cites childhood experience of violence as a reason for her murderous psychology, or at least not in isolation from other forms of brutalization.

Another childhood experience with potential for brutalization, which many male serial killers have, is juvenile detention. Historically, there has been little distinction between children and adults in terms of how they were treated by the criminal justice system. Until children were recognized as a different legal category, they were tried as adults and subjected to the same punishments or incarceration. Secure residential facilities for young people are used when they are considered a threat to public safety or the court process. In the United Kingdom, several prison reform acts have limited this use to the most serious cases of criminal behaviour. However, the United States incarcerates more young people than any other country in the world, a reflection of the larger trends in incarceration practices in the United States (US Bureau of Justice Statistics, 2009). Several serial killers seem to have experienced a different form of detention than that described in official reports. Albert Fish, for example, stated that he was routinely beaten, and that this turned him into the sadistic father, grandfather, child molester and serial murderer that he became. Female serial killers do not seem to recount the experience of juvenile detention in the same way, possibly because they are more likely to experience severe psychiatric disorders that are different to those of their male counterparts (Cauffman, Lexcen, Goldweber, Shulman, & Grisso, 2007). Such disorders may mean that the more brutalizing effects of incarceration are either different for girls or not experienced as much as in male juvenile detention.

Childhood is an important time with respect to the development of adult criminal behaviour, including serial murder. However, explanations at the individual level are not always the most compelling arguments. Social explanations also come into play in serial murder. The more sociological in nature suggest that high crime rates are a result of societal problems and that serial murder is no exception. This may not hold completely true for some of the more lurid of the serial killers' behaviours, but a society that allows sex workers and runaways to remain unprotected may need to take some blame. In addition, inadequate socialization may be a direct result of a societal breakdown at a micro level. In 1962, Reinhardt reported on a high level of a lack of normal communication between serial killers (or least those studied) and a reasonable part of the social world. As such, they had no workable system of social or personal frames of reference. Many have commented that serial killers do not come from a background of understanding and caring, rather the experience of socialization has been one of abuse and neglect, teaching the child that his (or her) world is one of pain and rejection. Why, then, do so many abused children fail to become serial killers? The world should be rampant with hate. It is more likely that the experience of inadequate socialization feeds into a complex interaction between psychological and biological predispositions and development. There is, however, one societal position that begs to be considered in our examination of the serial killer.

Some of even the most notorious female serial killers are seen as subservient to their male partner. Rose West, Myra Hindley, Bonnie Parker all killed within partnerships; whilst they are viewed as monsters because they are women who kill, they are also viewed as less likely to be blamed for initiation of killing (Gavin, 2010). Other female serial killers are described as either the comfort type, ones who provided services to those they killed, or as healthcare workers taking mercy killing a little too literally. In this case, it would seem that many women have potential access to victim types that fit these typologies of female killers. So why are serial killers predominately male? Feminist positions suggest that violence against women is misuse of power by men socialized into thinking that control over women is a right (Walker, 2006). Serial killer victims are predominantly female and sexual murder is seen as an act of violence designed to override women's choice about sex, life or death, what Caputi (1989) calls a patriarchal act of sexual terrorism. The high levels of sexual sadism that is seen in male serial killers killing women is of the most revolting kind, but some suggest that this establishes in the male murderer a viable sense of his own worth (Dworkin, 1975). As such, it illustrates the difficulty of determining where violent behaviour originates: the family, peer groups or media. Wherever it is an inherent part of the learning about social interaction, the lack of a wave of female serial killers could be due to differential male and female socialization, with women/girls taught to be subservient at the various levels of social learning processes.

We cannot leave consideration of societal issues without examining the effect of the media. Gresswell and Hollin (1994) suggest that public interest and the glorification in infamy might add to or even overtake the original motivation for the killing. The FBI's sample of serial killers examined in 1988 included those that reported they followed the stories in the press about their killing and associated behaviour (such as armed robbery, kidnap, etc.). This served to maintain and heighten post-offence excitement. Sometimes killers involve themselves in the police investigation by leaving clues for investigators, writing to newspapers, even helping in searches and so on. The issue of media coverage of such crimes is termed 'glorification', because the killers glory in their fame. The public is fascinated by serial murder, and this is no different for female killers; indeed, there seems to be more prurient interest in women who kill.

Turning from society's involvement, explanations at individual levels include psychiatry, psychopathy, paraphilia and sexual dysfunction, and neurology.

Psychiatric explanations

Leonarda Cianciulli was born as a result of rape and was clearly not wanted by her mother. She had a desperately unhappy life; she attempted suicide twice, she married young, her marital home was destroyed by an earthquake and she had seventeen pregnancies, of which she miscarried three, and ten children died in infancy. She consulted fortune-tellers who variously told her all her children would die and that she would end her days in a criminal asylum. When her eldest son had to join the army in the Second World War, she decided that the only way to keep him safe was by human sacrifice. She killed three of her middle-aged female neighbours and turned their bodies into soap. She did indeed end her days in a criminal asylum at Pozzuoli in 1970.

There is an underlying assumption that anyone who kills repeatedly for obscure motivations must be insane, but a relatively small proportion of serial killers have a psychiatric history. Additionally, there is little to support the stereotype of the mentally ill person as violent and dangerous (Choe, Teplin, & Abram, 2008). Again, it is the male serial killers in whom we find any mental illness; the person suffering from a psychotic break with reality favoured by dramatic portrayal of killers in shows such as *Criminal Minds* is uncommon, and almost always male. This is odd, because, as Vronsky (2007) points out, the public at large believe women commit murder through self-defence, mental illness or the hormonal imbalances that the female physiology is prone to produce, however ill-constructed these perceptions are. Such misperceptions include the views of schizophrenia, dissociative disorders and neurotic disorders. Schizophrenia seems to have a very bad image; according to Angermeyer and Matschinger (2003), people with schizophrenia are seen as more dangerous and unpredictable than with any other mental illness. However, it is clear that the debilitating effects of mental illness are unlikely to assist in planning several murders and evading detection and capture.

Perri and Lichtenwald (2010) contend that myths about the mentally ill serial killer are more pervasive when considering women who kill, and this does a disservice to both the perpetrators and the burden on the mental health system. In fact, they go further and say that the supposedly psychotic female killer is much more likely to be psychopathic.

The role of psychopathy

Psychopathic personality disorder (PPD) is a persistent disorder or disability of mind, resulting in abnormally aggressive or irresponsible behaviour that is not the product of psychosis or other illness. The term 'sociopathy' is often used interchangeably with psychopathy, although there are some distinctions. Additionally, there is no classification in the DSM 5 for either psychopathy or sociopathy, although the diagnosis of antisocial personality disorder (ASPD) is very closely related to it. The DSM 5 description of ASPD is a set of behaviours in an individual over 18 years old, indicating a disregard of the rights of others and persistent violation of them. These behaviours may be non-conformity to social norms, especially lawful behaviours, deception, such as repeated lying or conning, impulsiveness, irritability and aggressiveness, including physical fights, risk-taking with self or others, irresponsibility and lack of remorse Any three of these behaviours, occurring since the individual was 15 years of age, and not associated with other disorders, are enough for the diagnosis of ASPD (APA, 2013).

Hence, some people with psychopathy/sociopathy behave in a socially unacceptable manner, and can be said to have ASPD, although some can also behave in socially acceptable ways. Many successful people are said to exhibit some of the characteristics of psychopathy, such as charm and good social intelligence. Couple this with remorselessness, ruthlessness, and it is easy to see how some can be successful in business and other arenas. However, it is the criminal psychopath of interest here. Psychopathy is particularly associated with a propensity for violent crime (e.g., Serin, 1991), and serial murder, as the most extreme criminal behaviour, fits well with the psychopath as remorseless killer. But we still have no clue as to causality: does psychopathy cause some to become serial killers, and is serial murder simply an extreme form of antisocial behaviour, or do serial killers simply happen to share common characteristics with the personality disorder? Does the personality disorder cause the serial killing, or is there simply a coincidental match? The word psychopath is overused and mis-used to describe murderers, and appears to be a label for those of whom we have no understanding. Egger (1994) even suggests that psychologists use the term to describe serial murderers who appear to have no motive. However, motive is there, whether we understand it or not. Thrill of killing, sexual gratification or expression of dominance may seem alien to most of us but they are still motives.

So, are female serial killers psychopaths? Men are much more likely to be seen as showing the characteristics of psychopathy, but from the beginning of systematic study of the issue, women have numbered amongst the cases. The problems here is that experts agree women can show the full range of both ASPD and psychopathy, but no one is looking at them in the same way as the men because there are so few female serial killers anyway (Perri & Lichtenwald, 2010) and because there is still a persistent lack of ability to step outside of the rigid sex role/gender role stereotypes, even in the psychological/psychiatric community. This adherence to stereotypes may mean that women are not being labelled with antisocial personality disorders, but with the alternative histrionic disorders. Histrionic personality disorder (HPD) is characterized by attention-seeking behaviours, including inappropriate sexual seductiveness and exaggerated or shallow emotions, but not necessarily antisocial behaviour. Calling women manipulative, narcissistic, remorseless, callous, parasitic or irresponsible is difficult if they are always viewed as passive, emotional, nurturing and self-sacrificing, with the assumption that any criminal behaviour is the result of a psychiatric instability (Perri & Lichtenwald, 2010). Such perceived instability negates accountability. However, if female psychopaths are compared to male counterparts, there is a relatively equal set of irresponsible lifestyle behaviours, such as unemployment and relationship instability, but this is manifested in males as of unlawful behaviour and violent crimes (Salekin, Rogers, Ustad, & Sewell, 1998). As such, it is proposed that female psychopaths exist, but their antisocial behaviour is gender-specific (Cruise, Colwell, Lyons, & Baker, 2003). Female psychopaths therefore tend to rely on different means to achieve their goals, using manipulation and seduction rather than brute force (Forouzan & Cooke, 2005). Hence, the female serial killer may use different means to achieve the end she requires, the death of someone else, and the escalating need to achieve the same thrill. This is particularly evident when the sexual nature of serial killing is considered. The role of sexual deviancy in serial homicide is quite clear, but is this so for the female killer?

The role of paraphilias

According to Stone (2001), when we think of serial killers, the image we have is of serial sexual homicide, compulsive killing for sexual release of one nature or another. Paraphilia features strongly in the serial-killer population; Prentky, Burgess, Rokous and Lee (1989) identified high incidence of paraphilia and paraphiliac fantasy in serial killers, and Dietz, Hazelwood and Warren (1990) suggested that a large proportion of serial killers exhibit more than one paraphilia. Whilst some paraphilias can be relatively harmless, such as fetishism and transvestism (unless they cause distress to participants), there are clearly some that involve death, dying and murder, and the possibility of serial murder. Necrophilia and erotophonophilia feature largely in the life histories of some serial killers, but are they equally attractive to the female serial sexual murderer?

Necrophilia in females is extremely rare; notwithstanding any practical difficulties (which are reportedly possible to surmount), women are either not sexually molesting dead bodies or they are not getting caught doing it. There is no recorded instance of a female necrophile killing to achieve her goal of a dead, and supremely compliant, partner, unlike the men who litter the pages of lurid tabloids and academic journals alike. There is no female equivalent of Jeffrey Dahmer or Ed Gein. The closest we come to finding one is Elizabeth Bathory, the accusation against whom included bathing in the blood of her virgin housemaids and elements of necrophilia, but none are substantiated by anything other than unreliable accounts.

Are there female erotophonophiles? Erotophonophilia is a paraphilia dependent on erotic satisfaction from killing. The signature component of the crime is sexual fantasies and acting on those fantasies with the victim and their body. The symptoms of erotophonophilia include sexual arousal from killing, an abnormal amount of time spent thinking about killing someone, recurring intense sexual fantasies and urges involving killing. It is closely linked to sexual sadism. Where the sadist is female, it is thought that the onset is later than in men, so developmental theories may not be as compelling an explanation, and is often triggered by relationships with men who want to be dominated.

Thus, lust murder represents the integration of sexualized violence and murder. Evidence of peri-mortem mutilation is common, with methods of torture using a large range of weapons. Bite marks, vampirism or cannibalism are sometimes reported. Freudian concepts of unresolved sexual conflict, infantilization and maternal overprotection or rejection are used in explanation, with the conflict between the *id* and the *superego* a major element, due to unresolved childhood experiences. Hatred of a significant female (usually the mother) and/or Oedipal complexes have also been reported by many serial killers. Ed Kemper maintained that if he had killed his mother first, his other victims might have been spared. Alternative explanations from learning theory would name access to violent pornography and subsequent orgasmic conditioning as the culprits. None of these psychological positions suggests that women would be included in the pantheon of erotophonophiles. There are very few female killers that exhibit sexual arousal from the act of killing, possibly only the previously discussed Jane Toppan. Silvio, McCloskey and Ramos-Grenier (2006) suggest that such women are overwhelmingly found within killing teams, rather than as solo killers. They present gender-role socialization as the most likely theoretical explanation of this finding.

There must then be some explanation for why we cannot find women providing sexual reasons for serial killing. Are men and women just so bio-logically different that they cannot kill in the same way and for the same reasons? Evolutionary theories of aggression have been considered in chapter 2 but have not yet been called on to explain serial murder and the female killer. If violence is a complex behavioural adaptation, can it explain serial murder? Unlikely, as there is no evolutionary or genetic advantage to be gained from killing the types of victim seen here. It also does not explain any female serial murderer, as it is male humans who have evolved the physiological and psychological means to effect personal violence of this nature. It is also difficult to draw any comparative biological evaluation of murderous violence in a modern society when distinctions in sex roles are becoming blurred. However, there are other biological hypotheses to consider in serial murder.

Neurological contributions

A considerable minority of male serial killers have shown a history of head trauma and abnormality. For example, abnormality in brain areas associated with emotion and impulsiveness and inhibitory control are well documented. Money (1990) suggests that there may be a pathological confusion or conflation of sexual arousal and attack messages along certain neurological pathways. In addition, the thalamus and hypothalamus may have a direct role in aggression, as well as the ability to distinguish negative and positive stimuli. Abnormality here may explain the inability to form close personal relationships (Sears, 1991). The hypothalamus also interacts with the reticular activating system (RAS), and abnormality may mean that otherwise stimulating activity does not reach the cortex, explaining chronic under-arousal in the psychopath. Antisocial behaviour then follows in order to increase cortical levels of arousal; does this mean that thrill-oriented serial murder, and escalation of intensity and frequency of murders, is a manipulation of the environment in order to seek arousal? It might be, as Sears (1991) points out, since many serial murderers become compliant and biddable in captivity, contrasting with the arousal-seeking hypotheses.

Perhaps a clear picture can be drawn at the neurochemical level of examination. As discussed in chapter 1, endogenous hormones and neurochemicals are implicated in aggression, and show clear sex differences in both production and action. This position can be extended to include serial murder, but hypotheses of similarity in biochemistry of male and female serial murderers have never been tested.

We are not getting very far in either an explanation for serial murder, or an examination of female serial killers. Perhaps the rarity of female killers is something that should be examined, rather than why they are different to men. Two of the largest categories of our female killers have not yet been considered. The famous cases of rage leading to serial shootings, as seen in Aileen Wuornos, or those with what might be seen as perverse overtones, such as Jane Toppan or Elizabeth Bathory, are extremely rare. Our ladies are more likely to fall into categories that fit gender stereotypes.

Female Serial Killers

As well as Bathory, there have been several notable female serial killers throughout history. The first recorded was Locusta, who carried out her murder in the first century AD. She may have been a hired assassin, as she is said to have poisoned the Emperor Claudius at the behest of Agrippina the Younger, and she was given immunity from execution by Nero (Suetonius, 2007).

Some female killers have contributed to forensic science, albeit unwittingly. Arsenic has been a favourite poison through the ages; there is a fine line to draw between its medical use and its agency for death. Arsenical poisoning results in stomach pains, cramps, vomiting, diarrhoea, coma and death. For centuries it was used to kill but could not be identified in bodies, so it was a favourite poison for those with nefarious motives. In 1787, Johann Daniel Metzger described a method for identifying arsenic in solution – heating arsenious oxide in charcoal produces a black mirror-like substance. However, it was not until the 1800s when Valentin Rose showed how arsenic could be detected in human organs by extraction. This discovery was actually made during the investigation of the death of the husband, aunt and lover of Sophie Ursinus (Hale & Bolin, 1998). She was arrested in 1803 on suspicion of having poisoned her husband. His body was exhumed but arsenic poisoning could not be confirmed. She was next charged with murdering her aunt, who had left her a large inheritance. Unfortunately for Ursinus, by the time this trial came around, the test for arsenic could not be disputed, and she was convicted of murder. In addition to making forensic scientific history, Ursinus's case was clearly one of killing for profit.

Comfort serial killers

Comfort serial murderers kill for profit in order to fund a comfortable lifestyle, but they can also be said to be providing comfort as a means to ensnare victims. A review of the writings on female serial killers by Frei, Völlm, Graf and Dittman (2006) showed that, amongst the very sparse literature, it is difficult to categorize by patterns and/or motives, but the most common motive identified is material gain or similar gratification, while the hedonistic needs of the male serial killer are very rare. Hence, there is no consistent theory to be generated, although psychopathic personality traits and abusive childhood experiences regularly appear in case histories.

Therefore, the most common motive for female serial killing is gain. Perhaps the most vilified profit killings are those done by women who were trusted with the lives, literally, of the vulnerable. During the 1980s, Dorothea Puente ran a boarding house for elderly or mentally handicapped residents in Sacramento, California. She was, however, pocketing a large portion of their monthly benefits payments. This deception was netting her somewhere in the region of US$6,000 a month. Some of the tenants started to disappear, and Puente's handyman was called on to move large wooden boxes, to take soil away from the basement of the boarding house and to cover over the floor with concrete. Soon he disappeared too. On 11 November 1988, police calling to enquire after one missing tenant found the body of another in the house, and seven others in the garden and basement. No one thought Puente could be implicated, and she was allowed to wander off during the digging, ending up in Los Angeles, where she was recognized and turned in. She was convicted of three murders and died of natural causes in prison in 2011.

Comfort serial killers include the black widow category described in chapter 8. Sometimes these rather dangerous wives or girlfriends become serial killers. Forty-one-year-old Japanese businessman Yoshiyuki Oide was happily planning his wedding when he was found dead in his car from carbon monoxide poisoning. He had transferred five million yen (about £42,000 or US$65,000) to his fiancée days before his death, so something seemed suspicious. He was also found to have high levels of sleeping drugs in his system. His fiancée Kanae Kijima was subsequently charged with his murder and is suspected of involvement in the murders of up to six other men. She was originally arrested for defrauding two middle-aged men after meeting them on websites for people seeking marriage. She allegedly told them that she needed 3.2 million yen to pay her college tuition fees and promised to marry them after she graduated. In addition, 80-year-old Kenzo Ando died in a fire after Kijima visited him and withdrew money with his debit card. According to the English-language news site of Japan's *Mainichi* newspaper, her father was found dead in a car on her home island of Hokkaido several years ago. At the time of writing, her trial is set to start.

Despite the perception, borne out by figures, that there are low numbers of female serial killers, it is in the black widow serial killer area that we see higher numbers. A woman who kills for profit is much more common than a woman who kills for sexual gratification or sheer revenge. The lone female killer is even rarer than another, the woman who kills with a partner.

Couples Who Kill

On 23 May 1934, Clyde Barrow and Bonnie Parker were shot to death by police in Louisiana, the culmination of one of the most spectacular manhunts of the time. They were understood to have committed thirteen murders, usually during the commission of armed robberies. Barrow was also suspected of killing two police officers and kidnapping a couple in Louisiana (FBI, 2011). When Parker met Barrow, she was already married to an imprisoned killer; it is clear that she was attracted to Barrow because he was a dangerous person. The paraphilia of being sexually aroused by someone who has committed an outrageous or horrific crime is called hybristophilia but it has also been dubbed the 'Bonnie and Clyde syndrome'.

Some women do attach themselves to such men and fall into a downward spiral of behaviour that the world sees as depravity. Myra Hindley and Ian Brady, known as the Moors Murderers, abducted, sexually assaulted, tortured and murdered at least five children between July 1963 and October 1965. At least one body, that of 12-year-old Keith Bennett, lies hidden to this day. When Brady was arrested, after an emergency phone call made by Hindley's horrified brother-in-law, Hindley was allowed to remain free for five days, as no-one believed a woman could be implicated in such horrific crimes. Throughout the investigation and trial, Hindley remained steadfastly loyal to Brady; not so he to her. The trial revealed sickening evidence. A luggage locker was found with two suitcases containing sadistic pornography. These included nine photographs of 10-year-old Lesley Ann Downey, showing her naked, bound and gagged in Hindley's bedroom. A tape recording was also found in the luggage locker. On it, the voice of a young girl could be heard screaming, crying, and begging for her mother, and her life. What was most shocking in 1960s' Britain was one of the adult voices on the tape was female; Hindley could be heard taunting and threatening the terrified child. Both were sentenced to life imprisonment; Hindley died on 15 November 2002 after a heart attack, her press obituary dubbing her 'the most hated woman in Britain'. She had spent 37 years in custody, becoming Britain's longest-detained female prisoner and one of just two women to receive whole-life tariffs. Some still feel that Hindley was simply under Brady's spell during the time of the murders and, if she had never met him, she would never have been involved in such horrific acts.

The world is fascinated by Hindley, much more so than by Brady. The Moors Murders case is regarded as having a huge impact on life in Britain, the ending of a supposed innocence when it was thought to be safe to allow children out alone. It was certainly the first high-profile case of a woman being involved in serial child-sex murders. Hindley's part in the killings produces bewilderment, and is seen as especially deplorable.

The other female prisoner to receive a whole-life tariff was Rosemary West. Rosemary (or Rose) and her husband Fred West were accused of raping and murdering ten young women and girls over a 20-year period. They lured vulnerable runaways with offers of rides, lodging or jobs as nannies. Once inside their home, the girls were stripped, bound with tape, raped, tortured, killed, dismembered and buried, either in the garden, under the patio or under the house at 25 Cromwell Street, Gloucester. It also emerged that at least one of their own children had met the same fate. In 1994, their remaining children were taken into care after accusations of sexual abuse. Police, armed with a search warrant, dug up the remains of their 16-year-old daughter Heather, who had vanished in 1987.

Further excavations under the house and in the garden produced eight more female bodies. More bodies were found under the kitchen of a former home at 25 Midland Road, Gloucester. This was where the body of Charmaine was found. She was the daughter of Fred's first wife, Rena, a mixed-race child. Rena was also a victim of Fred's sexual violence and murderous urges. She was found buried in a field near Fred's parents' home.

Fred hanged himself in Winston Green Prison in Birmingham on New Year's Day in 1995. Rosemary still maintains her innocence. However, on 22 November 1995, she was convicted of ten murders and sentenced to life imprisonment. The Lord Chief Justice later decided that West should spend at least 25 years in prison, but, in July in 1997, the then Home Secretary Jack Straw subjected West to a whole-life tariff.

Killer couples are not confined solely to Britain of course. Canadian Karla Homolka adored her husband Paul Bernardo and would do anything for him. She was desperately sorry that she was not a virgin when she met Paul, as he so wanted to deflower a young woman. Karla worked at a veterinary surgery and stole some anaesthetic, halothane. On 23 December 1990, she drugged her younger sister Tammy and gave her to Paul as a Christmas present. Whilst Paul was raping her, Tammy, still unconscious, vomited and choked. Her death was ruled an accident. Bernardo then went on to pick up and rape female hitchhikers in the home he shared with Homolka. On 14 June 1991, Bernardo met Leslie Mahaffy, who was locked out; he drove her to his house where the couple kept her as a sex slave, videotaping the assaults as a reminder. They killed her in their basement. Paul cut up her body with a circular saw and Karla washed the body parts before setting them in concrete. Bernardo is confirmed as the Scarborough rapist, responsible for a horrific set of sexual assaults that took place in Scarborough, Ontario, in 1987–90. But the couple assaulted and killed several young women in addition to Tammy. Bernardo tried to pin the whole blame for the killings on Homolka who in turn tried to make a battered-wife defence. The videotapes they had made proved both of them were full and willing partners in the rape and murder of their young victims (Pron, 2005). Homolka testified against her husband and was sentenced to 12 years in prison. Bernardo was sentenced to life in prison without parole. Homolka has undergone psychiatric evaluation, with inconclusive diagnoses, although Williams (1996) suggested that a psychiatrist retained by Homolka's defence lawyer identified her as a classic example of hybristophilia. On 4 July 2005, Homolka was released.

Couples who kill are not exclusively heterosexual. Gwendolyn Graham and Cathy Wood met when they both worked as nurse's aides in the Alpine Moor nursing home, Walker, Michigan. They became lovers, practising sexual asphyxia to achieve a better orgasm, but also considered committing murder as a sexual game. Graham made several attempts to kill elderly women in the home, but chose the wrong victims as they fought back. Finally, in January 1987, Graham found one too feeble and she became the first victim, her death being ruled natural. Five more murders later, Graham decide to try to make the game more fun by selecting victims whose initials spelled MURDER. They openly boasted about the murders, but no one believed them, except Wood's ex-husband, who contacted the police. Wood made a plea bargain, claiming all the murders were carried out by Graham, and that she, Wood, had merely acted as lookout. Graham was convicted of five murders and sentenced to five life sentences. Wood was charged with one count of second-degree murder and one count of conspiracy to commit second-degree murder. She was sentenced to 20 years imprisonment (Buhk & Cohle, 2008).

Nurses feature prominently in our final category of female serial killer, the so-called angels of mercy, or angels of death. This is a type of serial killer who is employed as a caregiver in some capacity, and intentionally harms or kills the person/people in their care. This is murder from a position of power, and the 'angel' often claims that their victims were suffering and they ended their lives in an act of mercy. Neutralization theory, first developed by Sykes and Matza in 1957, has applications here, as the killers understand what they are doing is wrong but that the helping behaviour neutralizes the wrongdoing. An alternative explanation returns us to the issue of mental health in killers. In 1991, Beverley Allit killed four children and attempted to kill a further three. She was also convicted of using grievous bodily harm to another six children. The children were all patients in the Grantham and Kesteven Hospital, Lincolnshire, England, where Allitt was a nurse. She administered large doses of insulin or injected air into her victims. She received thirteen life sentences, being deemed a serious danger, and was detained in a secure psychiatric hospital. She is in hospital and not prison as she has been identified as being mentally ill. The diagnosis may be a factitious disorder (a condition in which a person acts as if he or she has an illness by deliberately producing, feigning or exaggerating symptoms), known as Munchausen syndrome by proxy. This is a controversial diagnosis, as the disorder is not formally listed in the DSM–IV–TR, although it can be included in the general criteria for factitious disorders. Munchausen syndrome by proxy involves a pattern of abuse in which a perpetrator ascribes to, or physically falsifies, illnesses in someone under their care in order to attract attention (Marks & Richmond, 2008). A case of a vulnerable person killing other vulnerable victims, or one of sheer negligence on the part of the medical field? Who can tell?

Conclusion

This brings us full circle to the idea that murderers are a breed apart, that they are mentally ill and that they are out for everything they can get. Do any of our examples or theories fully explain female serial killers?

Holmes and Holmes (1997) agree that the most likely motive for a female serial killer is financial gain and security. They do, however, attempt to suggest that there are typologies that include gain but that also include the person who has visions (generally agreed to be experiencing a psychotic break from reality), the rare hedonistic pleasure-seeker and the 'disciple' who kills to please a charismatic leader or partner. Always there are cases that can be found that are completely outside of these categories; what is most abundantly clear is that the female serial killer is a rare and unusual creature.

10

Conclusion

This book started with an attempt to place current definitions of and theories and research about aggression within a female perspective. Aggression and violence are still perceived as predominantly male issues, and it can appear that female aggression is seen as simply something that is a pale imitation of that behaviour. However, if, as seems to be the case in many countries, the only crime rate that is increasing is female-perpetrated violence, then dismissing it, or subsuming female aggression into male, may be a dangerous position. Examining it, and the theoretical positions attempting to explain it, is the first step to discovering what it is and how we can address it.

The broad examination of aggression covers every theoretical aspect of social and biological sciences. There are sociological, psychological, biological and neurological theories to be considered when investigating such a human aspect. There may even be economic, legislative and political factors to take into account. For example, Heidensohn and Gelsthorpe (2012) suggest that the perceived change in offences and arrest rates are an artefact of policy changes that reflect cultural changes in the perception of gender roles and gendered behaviour. An examination of shifts in rates of female-perpetuated violent crime in countries where women have gained some measure of legislatively coded freedoms has yet to be carried out. What this book has attempted to do is open up the possibilities of such investigations by starting to examine the question of female aggression.

Theories examined here have included the evolution of aggression and the ways in which women have developed or repressed aggressive and

Female Aggression, First Edition. Helen Gavin and Theresa Porter.
© 2015 John Wiley & Sons, Ltd. Published 2015 by John Wiley & Sons, Ltd.

violent urges during human development. Evolutionary science is based upon the idea that systems change as adaptation to the environments in which they grow, and successful adaptations are inherited by the next generation. This is true of behavioural and psychological adaptations as much as physical ones, hence evolutionary psychology is important in the consideration of the human condition. Aggression as an evolved adaptation is obvious as a need for survival when fighting predators or competitors is necessary. The differences in male and female aggression can therefore be explained if we consider that the male needed to protect and feed his mate (and their joint offspring) and that female behavioural evolution is one of nurturing, not violence. As a modern set of behaviours, it would be thought that the lack of necessity in most societies to fight for food would negate the need for aggression. A simple examination shows that male aggression is not receding, and that female aggression is actually growing. Therefore, evolutionary science, whilst it has clear value in examining the development of human aggression, tells us only part of the picture of modern-day female aggression.

If women are no less capable of aggressive thoughts and acts, an examination of the ways in which women express their aggression is fruitful when attempting to consider ways in which the outcome of aggression and its perpetration can be combated. The chapters in this book, detailing the different forms of aggression/violence that can be carried out and the ways in which specifically women do this, have considered it in ever escalating forms. From indirect aggression to serial murder, women are able to behave aggressively, albeit less frequently than men. There are forms, such as indirect aggression (chapter 3), that are particularly seen in female hands. Indirect aggression has not been studied in the same depth as the more physically violent forms, but is no less important. Emotional abuse, one form of indirect aggression for example, can have far-reaching and devastating results (Gavin, 2011). If, as this research seems to suggest, childhood emotional abuse is carried out by the mother or other female caregiver, then such behaviour and its outcomes needs to be considered. Other forms of indirect aggression appear to be suited to expressing women's hostile urges, and this is particularly evident with school-level bullying, the use of social media and the internet. Cyber aggression affords the aggressor a level of anonymity not seen elsewhere, except possibly with its non-electronic equivalent, the poison pen letter. The latter has disadvantages for the perpetrator in comparison with the internet in that it does not have the same instantaneous nature of electronic media and, possibly, their relentlessness. This aspect, along with issues such as adult female perpetrators, has not been researched to any great extent, concentrating instead on the school-level offender. The adult perpetrator is obviously more difficult to access and observe; although no less problematic and severe in outcome, child studies do not necessarily reflect the behaviour in the adult world. Such research, and all forms of research on indirect aggression by women, is only lately beginning to reflect the need to deal with the problem other than in school and workplace programmes.

Women remain the gender that is tasked with the care of children, almost exclusively in some parts of the world, yet it is clear that some women abuse and neglect children in high numbers. Whilst this is often dismissed as the outcome of mental illness or other mitigations, there are many instances when it is a function of the woman's tendency for aggression. As such, the current training for safeguarding agencies may need to be altered, particularly in the light of studies such as Campbell, Cook, LaFleur and Keenan (2010), revealing that the risk assessment of families may be underestimating the threat. A way to overcome this might be to turn to evidence-based treatments focusing on increasing positive interactions between parents and children. In this way, parents, and specifically mothers, can learn new ways to think about and interact with their children. The evidence presented in this book also suggests that educative and public information programmes would be fruitful venues to pursue.

Domestic violence has traditionally seen the woman as victim, not per-petrator, but increasingly the evidence suggests women are just as likely to be the abusive partner in a relationship, whether physically, psychologically or emotionally. The broadening definition of domestic violence (Walker & Gavin, 2011) means that there are opportunities to look at abuse within relationships that do not follow the pattern of male aggressor and female victim. Inclusive terms provide better opportunities for research and practice to counteract bias and not to ignore hitherto hidden populations of victims, including those victimized at female hands. Chapter 5 examines these positions and attempts to suggest ways in which policy can be education- and research-driven.

Domestic violence or intimate partner abuse is inextricably linked to the issue of sexual behaviour and sexualized violence. Sexual violence and sexual offending by women is only recently becoming an issue that is addressed by support agencies, the police and governmental policy. The cultural resistance to this issue, as discussed in chapter 6, is difficult to overcome, but attitudes are changing. However, there is still the doubly deviant perception to overcome, in that women who offend sexually are offending against their gender as well as their victim. Nowhere is this more apparent than when considering women who kill. Men are still the major perpetrators of homicide of whatever type, as described in chapter 8, but women and girls do kill. Additionally, they do not only kill in self-defence and their victims are not only abusive husbands on unwanted infants. The problem arises when female killers either are demonized, due to their gender, or are automatically assumed to be victims themselves. This is unhelpful either for research about women killing or for the services, such as police and prison services, who need to investigate the crimes and deal with offenders; chapter 9 attempts a look at those who have killed several victims over time. Women kill for the same reasons men do – greed, love or the sheer pleasure derived from killing. The female serial killer is rare but not non-existent, and their cases have all the salaciousness associated with them that the media love to focus on: sex, sexuality, lust and greed, with a little psychopathy and psychopathology thrown in. The theory and research presented in chapter 9 shows that the most likely reason for a woman killing multiple times is financial or related to her own security but that there are elements of psychosis to consider.

What we have attempted to do in this book is to examine a broad range of theoretical positions and real-life research associated with the idea and fact of female aggression in the hope that this influences attitudes to women who behave aggressively, in terms of recognizing this behaviour, and that it inspires more research into the area.

References

Abel, E. L. (1986). Childhood homicide in Erie County, New York. *Pediatrics,* 77(5), 709–713.

Abel, G., & Wiegel, M. (2009). Visual reaction time: Development, theory, empirical evidence and beyond. In F. M. Saleh (Eds.), *Sex Offenders: Identification, Risk Assessment, Treatment, and Legal Issues* (pp. 101–118). Oxford: Oxford University Press.

Adler, R. N., Loyle, C. E., & Globerman, J. (2007). A calamity in the neighborhood: Women's participation in the Rwandan genocide. *Genocide Studies and Prevention, 2*(3), 209–233.

Adshead, G., & Bluglass, K. (2005). Attachment representations in mothers with abnormal illness behaviour by proxy. *The British Journal of Psychiatry, 187*(4), 328–333.

Adshead, G., Brooke, D., Samuels, M., Jenner, S., & Southall, D. (2000). Maternal behaviours associated with smothering: A preliminary descriptive study. *Child Abuse & Neglect, 24*(9), 1175–1183.

Aggarwal, K., Bhullar, D., & Sharma, M. (2010). A case study of serial killers. *Medico-Legal Update – An International Journal, 10*(1).

Aggrawal, A. (2005). Mass murder. *Encyclopedia of Forensic and Legal Medicine, 3,* 216–223.

Agrawal, P., Bhatia, M., & Malik, S. (1997). Postpartum psychosis: A clinical study. *International Journal of Social Psychiatry, 43*(3), 217–222.

Aizenman, M., & Kelley, G. (1988). The incidence of violence and acquaintance rape in dating relationships among college men and women. *Journal of College Student Development, 29*(4), 305–311.

Alder, C., & Baker, J. (1997). Maternal filicide: More than one story to be told. *Women and Criminal Justice, 9*(2), 15–39.

Female Aggression, First Edition. Helen Gavin and Theresa Porter.
© 2015 John Wiley & Sons, Ltd. Published 2015 by John Wiley & Sons, Ltd.

Allen, C. M. (1991). *Women and Men who Sexually Abuse Children: A Comparative Analysis.* Orwell, VT: Safer Society Press.

Allen, P. (2010, July 20). I killed my eight babies because I didn't want to use contraception: French mother confessed to murdering newborns. *The Mail.* Retrieved from www.dailymail.com.

Anand, S. (2010). Rationalizing infanticide: A medico-legal assessment of the criminal code's child homicide offence. *Alberta Law Review, 47*(3), 706–728.

Anderson, C. A., & Bushman, B. (2002). Human aggression. *Annual Review of Psychology, 53*(1), 27–51.

Anderson, C. A., Anderson, K. B., Dorr, N., DeNeve, K. M., & Flanagan, M. (2000). Temperature and aggression. *Advances in Experimental Social Psychology, 32*, 63–129.

Anderson, P. B. (1998). Variations in college women's self-reported heterosexual aggression. *Sexual Abuse: A Journal of Research and Treatment, 10*(4), 283–292.

Anderson, P. B., & Struckman-Johnson, C. (Eds.). (1998). *Sexually Aggressive Women: Current Perspectives and Controversies.* New York: Guilford Press.

Angermeyer, M. C., & Matschinger, H. (2003). The stigma of mental illness: Effects of labelling on public attitudes towards people with mental disorder. *Acta Psychiatrica Scandinavica, 108*(4), 304–309.

APA (American Psychiatric Association). (2013). *Diagnostic and Statistical Manual of Mental Disorder* (5th ed.). Arlington, VA: American Psychiatric Association.

Araji, S. K., & Carlson, J. (2001). Family violence including crimes of honor in Jordan: Correlates and perceptions of seriousness. *Violence Against Women, 7*(5), 586–621.

Archer, J. (2002). Sex differences in physically aggressive acts between heterosexual partners: A meta-analytic review. *Aggression and Violent Behavior, 7*(4), 313–351.

Archer, J. (2004). Sex differences in aggression in real-world settings: A meta-analytic review. *Review of General Psychology, 8*(4), 291–322.

Archer, J. (2006). Cross-cultural differences in physical aggression between partners: A social-role analysis. *Personality and Social Psychology Review, 10*(2), 133–153.

Archer, J., & Coyne, S. M. (2005). An integrated review of indirect, relational, and social aggression. *Personality and Social Psychology Review, 9*(3), 212–230.

Archer, J., & Ray, N. (1989). Dating violence in the United Kingdom: A preliminary study. *Aggressive Behavior, 15*(5), 337–343.

Arehart-Treichel, J. (2007). Men shouldn't be overlooked as victims of partner violence. *Psychiatric News, 42*(15), 31.

Awwad, A. M. (2001). Gossip, scandal, shame and honor killing: A case for social constructionism and hegemonic discourse. *Social Thought & Research, 24*(1–2), 39–52.

Azar, S. T., Nix, R. L., & Makin-Byrd, K. N. (2005). Parenting schemas and the process of change. *Journal of Marital and Family Therapy, 31*(1), 45–58.

Babcock, J. C., Jacobson, N. S., Gottman, J. M., & Yerington, T. P. (2000). Attachment, emotional regulation, and the function of marital violence: Differences between secure, preoccupied, and dismissing violent and nonviolent husbands. *Journal of Family Violence, 15*(4), 391–409.

Babcock, J. C., Miller, S. A., & Siard, C. (2003). Toward a typology of abusive women: Differences between partner-only and generally violent women in the use of violence. *Psychology of Women Quarterly, 27*(2), 153–161.

Bader, S. M., Scalora, M. J., Casady, T. K., & Black, S. (2008). Female sexual abuse and criminal justice intervention: A comparison of child protective service and criminal justice samples. *Child Abuse & Neglect, 32*(1), 111–119.

Bader, S. M., Welsh, R., & Scalora, M. J. (2010). Recidivism among female child molesters. *Violence and Victims, 25*(3), 349–362.

Baer, J. C., and Martinez, C. D. (2006). Child maltreatment and insecure attachment: A meta-analysis. *Journal of Reproductive and Infant Psychology, 24*(3), 187–197.

Bajanowski, T., Vennemann, M., Bohnert, M., Rauch, E., Brinkmann, B., & Mitchell, E. A. (2005). Unnatural causes of sudden unexpected deaths initially thought to be sudden infant death syndrome. *International Journal of Legal Medicine, 119*(4), 213–216.

Balakrishnan, C., Imel, L. L., Bandy, A. T., & Prasad, J. K. (1995). Perineal burns in males secondary to spouse abuse. *Burns, 21*(1), 34–35.

Banning, A. (1989). Mother–son incest: Confronting a prejudice. *Child Abuse & Neglect, 13*(4), 563–570.

Bard, P., & Mountcastle, V. B. (1948). Some forebrain mechanisms involved in expression of rage with special reference to suppression of angry behavior. *Research Publications –Association for Research in Nervous and Mental Disease, 27*, 362–404.

Bardone, A. M., Moffitt, T. E., Caspi, A., Dickson, N., & Silva, P. A. (1996). Adult mental health and social outcomes of adolescent girls with depression and conduct disorder. *Development and Psychopathology, 8*(04), 811–829.

Barratt, E. S., Stanford, M. S., Dowdy, L., Liebman, M. J., & Kent, T. A. (1999). Impulsive and premeditated aggression: A factor analysis of self-reported acts. *Psychiatry Research, 86*(2), 163–173.

BBC (2006). Mother jailed after baby's death. Retrieved from www.bbc.co.uk

BBC (2008). Spotlight on domestic abuse laws. Retrieved from www.bbc.co.uk

BBC (2010). University of Alabama shooting suspect 'killed brother'. Retrieved from www.bbc.co.uk

BBC (2011). Theresa Riggi jailed for killing her three children. Retrieved from www.bbc.co.uk

BBC News (2006, June 1). German convicted over baby deaths. Retrieved from http://news.bbc.co.uk/2/hi/5037158.stm

Beaver, K. M. (2011). Genetic influences on being processed through the criminal justice system: Results from a sample of adoptees. *Biological Psychiatry, 69*(3), 282–287.

Beck, A. J., & Harrison, P. M. (2008). *Sexual Victimization in State and Federal Prisons Reported by Inmates, 2007*. US Department of Justice, Office of Justice Programs, Bureau of Justice Statistics.

Beck, A. J., & Johnson, C. (2012). *Sexual Victimization Reported by Former State Prisoners, 2008*. US Department of Justice, Office of Justice Programs, Bureau of Justice Statistics.

Beech, A. R., Parrett, N., Ward, T., & Fisher, D. (2009). Assessing female sexual offenders' motivations and cognitions: An exploratory study. *Psychology, Crime & Law, 15*(2–3), 201–216.

Behrendt, N., Buhl, N., & Seidl, S. (2002). The lethal paraphiliac syndrome: Accidental autoerotic deaths in four women and a review of the literature. *International Journal of Legal Medicine, 116*(3), 148–152.

Beier, K. M., Wille, R., & Wessel, J. (2006). Denial of pregnancy as a reproductive dysfunction: A proposal for international classification systems. *Journal of Psychosomatic Research, 61*(5), 723–730.

Belanger, S. (2007). *Three Studies of Sexual Offenders: Female Perpetrated Sexual Victimization, Comparison of Male and Female Perpetrated Sexual Victimization, and Escalation Histories* (unpublished thesis). Smith College, MA, USA.

Benenson, J. F., Markovits, H., Thompson, M. E., & Wrangham, R. W. (2011). Under threat of social exclusion, females exclude more than males. *Psychological Science, 22*(4), 538–544.

Bennett, M. D., Hall J., Frazier L., Patel N., Barker L., & Shaw, K. (2006). Homicide of children aged 0–4 years, 2003–2004: Results from the national violent death reporting system. *Injury Prevention, 12*(2), 39–43.

Bennett, W. (1996). Sara Thornton is cleared of murder. Retrieved from www.independent.co.uk

Bent, J., Gavin, H. & Porter, T. (2014). Sugar and spice, but not very nice: Representations of evil little 'girls' in cartoons and comic books/strips. In H. Priest (Ed.), *The Female of the Species: Cultural Constructions of Evil, Women and the Feminine*. Oxford: Inter-disciplinary Press.

Berkowitz, L. (1989). Frustration-aggression hypothesis: Examination and reformulation. *Psychological Bulletin, 106*(1), 59–73.

Beyer, K., Mack, S. M., & Shelton, J. L. (2008). Investigative analysis of neonaticide: An exploratory study. *Criminal Justice and Behaviour, 35*(4), 522–535.

Billingham, R. E., & Sack, A. R. (1986). Courtship violence and the interactive status of the relationship. *Journal of Adolescent Research, 1*(3), 315–325.

Bjorklund, D. F., & Pellegrini, A. D. (2000). Child development and evolutionary psychology. *Child Development, 71*(6), 1687–1708.

Bjorkqvist, K. (2001). Social defeat as a stressor in humans. *Physiology & Behavior, 73*(3), 435–442.

Bjorkqvist, K., & Niemela, P. (1992). *Of Mice and Women: Aspects of Female Aggression.* Academic Press.

Bjorkqvist, K., Lagerspetz, K. M., & Kaukiainen, A. (1992). Do girls manipulate and boys fight? Developmental trends in regard to direct and indirect aggression. *Aggressive Behavior, 18*(2), 117–127.

Björkqvist, K., Österman, K., & Kaukiainen, A. (2000). Social intelligence − empathy = aggression? *Aggression and Violent Behavior, 5*(2), 191–200.

Bland, R. C., & Orn, H. (1986). Family violence and psychiatric disorder. *The Canadian Journal of Psychiatry/La Revue canadienne de psychiatrie, 31*(2), 129–137.

Block, C. R., Blokland, A. A., van der Werff, C., van Os, R., & Nieuwbeerta, P. (2010). Long-term patterns of offending in women. *Feminist Criminology, 5*(1), 73–107.

Bloom, M. (2007). Dying to kill: Motivations for suicide terrorism. In A. Pedahzur (Ed.), *Root Causes of Suicide Terrorism: The Globalization of Martyrdom.* New York: Routledge.

Bohnert, M., Grosse Perdekamp, M., & Pollak, S. (2003). Three subsequent infanticides covered up as SIDS. *International Journal of Legal Medicine, 119*(1), 31–34.

Bonanno, G. A. (2004). Loss, trauma, and human resilience: Have we underestimated the human capacity to thrive after extremely aversive events? *American Psychologist, 59*(1), 20–28.

Boroughs, D. S. (2004). Female sexual abusers of children. *Children and Youth Services Review, 26*(5), 481–487.

Bosquet, M., & Egeland, B. (2000). Predicting parenting behaviors from antisocial practices content scale scores of the MMPI-2 administered during pregnancy. *Journal of Personality Assessment, 74*(1), 146–162.

Botje, C., Schlöfke, D., Nedopil, N., and Hossler, F. (2011). Kindst÷tungen. Soziale und gutachterliche Aspekte. [Infanticide: Social and forensic aspects]. *Nervenarzt, 82*(7), 873–9.

Bouchard, T. J., Lykken, D. T., McGue, M., Segal, N. L., & Tellegen, A. (1990). Sources of human psychological differences: The Minnesota study of twins reared apart. *Science, 250*(4978), 223–228.

Bourget, D., & Gagné, P. (2005). Paternal filicide in Quebec. *Journal of the American Academy of Psychiatry and the Law Online, 33*(3), 354–360.

Bourget, D., Grace, J., & Whitehurst, L. (2006). A review of maternal and paternal filicide. *Journal of the American Academy of Psychiatry and the Law Online, 35*(1), 74–82.

Bourke, J. (2008). *Rape: A History from 1860 to the Present.* Virago Press, p. 221.

Bowen, E. L. (2008). *Domestic Violence Treatment for Abusive Women: A Treatment Manual.* New York: Routledge.

Bowie, B. H. (2007). Relational aggression, gender, and the developmental process. *Journal of Child and Adolescent Psychiatric Nursing, 20*(2), 107–115.

Boyes, R. (2007). 'Dump your children here' box to stop mothers killing their babies. *The Sunday Times.* Retrieved from www.timesonline.co.uk

Brand, P. A., & Kidd, A. H. (1986). Frequency of physical aggression in heterosexual and female homosexual dyads. *Psychological Reports, 59*(3), 1307–1313.

Branson-Trent, G. (2010). *Vampires Among Us: The Children of the Night.* New Image Productions.

Brent, D., Oquendo, M., Nirmaher, B., Greenhill, L., Kolko, D. Stanley, B., . . . Mann, J. (2003). Peripubertal suicide attempts in offspring of suicide attempters with siblings concordant for suicidal behaviour. *American Journal of Psychiatry, 160* (August), 1486–1493.

Briggs, F., & Hawkins, R. M. (1996). A comparison of the childhood experiences of convicted male child molesters and men who were sexually abused in childhood and claimed to be non-offenders. *Child Abuse & Neglect, 20*(3), 221–233.

Brinich, P. M. (1980). Some potential effects of adoption on self and object representation. *Psychoanalytic Study of the Child, 35*, 107–133.

Brinkerhoff, M. B., & Lupri, E. (1988). Interspousal violence. *Canadian Journal of Sociology/Cahiers canadiens de sociologie, 13*(4), 407–434.

Brookman, F., & Nolan, J. (2006). The dark figure of infanticide in England and Wales: Complexities of diagnosis. *Journal of Interpersonal Violence, 21*(7), 869–889.

Brown, M. (1979). Viewing time of pornography. *The Journal of Psychology, 102*(1), 83–95.

Brownmiller, S. (1989, February 2). Hedda Nussbaum, hardly a heroine. . . *New York Times.* R Retrieved from http://www.nytimes.com/1989/02/02/opinion/hedda-nussbaum-hardly-a-heroine.html

Brunner, C. (2007). Occidentalism meets the female suicide bomber: A critical reflection on recent terrorism debates: A review essay. *Signs, 32*(4), 957–971.

Brunner, H. G., Nelen, M., Breakefield, X. O., Ropers, H. H., & van Oost, B. A. (1993). Abnormal behavior associated with a point mutation in the structural gene for monoamine oxidase A. *Science, 262*, 578–580.

Buchanan, A. (1996). *Cycles of Child Maltreatment: Facts, Fallacies, and Interventions.* West Sussex: Wiley-Blackwell.

Bugental, D. B., Ellerson, P. C., Lin, E. K., Rainey, B., Kokotovic, A., & O'Hara, N. (2010). A cognitive approach to child abuse prevention. *Psychology of Violence, 1*(S), 84–106.

Buhk, T. T., & Cohle, S. D. (2008). *Skeletons in the Closet: Stories from the County Morgue*. New York: Prometheus Books.

Bunting, L. (2005). *Females who Sexually Offend against Children: Responses of the Child Protection and Criminal Justice Systems*. London: National Society for the Prevention of Cruelty to Children.

Bureau of Justice Statistics (2010, January). *Sexual Victimization in Juvenile Facilities Reported by Youth, 2008–2009*. Special Report, NCJ 228416.

Burgess, A. W., Hartman, C. R., & McCormack, A. (1987). Abused to abuser: Antecedents of socially deviant behaviors. *American Journal of Psychiatry, 144*(11), 1431–1436.

Burke, P. J., Stets, J. E., & Pirog-Good, M. A. (1988). Gender identity, self-esteem, and physical and sexual abuse in dating relationships. *Social Psychology Quarterly, 51*(3), 272–285.

Busch, F. (1997, September 14). A mother on trial. *New York Times*. Retrieved from http://www.nytimes.com/1997/09/14/books/a-mother-on-trial.html

Bushman, B. J., & Anderson, C. A. (2001). Is it time to pull the plug on hostile versus instrumental aggression dichotomy? *Psychological Review, 108*(1), 273–279.

Buss, A. H., & Durkee, A. (1957). An inventory for assessing different kinds of hostility. *Journal of Consulting Psychology, 21*(4), 343–349.

Buss, A. H., & Perry, M. (1992). Personality processes and individual differences. *Journal of Personality and Social Psychology, 63*(3), 4S9.

Buss, D. M., & Duntley, J. D. (2008). Adaptations for exploitation. *Group Dynamics: Theory, Research, and Practice, 12*(1), 53–62.

Butler, J. (2010). Musical works, cover versions and *Strange Little Girls*. *La revue des musiques populaires, 7*(1), 42–72.

Byard, R. W., Hucker, S. J., & Hazelwood, R. R. (1993). Fatal and near-fatal autoerotic asphyxial episodes in women: Characteristic features based on a review of nine cases. *The American Journal of Forensic Medicine and Pathology, 14*(1), 70–73.

Campbell, A. (1984). The girls in the gang. *New Society, 69*(1135), 308–311.

Campbell, A. (1991). On the invisibility of the female delinquent peer group. *Women & Criminal Justice, 2*(1), 41–62.

Campbell, A. (1995). A few good men: Evolutionary psychology and female adolescent aggression. *Ethology and Sociobiology, 16*(2), 99–123.

Campbell, A., & Muncer, S. (2009). Can 'risky' impulsivity explain sex differences in aggression? *Personality and Individual Differences, 47*(5), 402–406.

Campbell, K. A., Cook, L. J., LaFleur, B. J., & Keenan, H. T. (2010). Household, family, and child risk factors after an investigation for suspected child maltreatment: A missed opportunity for prevention. *Archives of Pediatrics & Adolescent Medicine, 164*(10), 943–949.

Campbell, S. B., & Cohn, J. F. (1991). Prevalence and correlates of postpartum depression in first-time mothers. *Journal of Abnormal Psychology, 100*(4), 594–599.

Capaldi, D. M., & Clark, S. (1998). Prospective family predictors of aggression toward female partners for at-risk young men. *Developmental Psychology, 34*(6), 1175–1188.

Capaldi, D. M., Kim, H. K., & Shortt, J. W. (2004). Women's involvement in aggression in young adult romantic relationships: A developmental systems model. In M. Putallaz & K. L. Birman (Eds.), *Aggression, Antisocial Behavior and Violence Among Girls: A Developmental Perspective* (pp. 223–241). New York: Guilford.

Caputi, J. (1989). The sexual politics of murder. *Gender & Society, 3*(4), 437–456.

Carangelo, L. (2002). *Chosen Children: Billion Dollar Babies in America's Foster Care, Adoption, and Prison Systems.* Rochester, VT: Schenkman Books.

Card, C. (2003). Genocide and social death. *Hypatia, 18*(1), 63–79.

Carlsmith, K. M., Wilson, T. D., & Gilbert, D. T. (2008). The paradoxical consequences of revenge. *Journal of Personality and Social Psychology, 95*(6), 1316–1324.

Carlson, V., Cicchetti, D., Barnett, D., & Braunwald, K. (1989). Disorganized/disoriented attachment relationships in maltreated infants. *Developmental Psychology, 25*(4), 525–531.

Carney, M. M., & Buttell, F. P. (2004). A multidimensional evaluation of a treatment program for female batterers: A pilot study. *Research on Social Work Practice, 14*(4), 249–258.

Cashdan, E. (1996). Women's mating strategies. *Evolutionary Anthropology, 5,* 134–143.

Cashdan, E. (2003). Hormones and competitive aggression in women. *Aggressive Behavior, 29*(2), 107–115.

Carrado, M., George, M. J., Loxam, E., Jones, L., & Templar, D. (1996). Aggression in British heterosexual relationships: A descriptive analysis. *Aggressive Behavior, 22*(6), 401–415.

Cascardi, M., Langhinrichsen, J., & Vivian, D. (1992). Marital aggression: Impact, injury, and health correlates for husbands and wives. *Archives of Internal Medicine, 152*(6), 1178–1184.

Castella, T., & McClatchey, C. (2011). UK riots: What turns people into looters? *BBC News.* Retrieved from www.bbc.co.uk/news/magazine-14463452.

Cauffman, E., Lexcen, F. J., Goldweber, A., Shulman, E. P., & Grisso, T. (2007). Gender differences in mental health symptoms among delinquent and community youth. *Youth Violence and Juvenile Justice, 5,* 287–307.

Chadwick, B. A., & Top, B. L. (1993). Religiosity and delinquency among LDS adolescents. *Journal for the Scientific Study of Religion, 33,* 51–67.

Chaffin, M., & Friedrich, B. (2004). Evidence-based treatments in child abuse and neglect. *Children and Youth Services Review, 26*(11), 1097–1113.

Chagnon, N. A. (2000). Yanomamö: The last days of Eden. In C. Gowans (Ed.), *Moral Disagreements: Classic and Contemporary Readings* (pp. 91–101). New York: Routledge.

Chesler, P. (2009). *Woman's Inhumanity to Woman.* Chicago: Lawrence Hill Books.

Chesney-Lind, M., & Brown, M. (1999). Girls and violence: An overview. In D. J. Flannery and C. R. Huff (Eds.), *Youth Violence: Prevention, Intervention, and Social Policy.* Washington, DC: American Psychiatric Press.

Chesney-Lind, M., & Eliason, M. (2006). From invisible to incorrigible: The demonization of marginalized women and girls. *Crime Media Culture, 2*(1), 29–47.

Chivers, M. L., & Bailey, J. M. (2005). A sex difference in features that elicit genital response. *Biological Psychology, 70*(2), 115–120.

Chivers, M. L., Rieger, G., Latty, E., & Bailey, J. M. (2004). A sex difference in the specificity of sexual arousal. *Psychological Science, 15*(11), 736–744.

Chivers, M. L., Seto, M. C., & Blanchard, R. (2007). Gender and sexual orientation differences in sexual response to sexual activities versus gender of actors in sexual films. *Journal of Personality and Social Psychology, 93*(6), 1108–1121.

Clements-Schreiber, M. E., Rempel, J. K., & Desmarais, S. (1998). Women's sexual pressure tactics and adherence to related attitudes: A step toward prediction. *Journal of Sex Research, 35*(2), 197–205.

Clutton-Brock, T. (2007). Sexual selection in males and females. *Science, 318*(5858), 1882–1885.

CNN (2009). Issues with Jane Velez-Mitchell encore: Cases that changed America – Human Hunters. *CNN.* Retrieved from http://transcripts.cnn.com/TRANSCRIPTS/0909/07/ijvm.01.html

Coccaro, E. F. (1998). Impulsive aggression: A behavior in search of clinical definition. *Harvard Review of Psychiatry, 5*(6), 336–339.

Coccaro, E. F., Berman, M. E., & Kavoussi, R. J. (1997). Assessment of life history of aggression: Development and psychometric characteristics. *Psychiatry Research, 73*(3), 147–157.

Coccaro, E. F., Berman, M. E., Kavoussi, R. J., & Hauger, R. L. (1996). Relationship of prolactin response to d-fenfluramine to behavioral and questionnaire assessments of aggression in personality-disordered men. *Biological Psychiatry, 40*(3), 157–164.

Cohen, R., Hsueh, Y., Russell, K. M., & Ray, G. E. (2006). Beyond the individual: A consideration of context for the development of aggression. *Aggression and Violent Behavior, 11*(4), 341–351.

Coke, E. (1997[c. 1698]). The Third Part of the Institutes of the Laws of England: Concerning High Treason, and Other Pleas of the Crown and Criminal Causes.

Cited in A. D. Boyer (Ed.), Ciceronianus: Classical rhetoric and the common law tradition. *Revue internationale de semiotique juridique, 10*(1), 3–36.

Collins, A. M., & Loftus, E. F. (1975). A spreading-activation theory of semantic processing. *Psychological Review, 82*(6), 407–428.

Connelly, C. D., & Straus, M. A. (1992). Mother's age and risk for physical abuse. *Child Abuse & Neglect, 16*(5), 709–718.

Condy, S. R., Templer, D. I., Brown, R., & Veaco, L. (1987). Parameters of sexual contact of boys with women. *Archives of Sexual Behavior, 16*(5), 379–394.

Coney, N. S., & Mackey, W. C. (1997). A reexamination of Gilligan's analysis of the female moral system. *Human Nature, 8*(3), 247–273.

Conradi, L., Geffner, R., Kevin Hamberger, L., & Lawson, G. (2009). An exploratory study of women as dominant aggressors of physical violence in their intimate relationships. *Journal of Aggression, Maltreatment & Trauma, 18*(7), 718–738.

Cook, W. W., & Medley, D. M. (1954). Proposed hostility and pharisaic-virtue scales for the MMPI. *Journal of Applied Psychology, 38*(6), 414–418.

Cooper, A. J., Swaminath, S., Baxter, D., & Poulin, C. (1990). A female sex offender with multiple paraphilias: A psychologic, physiologic (laboratory sexual arousal) and endocrine case study. *The Canadian Journal of Psychiatry/La Revue canadienne de psychiatrie, 35*(4), 334–337.

Cooper, P. J., Campbell, E. A., Day, A., Kennerly, H., & Bond, A. (1988). Nonpsychotic psychiatric disorder after childbirth: A prospective study of prevalence, incidence, course and nature. *The British Journal of Psychiatry, 152*, 799–806.

Cortoni, F. (2010). Female sexual offenders: A special subgroup. In K. Harrison (Ed.), *Managing High-Risk Sex Offenders in the Community: Risk Management, Treatment and Social Responsibility* (pp. 159–173). Cullompton: Willan Publishing.

Couprie, D. L., Hahn, R., & Gerard, N. (2003). *Anaximander in Context: New Studies in the Origins of Greek Philosophy*. Albany: State University of New York Press.

Coyne, S. M., & Archer, J. (2004). Indirect aggression in the media: A content analysis of British television programs. *Aggressive Behavior, 30*(3), 254–271.

Cox, J., Murray, D., & Chapman G. (1993). A controlled study of the onset, duration and prevalence of postnatal depression. *British Journal of Psychiatry, 163*(1), 27–31.

Craft, A. W., & Hall, D. M. B. (2004). Munchausen syndrome by proxy and sudden infant death. *British Medical Journal, 328*(7451), 1309–1312.

Creighton, S. J. (1985). An epidemiological study of abused children and their families in the United Kingdom between 1977 and 1982. *Child Abuse & Neglect, 9*(4), 441–448.

Creighton, S. J., & Noyes, P. (1989). *Child Abuse Trends in England and Wales, 1983–1987*. London: National Society for the Prevention of Cruelty to Children.

Crick, N. R. (1995). Relational aggression: The role of intent attributions, feelings of distress, and provocation type. *Development and Psychopathology, 7*(2), 313–322.

Crimmins, S., Langley, S., Brownstein, H., & Spunt, B. (1997). Convicted women who have killed children: A self-psychology perspective. *Journal of Interpersonal Violence, 12*(1), 49–69.

Crittenden, P. M., & Craig, S. E. (1990). Developmental trends in the nature of child homicide. *Journal of Interpersonal Violence, 5*(2), 202–216.

Cruise, K. R., Colwell, L. H., Lyons, P. M., & Baker, M. D. (2003). Prototypical analysis of adolescent psychopathy: Investigating the juvenile justice perspective. *Behavioral Sciences & the Law, 21*(6), 829–846.

Crume, T. L., DiGuiseppi, C., Byers, T., Sirotnak, A. P., & Garrett, C. J. (2002). Underascertainment of child maltreatment fatalities by death certificates, 1990–1998. *Pediatrics, 110*(2), e18–e18.

Crumley, B. (2010, July 7). Why are French women killing their babies? *The Times*. Retrieved from www.thetimesonline

Cummings, P., Theis, M. K., Mueller, B.A., & Rivara, F. P. (1994). Infant injury death in Washington State, 1981 through 1990. *Archives of Pediatric and Adolescent Medicine, 148*(10), 1021–1026.

Curry, C. (2009). Bones of two infants found in car of baby Crystal's mom. *Rockford Register Star*. Retrieved from www.rrstar.com

Dale, M. C. (2010, October 25). Woman charged after five infant skeletons found: Tests reveal that at least four infants were born alive but killed, officials say. *Associated Press*. Retrieved from www.msnbc.com.

Dalley, M. (2000 [1997]). *The Killing of Canadian Children by a Parent(s) or Guardian(s): Characteristics and Trends 1990–1993*. Report prepared for the Royal Canadian Mounted Police Missing Children's Registry and National Police Services.

Daly, M., & Wilson, M. (1985). Child abuse and other risks of not living with both parents. *Ethology and Sociobiology, 6*(4), 197–210.

Daly, M., & Wilson, M. (1988). Evolutionary social psychology and family homicide. *Science, 242*(4878), 519–524.

Daly, M., & Wilson, M. (1994). Some differential attributes of lethal assaults on small children by stepfathers versus genetic fathers. *Ethology and Sociobiology, 15*(4), 207–217.

Daly, M., & Wilson, M. (2005). The 'Cinderella Effect' is no fairy tale. *Trends in Cognitive Sciences, 9*(11), 507–508.

Danner, C., Pacher, M., Ambach, E., & Brezinka, C. (2005). Anonymous birth and neonaticide in Tyrol. *Zeitschrift fur Geburtshilfe und Neonatologie, 209*(5), 192–198.

Dasgupta, S. D. (2002). A framework for understanding women's use of nonlethal violence in intimate heterosexual relationships. *Violence Against Women, 8*(11), 1364–1389.

da Veiga, C. P., Miczek, K. A., Lucion, A. B., & de Almeida, R. M. M. (2011). Social instigation and aggression in postpartum female rats: Role of 5-Ht1A and 5-Ht1B receptors in the dorsal raphe nucleus and prefrontal cortex. *Psychopharmacology, 213*(2–3), 475–487.

De Bellis, M. D., Broussard, E. R., Herring, D. J., Wexler, S., Moritz, G., & Benitez, J. G. (2001). Psychiatric co-morbidity in caregivers and children involved in maltreatment: A pilot research study with policy implications. *Child Abuse & Neglect, 25*(7), 923–944.

de Boer, F., & Koolhaas, J. (2005). 5-HT$_{1A}$ and 5-HT$_{1B}$ receptor agonists and aggression: A pharmacological challenge of the serotonin deficiency hypothesis. *European Journal of Pharmacology, 526*(1–3), 125–139.

de Bruxelles, S. (2009, October 2). Vanessa George and Angela Allen abused toddlers for Facebook 'friend' they never met. *The Times.* Retrieved from www.thetimes.co.uk/tto/news/uk/crime/article1877216.ece

Deering, R., & Mellor, D. (2009). Sentencing of male and female child sex offenders: Australian study. *Psychiatry, Psychology and Law, 16*(3), 394–412.

Deering, R., & Mellor, D. (2010). What is the prevalence of female-perpetrated child sexual abuse? A review of the literature. *American Journal of Forensic Psychology, 28*(3), 25–53.

Dees, M., Vernooij-Dassen, M., Dekkers, W., & van Weel, C. (2010). Unbearable suffering of patients with a request for euthanasia or physician-assisted suicide: An integrative review. *Psycho-Ontology, 19*(4), 339–352.

DeLeon-Granados, W., Wells, W., & Binsbacher, R. (2006). Arresting developments trends in female arrests for domestic violence and proposed explanations. *Violence Against Women, 12*(4), 355–371.

Denov, M. S. (2001). Culture of denial: Exploring professional perspectives on female sex offending. *Canadian Journal of Criminology, 43*(3), 303–329.

Denov, M. S. (2003). To a safer place? Victims of sexual abuse by females and their disclosures to professionals. *Child Abuse & Neglect, 27*(1), 47–61.

De Paul, J., & Guibert, M. (2008). Empathy and child neglect: A theoretical model. *Child Abuse & Neglect, 32*(11), 1063–1071.

De Paul, J., Pérez-Albeniz, A., Guibert, M., Asla, N., & Ormaechea, A. (2008). Dispositional empathy in neglectful mothers and mothers at high risk for child physical abuse. *Journal of Interpersonal Violence, 23*(5), 670–684.

Des Rosier, J. (2008). Little coffins: A history of infanticide. *Time Warner News.* Retrieved from http://capitolregion.ynn.com

DeWall, C., Bushman, B., Giancola, P., & Webster, G. (2010). The big, the bad, and the boozed-up: Weight moderates the effect of alcohol on aggression. *Journal of Experimental Social Psychology, 46*(4) (July), 619–623.

Diem, C., & Pizarro, J. M. (2010). Social structure and family homicides. *Journal of Family Violence, 23*(5), 521–532.

Dietrich, D., Berkowitz, L., Kadushin, A., & McGloin, J. (1990). Some factors influencing abusers' justification of their child abuse. *Child Abuse & Neglect, 14*(3), 337–345.

Dietz, P. E., Hazelwood, R. R., & Warren, J. (1990). The sexually sadistic criminal and his offenses. *Bulletin of the American Academy of Psychiatry and the Law, 18*(2), 163–178.

DiScala, C., Sege, R., Li, G., & Reece, R. M. (2000). Child abuse and unintentional injuries: A 10-year retrospective. *Archives of Pediatrics & Adolescent Medicine, 154*(1), 16–22.

Dix, T., Ruble, D. N., Grusec, J. E., & Nixon, S. (1986). Social cognition in parents: Inferential and affective reactions to children of three age levels. *Child Development, 57*(4), 879–894.

Dixon, L., Hamilton-Giachritsis, C., & Browne, K. (2005). Attributions and behaviours of parents abused as children: A mediational analysis of the intergenerational continuity of child maltreatment (part II). *Journal of Child Psychology and Psychiatry, 46*(1), 58–68.

Dobson, V., & Sales, B. D. (2000). The science of infanticide and mental illness. *Psychology, Public Policy and Law, 6*(4), 1098–1112.

Dodson, R., & Iredale, W. (2006, December 31). Office queen bees hold back women's careers. *The Sunday Times.* Retrieved from www.timesonline.co.uk

Dollard, J., Miller, N. E., Doob, L. W., Mowrer, O. H., & Sears, R. R. (1939). *Frustration and Aggression.* New Haven, CT: Yale University Press.

Dopke, C. A., Lundahl, B. W., Dunsterville, E., & Lovejoy, M. C. (2003). Interpretations of child compliance in individuals at high-and low-risk for child physical abuse. *Child Abuse & Neglect, 27*(3), 285–302.

d'Orbán, P. T. (1979). Women who kill their children. *British Journal of Psychiatry, 134*(6), 560–571.

Doroszewicz, K., & Forbes, G. B. (2008). Experiences with dating aggression and sexual coercion among Polish college students. *Journal of Interpersonal Violence, 23*(1), 58–73.

Dowd, L., & Leisring, P. A. (2008). A framework for treating partner aggressive women. *Violence and Victims, 23*(2), 249–263.

Dowd, L. S., Leisring, P. A., & Rosenbaum, A. (2005). Partner aggressive women: Characteristics and treatment attrition. *Violence and Victims, 20*(2), 219–233.

Drescher-Burke, K., Krall, J., & Penick, A. (2004). Discarded infants and neonaticide: A review of the literature. *National Abandoned Infants Assistance Resource Center, 1–13.*

Dubowitz, H., Hampton, R. L., Bithoney, W. G., & Newberger, E. H. (1987). Inflicted and non-inflicted injuries. *American Journal of Orthopsychiatry, 57*(4), 525–535.

Duke, L. M., & Desforges, D. M. (2007). Mock juror decision-making in sexual abuse cases. *Applied Psychology in Criminal Justice, 3*(2), 96–116.

Dulit, E. (2000). Girls who deny pregnancy: Girls who kill the neonate. *Adolescent Psychiatry, 25,* 219–236.

Duminy, F. J., & Hudson, D. A. (1993). Assault inflicted by hot water. *Burns, 19*(5), 426–428.

Duncan, L., & Owen-Smith, A. (2006). Powerlessness and the use of indirect aggression in friendships. *Sex Roles, 55*(7–8), 493–502.

Dutch News (2011). Prosecutor wants eight years jail for Geleen mother. Retrieved from www.dutchnews.nl/news/archives/2011/09/prosecutor_wants_eight_years_j.php

Dutton, D. G. (2006). *The Abusive Personality: Violence and Control in Intimate Relationships.* New York: Guilford Press.

Dutton, D. G. (2007). *The Psychology of Genocide, Massacres, and Extreme Violence: Why 'Normal' People Come to Commit Atrocities.* Westport, CN: Greenwood Publishing Group.

Dutton, D. G., Nicholls, T. L., & Spidel, A. (2006). Female perpetrators of intimate abuse. *Journal of Offender Rehabilitation, 41*(4), 1–31.

Dworkin, R. (1975). Hard cases. *Harvard Law Review, 88*(6), 1057–1109.

ECCC (2010). Closing orders of the Extraordinary Chambers of the courts of Cambodia. United Nations.

Egeland, B., & Sroufe, L. A. (1981). Attachment and early maltreatment. *Child Development, 52*(1), 44–52.

Egger, S. A. (1984). A working definition of serial murder and the reduction of linkage blindness. *Journal of Police Science and Administration, 12*(3), 348–357.

Ehrensaft, M. K., Cohen, P., Brown, J., Smailes, E., Chen, H., & Johnson, J. G. (2003). Intergenerational transmission of partner violence: A 20-year prospective study. *Journal of Consulting and Clinical Psychology, 71*(4), 741–753.

Ehrensaft, M. K., Moffitt, T. E., & Caspi, A. (2004). Clinically abusive relationships in an unselected birth cohort: Men's and women's participation and developmental antecedents. *Journal of Abnormal Psychology, 113*(2), 258–270.

Eisenberger, N., Way, B., Taylor, S., Welch, W., & Lieberman, M. (2007). Understanding genetic risk for aggression: Clues from the brain's response to social exclusion. *Biological Psychiatry, 61*(9), 1100–1108.

Elliott, I. A., & Ashfield, S. (2011). The use of online technology in the modus operandi of female sex offenders. *Journal of Sexual Aggression, 17*(1), 92–104.

Elliott, I. A., Eldridge, H. J., Ashfield, S., & Beech, A. R. (2010). Exploring risk: Potential static, dynamic, protective and treatment factors in the clinical histories of female sex offenders. *Journal of Family Violence, 25*(6), 595–602.

Everson, M. D., Smith, J. B., Hussey, J. M., English, D., Litrownik, A. J., Dubowitz, H., Thompson, R., Knight, E. & Runyan, D. K. (2008). Concordance between adolescent reports of childhood abuse and child protective service determinations in an at-risk sample of young adolescents. *Child Maltreatment, 13*(1), 14–26.

Ewigman, B., Kivlahan, C., & Land, G. (1993). The Missouri child fatality study: Underreporting of maltreatment fatalities among children younger than five years of age, 1983 through 1986. *Pediatrics, 91*(2), 330–337.

Ewing, C. P. (1997). *Fatal Families: The Dynamics of Intrafamilial Homicide.* Thousand Oaks, CA: Sage Publications.

Faller, K. C. (1987). Women who sexually abuse children. *Violence & Victims, 2*(4), 263–276.

Faller, K. (1995). A clinical sample of women who have sexually abused children. *Journal of Child Sexual Abuse, 4*(3), 13–30.

Famularo, R., Kinscherff, R., & Fenton, T. (1992). Psychiatric diagnoses of maltreated children: Preliminary findings. *Journal of the American Academy of Child & Adolescent Psychiatry, 31*(5), 863–867.

Fanetti, M., Kobayashi, I., & Mitchell, D. W. (2008). The effects of gender on decisions of guilt in cases of alleged child sexual abuse. *American Journal of Forensic Psychology, 26*(4), 31–40.

Farrington, D. P. (2005). Childhood origins of antisocial behavior. *Clinical Psychology & Psychotherapy, 12*(3), 177–190.

Farrington, D. P., Loeber, R., & Welsh, B. C. (2010). Longitudinal-experimental studies. In A. R. Piquero and D. Weisbird (Eds.), *Handbook of Quantitative Criminology* (pp. 503–518). New York: Springer.

Fawthrop, T., & Jarvis, H. (2005). *Getting Away with Genocide? Elusive Justice and the Khmer Rouge Tribunal.* UNSW Press.

Fazel, S., Sjöstedt, G., Grann, M., & Långström, N. (2010). Sexual offending in women and psychiatric disorder: A national case-control study. *Archives of Sexual Behavior, 39*(1), 161–167.

FBI (Federal Bureau of Investigation) (2011). Bonnie & Clyde. FBI Records: The Vault. Retrieved from http://vault.fbi.gov/Bonnie%20and%20OClyde

Fedoroff, J. P., Fishell, A., & Fedoroff, B. (1999). A case series of women evaluated for paraphilic sexual disorders. *Canadian Journal of Human Sexuality, 8*(2), 127–140.

Fehrenbach, P. A., & Monastersky, C. (1988). Characteristics of female adolescent sexual offenders. *American Journal of Orthopsychiatry, 58*(1), 148–151.

Feldman, M. D., & Brown, R. (2002). Munchausen by proxy in an international context. *Child Abuse & Neglect, 26*(5), 509–524.

Felson, R. B., & Outlaw, M. C. (2007). The control motive and marital violence. *Violence and Victims, 22*(4), 387–407.

Felson, R. B., & Paré, P. P. (2005). The reporting of domestic violence and sexual assault by non-strangers to the police. *Journal of Marriage and Family, 67*(3), 597–610.

Ferguson, M. (2012). You cannot leave it at the office: Spillover and crossover of coworker incivility. *Journal of Organizational Behavior, 33*(4), 571–588.

Ferguson, R. B. (2001). Materialist, cultural, and biological theories on why Yanomami make war. *Anthropological Theory, 1*(1), 96–116.

Fergusson, D. M., Horwood, L. J., & Ridder, E. M. (2005). Partner violence and mental health outcomes in a New Zealand birth cohort. *Journal of Marriage and Family, 67*(5), 1103–1119.

Fiebert, M. S., & Gonzalez, D. M. (1997). College women who initiate assaults on their male partners and the reasons offered for such behavior. *Psychological Reports, 80*(2), 583–590.

Finkelhor, D. (1994). Current information on the scope and nature of child sexual abuse. *Sexual Abuse of Children, 4*(2), 31–53.

Finkelhor, D. (1997). The homicides of children and youth: A developmental perspective. In J. Jasinski and G. K. Kantor (Eds.), *Out of the Darkness: Contemporary Perspectives on Family Violence* (pp. 17–34). Thousand Oaks, CA: Sage Publications.

Finkelhor, D., Mitchell, K. J., & Wolak, J. (2000). Online victimization: A report on the nation's youth. Washington: Department of Justice.

Finkelhor, D., Hotaling, G., Lewis, I., & Smith, C. (1990). Sexual abuse in a national survey of adult men and women: Prevalence, characteristics, and risk factors. *Child Abuse & Neglect, 14*(1), 19–28.

Finkelhor, D., & Ormrod, R. (2001). *Homicides of Children and Youth.* Washington, DC: US Department of Justice, Office of Juvenile Justice and Delinquency Prevention (report) www.jcjrs.gov/pdffiles1/ojjdp/187239.pdf

First, M. B., Spitzer, R. L., Gibbon, M., & Williams, J. B. W. (1997). Structured clinical interview for DSM-IV disorders (SCID-IV). Washington, DC: American Psychiatric Press.

Flinck, A., & Paavilainen, E. (2010). Women's experiences of their violent behavior in an intimate partner relationship. *Qualitative Health Research, 20*(3), 306–318.

Flynn, J. P., & Wasman, M. (1960). Learning and cortically evoked movement during propagated hippocampal afterdischarges. *Science, 131*, 1607–1608.

Follingstad, D. R., Wright, S., Lloyd, S., & Sebastian, J. A. (1991). Sex differences in motivations and effects in dating violence. *Family Relations, 40*(1), 51–57.

Ford, R. P., Tappin, D. M., Schluter, P. J., & Wild, C. J. (1997). Smoking during pregnancy: How reliable are maternal self-reports in New Zealand? *Journal of Epidemiology and Community Health, 51*(3), 246–251.

Forouzan, E., & Cooke, D. (2005). Figuring out la femme fatale: Conceptual and assessment issues concerning psychopathy in females. *Behavioral Sciences & the Law, 23*(6), 765–778.

Fox, J. A., & Zawitz, M. (2007). Homicide trends in the United States. Washington, DC: US Department of Justice: Bureau of Justice Statistics.

Frei, A., Völlm, B., Graf, M., & Dittman, V. (2006). Female serial killing: Review and case report. *Criminal Behaviour and Mental Health, 16*(3), 167–176.

French, J. R., Jr, & Raven, B. (1959). The bases of social power. In D. Cartwright (Ed.), *Studies in Social Power* (pp. 150–167). Ann Arbor, MI: Institute for Social Research.

Fromuth, M. E., & Conn, V. E. (1997). Hidden perpetrators: Sexual molestation in a nonclinical sample of college women. *Journal of Interpersonal Violence, 12*(3), 456–465.

Fromuth, M. E., & Holt, A. R. (2008). Perception of teacher sexual misconduct by age of student. *Journal of Child Sexual Abuse, 17*(2), 163–179.

Fried, S. (1998, January 17). Cradle to grave. *Philadelphia Magazine.* Retrieved from www.phillymag.com

Frieden, J. (2003). Female sexual abuse of boys often goes unreported. *Clinical Psychiatry News.*

Friedman, S. H., Heneghan, A., & Rosenthal, M. (2007). Characteristics of women who deny or conceal pregnancy. *Psychosomatics, 48*(2), 117–122.

Friedman, S. H., Hrouda, D. R., Holden, C. E., Noffsinger, S. G., & Resnick, P. J. (2005). Child murder committed by severely mentally ill mothers: An examination of mothers found not guilty by reason of insanity. *Journal of Forensic Sciences, 50*(6), 1466–1471.

Friedman, S. H., Resnick, P. J., & Rosenthal, M. (2009). Postpartum psychosis: Strategies to protect infant and mother from harm. *Current Psychiatry, 8*(2), 40–46.

Fromuth, M. E., & Burkhart, B. R. (1989). Long-term psychological correlates of childhood sexual abuse in two samples of college men. *Child Abuse & Neglect, 13*(4), 533–542.

Fujiwara, T., Barber, C., Schaechter, J., & Hemenway, D. (2009). Characteristics of infant homicides: Findings from a US multisite reporting system. *Paediatrics, 124*(2), 210–17.

Gair, S. (2008). The psychic disequilibrium of adoption: Stories exploring links between adoption and suicidal thoughts and actions. *The Australian e-Journal for the Advancement of Mental Health, 7*(3), 206–217.

Gakhal, B. K., & Brown, S. J. (2011). A comparison of the general public's, forensic professionals' and students' attitudes towards female sex offenders. *Journal of Sexual Aggression, 17*(1), 105–116.

Gannon, T. A., & Cortoni, F. (Eds.). (2010). *Female Sexual Offenders: Theory, Assessment and Treatment.* West Sussex: Wiley-Blackwell.

Gannon, T. A., & Rose, M. R. (2008). Female child sexual offenders: Towards integrating theory and practice. *Aggression and Violent Behavior, 13*(6), 442–461.

Gannon, T. A., & Rose, M. R. (2009). Offense-related interpretative bias in female child molesters: A preliminary study. *Sexual Abuse: A Journal of Research and Treatment, 21*(2), 194–207.

Gannon, T., Rose, M., & Ward, T. (2008, September). A descriptive model of the offense process for female sexual offenders. *Sex Abuse: A Journal of Research and Treatment, 20*, 352–374.

Gannon, T., Rose, M. R., & Ward, T. (2010). Pathways to female sexual offending: Approach or avoidance? *Psychology, Crime & Law, 16*(5), 359–380.

Gardner, D. (2011a, 20 June). Ten years ago today Andrea Yates drowned her five children . . . and she could be freed by the end of this year. *The Daily Mail.*

Gardner, D. (2011b, August 24). Civil rights workers fired after giving employees nicknames like Psycho, Monster and Teen Wolf. *The Daily Mail.*

Gaulin, S., & McBurney, D. (2003). *Evolutionary Psychology* (2nd ed.). Harlow, UK: Pearson.

Gavin, H. (2001). *The Third Person Effect and Perceptual Elements of Television.* Confidential Report for Hallmark Channel, London.

Gavin, H. (2006). Intrusive music: The perception of everyday music explored by diaries. *The Qualitative Report, 11*(3), 550–565.

Gavin, H. (2010). 'Mummy wouldn't do that': The perception and construction of the female sex offender. In M. Barrett (Ed.), *Grotesque Femininities: Evil, Women and the Feminine.* Oxford: Inter-Disciplinary Press.

Gavin, H. (2011). Sticks and stones may break my bones: An examination of the effects of emotional abuse. *Journal of Aggression, Maltreatment & Trauma, 20*(5), 503–529.

Gavin, H., & Bent, J. (2012). The damsel in distress: Not as sweet as she is painted? *Fourth Global Conference on Evil, Women and the Feminine.* Warsaw, Poland, May 4–6.

Gavin, H., & Hockey, D. (2010). Criminal careers and cognitive scripts: An investigation into criminal versatility. *The Qualitative Report, 15*(2), 389–410.

Geberth, V. (1998). Domestic violence homicides. *Law and Order, 46*(11), 51–54.

Gelles, R. J. (1972). *The Violent Home: A Study of Physical Aggression between Husbands and Wives.* Oxford: Sage.

Gelles, R. J. (1989). Child abuse and violence in single-parent families: Parent absence and economic deprivation. *American Journal of Orthopsychiatry, 59*(4), 492–501.

Gelles, R. J. (2007). The politics of research: The use, abuse, and misuse of social science data – The cases of intimate partner violence. *Family Court Review, 45*(1), 42–51.

George, C. (1996). A representational perspective of child abuse and prevention: Internal working models of attachment and caregiving. *Child Abuse & Neglect, 20*(5), 411–424.

George, M. J. (1999). A victimization survey of female-perpetrated assaults in the United Kingdom. *Aggressive Behavior, 25*(1), 67–79.

George, M. J. (2003). Invisible touch. *Aggression and Violent Behavior, 8*(1), 23–60.

Gheorghe, A., Banner, J., Hansen, S. H., Stolborg, U., & Lynnerup, N. (2011). Abandonment of newborn infants: A Danish forensic medical survey 1997–2008. *Forensic Science, Medicine, and Pathology, 7*(4), 317–321.

Giancola, P., Levinson, C., Corman, M., Godlaski, A., Morris, D., Phillips, J., & Holt, J. (2009). Men and women, alcohol and aggression. *Experimental and Clinical Psychopharmacology, 17*(3) (June), 154–164.

Gilbert, R., Widom, C. S., Browne, K., Fergusson, D., Webb, E., & Janson, S. (2009). Burden and consequences of child maltreatment in high-income countries. *The Lancet, 373*(9657), 68–81.

Gillenwater, J. M., Quan, L., & Feldman, K. W. (1996). Inflicted submersion in childhood. *Archives of Paediatric and Adolescent Medicine, 15*(3), 298–303.

Gilroy, P. J., & Carroll, L. (2009). Woman to woman sexual violence. *Women & Therapy, 32*(4), 423–435.

Giordano, P. C., Millhollin, T. J., Cernkovich, S. A., Pugh, M. D., & Rudolph, J. L. (1999). Delinquency, identity, and women's involvement in relationship violence. *Criminology, 37*(1), 17–40.

Girla, L. (2005). *Neonaticide: Penal and Criminological Research* (thesis). Retrieved from www.cnaa.md/en/thesis/2140

Girshick, L. B. (2002a). No sugar, no spice reflections on research on woman-to-woman sexual violence. *Violence Against Women, 8*(12), 1500–1520.

Girshick, L. B. (2002b). *Woman-to-Woman Sexual Violence: Does She Call it Rape?* (The Northeastern Series on Gender, Crime, and the Law). Boston: Northeastern University Press.

Glass, N., Perrin, N., Hanson, G., Bloom, T., Gardner, E., & Campbell, J. C. (2008). Risk for re-assault in abusive female same-sex relationships. *American Journal of Public Health, 98*(6), 1021–1027.

Glasser, M., Kolvin, L., Campbell, D., Glasser, A., Leitch, I., & Farrelly, S. (2001). Cycle of child sexual abuse: Links between being a victim and becoming a perpetrator. *British Journal of Psychiatry, 179*, 482–494.

Glazer, I. M., & Ras, W. A. (1994). On aggression, human rights, and hegemonic discourse: The case of a murder for family honor in Israel. *Sex Roles, 30*(3–4), 269–288.

Glendinning, L. (2003). Inside the mind of a killer mother. *The Age*. Retrieved from www.theage.com.au

Global Post (2011). Dutch mother convicted of killing her four newborns. Retrieved from www.globalpost.com

Goetting, A. (1987). Homicidal wives: A profile. *Journal of Family Issues, 8*(3), 332–341.

Goetz, A. T. (2010). The evolutionary psychology of violence. *Psicothema, 22*(1), 15–21.

Goodson, S., Pearson, S., & Gavin, H. (2010). Violent video games: The media scapegoat for an aggressive society. *The Inter-Disciplinary Conference for Videogame Cultures and the Future of Interactive Entertainment.* Oxford, UK (July).

Goodwin, J. M., & Sachs, R. G. (1996). Child abuse in the etiology of dissociative disorders. In L. Michelson & W. Ray (Eds.), *Handbook of Dissociation* (pp. 91–105). New York: Springer.

Grabe, M. E., & Kamhawi, R. (2006). Hard wired for negative news? Gender differences in processing broadcast news. *Communication Research, 33*(5), 346–369.

Grace, A. (2011). *Dark Angels Revealed: From Dark Rogues to Dark Romantics, the Most Mysterious and Mesmerizing Vampires and Fallen Angels from Count Dracula to Edward Cullen Come to Life.* Fair Winds Press.

Graham, S., Weiner, B., Cobb, M., & Henderson, T. (2001). An attributional analysis of child abuse among low-income African American mothers. *Journal of Social and Clinical Psychology, 20*(2), 233–257.

Graham-Kevan, N. (2009). The psychology of women's partner violence: Characteristics and cautions. *Journal of Aggression, Maltreatment & Trauma, 18*(6), 587–603.

Graham-Kevan, N. & Archer, J. (2005). Investigating three explanations of women's relationship aggression. *Psychology of Women Quarterly, 29*(3), 270–277.

Grayston, A. D., & De Luca, R. V. (1999). Female perpetrators of child sexual abuse: A review of the clinical and empirical literature. *Aggression and Violent Behavior, 4*(1), 93–106.

Greenwood, D. N. (2007). Are female action heroes risky role models? Character identification, idealization, and viewer aggression. *Sex Roles, 57*(9–10), 725–732.

Gresswell, D., & Hollin, C. (1994). Multiple murder: A review. *British Journal of Criminologybjc.oxfordjournals.org British Journal of Criminology, 34*(1): 1–14.

Grier, P. E., Clark, M., & Stoner, S. B. (1993). Comparative study of personality traits of female sex offenders. *Psychological reports, 73*(3f), 1378–1378.

Griskevicius, V., Tybur, J. M., Gangestad, S. W., Perea, E. F., Shapiro, J. R., & Kenrick, D. T. (2009). Aggress to impress: Hostility as an evolved context-dependent strategy. *Journal of Personality and Social Psychology, 96*(5), 980–994.

Groth, A. N., & Burgess, A. W. (1979). Sexual trauma in the life histories of rapists and child molesters. *Victimology, 4*(1), 10–16.

Guileyardo, J. M., Prahlow, J. A., & Barnard, J. J. (1999). Familial filicide and filicide classification. *The American Journal of Forensic Medicine and Pathology, 20*(3), 286–292.

Guterman, N. B., Lee, Y., Lee, S. J., Waldfogel, J., & Rathouz, P. J. (2009). Fathers and maternal risk for physical child abuse. *Child Maltreatment, 14*(3), 277–290.

Haapasalo, J., & Petaja, S. (1999). Mothers who killed or attempted to kill their child: Life circumstances, childhood abuse, and types of killing. *Violence and Victims, 14*(3), 219–239.

Hale, R., & Bolin, A. (1998). The female serial killer. In R. Holmes & S. Holmes (Eds.), *Contemporary Perspectives on Serial Murder* (pp. 33–58). London: Sage Publications.

Hamberger, L. K. (1997). Female offenders in domestic violence: A look at actions in their context. *Journal of Aggression, Maltreatment & Trauma, 1*(1), 117–129.

Hamel, J. (Ed.). (2005). *Gender Inclusive Treatment of Intimate Partner Abuse: A Comprehensive Approach.* New York: Springer Publishing Company.

Hardy, A. (1960). Was man more aquatic in the past? *New Scientist, 7*(642), 5.

Harris, B. (1994). Biological and hormonal aspects of post-partum depressed mood: Working towards strategies for prophylaxis and treatment. *The British Journal of Psychiatry, 164*, 288–292.

Hart, J. L., & Helms, J. L. (2003). Factors of parricide: Allowance of the use of battered child syndrome as a defense. *Aggression and Violent Behavior, 8*(6), 671–683.

Hay, P. J. (2009). Post-partum psychosis: Which women are at higher risk? *PLoS Medicine, 6*(2).

Heide, K. M. (1992). *Why Kids Kill Parents: Child Abuse and Adolescent Homicide.* Columbus, OH: Ohio State University Press.

Heide, K. M., & Solomon, E. P. (2009). Female juvenile murderers: Biological and psychological dynamics leading to homicide. *International Journal of Law and Psychiatry, 32*(4), 244–252.

Heide, K. M., Solomon, E. P., Sellers, B. G., & Chan, H. C. (2011). Male and female juvenile homicide offenders: An empirical analysis of US arrests by offender age. *Feminist Criminology, 6*(1), 3–31.

Heidensohn, F., & Gelsthorpe, L. (2012). Gender and crime. In R. Morgan, M. Maguire & R. Reiner (Eds.), *The Oxford Handbook of Criminology* (pp. 336–369). Oxford University Press.

Henderson, K. K., & King, K. (1998). Recreation programming for adolescent girls: Rationale and foundations. *Journal of Park and Recreation Administration, 16*(2), 1–14.

Hendriks, J., & Bijleveld, C. C. J. H. (2006). Female adolescent sex offenders: An exploratory study. *Journal of Sexual Aggression, 12*(1), 31–41.

Hendrix, C., & Schumm, W. (1990). Reliability and validity of the Abusive Violence Scale. *Psychological Reports, 66*(3c), 1251–1258.

Henning, K., & Feder, L. (2004). A comparison between men and women arrested for domestic violence: Who presents a greater threat? *Journal of Family Violence, 19*(2), 69–80.

Henning, K., Martinsson, R., & Holdford, R. (2009). Gender differences in risk factors for intimate partner violence recidivism. *Journal of Aggression, Maltreatment & Trauma, 18*(6), 623–645.

Henson, J. R., & Olson, L. N. (2010). The monster within: How male serial killers discursively manage their stigmatized identities. *Communication Quarterly, 58*(3), 341–364.

Herman, H. (2010, October 31). Mystery of Michele Kalina: Reading infant homicides baffle experts. *Reading Eagle*. Retrieved from http://www2.readingeagle.com/article.aspx?id=260505 3.2.11.

Herman-Giddens, M. E., Smith, J. B., Mittal, M., Carlson, M., & Butts, J. D. (2003). Newborns killed or left to die by a parent. *The Journal of the American Medical Association, 289*(11), 1425–1429.

Herrenkohl, T. I., Sousa, C., Tajima, E. A., Herrenkohl, R. C., & Moylan, C. A. (2008). Intersection of child abuse and children's exposure to domestic violence. *Trauma, Violence, & Abuse, 9*(2), 84–99.

Hess, N. H., & Hagen, E. H. (2006). Sex differences in indirect aggression: Psychological evidence from young adults. *Evolution and Human Behavior, 27*(3), 231–245.

Hetherton, J., & Beardsall, L. (1998). Decisions and attitudes concerning child sexual abuse: Does the gender of the perpetrator make a difference to child protection professionals? *Child Abuse & Neglect, 22*(12), 1265–1283.

Hettrich, E., & O'Leary, K. (2007). Females' reasons for their physical aggression in dating relationships. *Journal of Interpersonal Violence, 22*(9), 1131–1143.

Heyman, R. E., & Neidig, P. H. (1999). A comparison of spousal aggression prevalence rates in US army and civilian representative samples. *Journal of Consulting and Clinical Psychology, 67*(2), 239–242.

Higgins, C., & Ireland, C. (2009). Attitudes towards male and female sex offenders: A comparison of forensic staff, prison officers and the general public in Northern Ireland. *British Journal of Forensic Practice, 11*(1), 14–19.

Hines, D. A. (2007). Predictors of sexual coercion against women and men: A multilevel, multinational study of university students. *Archives of Sexual Behavior, 36*(3), 403–422.

Hines, D. A. (2008). Borderline personality traits and intimate partner aggression: An international multisite, cross-gender analysis. *Psychology of Women Quarterly, 32*(3), 290–302.

Hines, D. A., & Douglas, E. M. (2009). Women's use of intimate partner violence against men: Prevalence, implications, and consequences. *Journal of Aggression, Maltreatment & Trauma, 18*(6), 572–586.

Hines, D. A., & Malley-Morrison, K. (2001). Psychological effects of partner abuse against men: A neglected research area. *Psychology of Men & Masculinity, 2*(2), 75–85.

Hines, D. A., Brown, J., & Dunning, E. (2007). Characteristics of callers to the domestic abuse helpline for men. *Journal of Family Violence, 22*(2), 63–72.

Hodgkins, S., & M. Dube (1995). Parents who kill their children: A cohort study. In M. Riedel & J. Boulahanis (Eds.), *Lethal Violence: Proceedings of the 1995 Meeting of the Homicide Research Working Group.* National Institute of Justice, Ottawa, Canada.

Hoffman, B. (2003). Al Qaeda, trends in terrorism, and future potentialities: An assessment. *Studies in Conflict & Terrorism, 26*(6), 429–442.

Holmes, R., & Holmes, S. (Eds.) (1997). *Contemporary Perspectives on Serial Murder.* London: Sage Publications.

Holt, M. K., & Espelage, D. L. (2005). Social support as a moderator between dating violence victimization and depression/anxiety among African American and Caucasian adolescents. *School Psychology Review, 34*(3), 309–328.

Holtzworth-Munroe, A., & Stuart, G. L. (1994). Typologies of male batterers: Three subtypes and the differences among them. *Psychological Bulletin, 116*(3), 476–497.

Hornung, C. A., McCullough, B. C., & Sugimoto, T. (1981). Status relationships in marriage: Risk factors in spouse abuse. *Journal of Marriage and the Family, 43*(3), 675–692.

Howell, J. L., Egan, P. M., Giuliano, T. A., & Ackley, B. D. (2011). The reverse double standard in perceptions of student–teacher sexual relationships: The role of gender, initiation, and power. *The Journal of Social Psychology, 151*(2), 180–200.

Huesmann, L. R. (1998). The role of social information processing and cognitive schema in the acquisition and maintenance of habitual aggressive behavior. In R. G. Geen & E. Donnerstein (Eds.), *Human Aggression: Theories, Research, and Implications for Policy* (pp. 73–109). New York: Academic Press.

Hughes, F. M., Stuart, G. L., Gordon, K. C., & Moore, T. M. (2007). Predicting the use of aggressive conflict tactics in a sample of women arrested for domestic violence. *Journal of Social and Personal Relationships, 24*(2), 155–176.

Huizinga, D., & Elliott, D. S. (1986). Reassessing the reliability and validity of self-report delinquency measures. *Journal of Quantitative Criminology, 2*(4), 293–327.

Human Rights Watch (1999). *World Report 2000: The Events of 1999.* Human Rights Watch.

Hunter, J. A., Jr, Lexier, L. J., Goodwin, D. W., & Dennis, C. (1993). Psychosexual, attitudinal, and developmental characteristics of juvenile female sexual perpetrators in a residential treatment setting. *Journal of Child and Family Studies, 2*(4), 317–326.

Hunter, R. S., Kilstrom, N., Kraybill, E. N., & Loda, F. (1978). Antecedents of child abuse and neglect in premature infants: A prospective study in a newborn intensive care unit. *Pediatrics, 61*(4), 629–635.

Husain, S. A., & Daniel, A. (1984). A comparative study of filicidal and abusive mothers. *The Canadian Journal of Psychiatry/La Revue Canadienne de Psychiatrie, 29*(7), 596–598.

Iacovetta, F., & Valverde, M. (2002). *Gender Conflicts: New Essays in Women's History.* University of Toronto Press.

Israel, E., & Strassberg, D. S. (2009). Viewing time as an objective measure of sexual interest in heterosexual men and women. *Archives of Sexual Behavior, 38*(4), 551–558.

Jankowski, M. K., Leitenberg, H., Henning, K., & Coffey, P. (1999). Intergenerational transmission of dating aggression as a function of witnessing only same sex parents vs. opposite sex parents vs. both parents as perpetrators of domestic violence. *Journal of Family Violence, 14*(3), 267–279.

Janus, M. D., Archambault, F. X., Brown, S. W., & Welsh, L. A. (1995). Physical abuse in Canadian runaway adolescents. *Child Abuse & Neglect, 19*(4), 433–447.

Jason, J., Carpenter, M. M., & Tyler, C. W. (1983). Under-recording of infant homicide in the United States. *American Journal of Public Health, 73*(2), 195–197.

Jennings, D, Ross, K, Popper, S., & Elmore, M. (1999). Thoughts of harming infants in depressed and non-depressed mothers. *Journal of Affective Disorders, 54*(1), 21–28.

Johansson-Love, J., & Fremouw, W. (2009). Female sex offenders: A controlled comparison of offender and victim/crime characteristics. *Journal of Family Violence, 24*(6), 367–376.

Jones, I., & Craddock, N. (2001). Familiality of the puerperal trigger in bipolar disorder: Results of a family study. *American Journal of Psychiatry, 158*(6), 913–917.

Jones, O. D. (2006). Behavioral genetics and crime, in context. *Law and Contemporary Problems, 69*, 81–100.

Joshi, S. (2007). *Icons of Horror and the Supernatural: An Encyclopedia of Our Worst Nightmares, Vol. 2.* Westport, CT: Greenwood Press.

Kalders, A., Inkster, H., & Britt, E. (1997). Females who offend sexually against children in New Zealand. *Journal of Sexual Aggression, 3*(1), 15–29.

Kaplan, S. J., Sunday, S. R., Labruna, V., Pelcovitz, D., & Salzinger, S. (2009). Psychiatric disorders of parents of physically abused adolescents. *Journal of Family Violence, 24*(5), 273–281.

Karakus, M, Ince, H., Ince, N., Arican, N., & Sozen, S. (2003). Filicide cases in Turkey, 1995–2000. *Croatian Medical Journal, 44*(5), 592–595.

Kates, E. J. (2010). Statistics: Male versus female: Who is more likely to perpetrate child abuse? The Liz Library. Retrieved from www.thelizlibrary.org/liz/statistics.html

Kaufman, K. L., Wallace, A. M., Johnson, C. F., & Reeder, M. L. (1995). Comparing female and male perpetrators' modus operandi: Victims' reports of sexual abuse. *Journal of Interpersonal Violence, 10*(3), 322–333.

Kaukiainen, A., Bjorkqvist, K., Lagerspetz, K., Osterman, K., Salmivalli, C., Rothberg, S., & Ahlbom, A. (1999). The relationships between social intelligence, empathy, and three types of aggression. *Aggressive Behavior, 25*(2), 81–89.

Kauppi, A., Kumpulainen, K., Karkola, K., Vanamo, T., & Merikanto, J. (2010). Maternal and paternal filicides: A retrospective review of filicides in Finland. *Journal of the American Academy of Psychiatry and the Law Online, 38*(2), 229–238.

Kauppi, A., Kumpulainen, K., Vanamo, T., Merikanto, J., & Karkola, K. (2008). Maternal depression and filicide: Case study of ten mothers. *Archives of Women's Mental Health, 11*(3), 201–206.

Kaura, S. A., & Allen, C. M. (2004). Dissatisfaction with relationship power and dating violence perpetration by men and women. *Journal of Interpersonal Violence, 19*(5), 576–588.

Kelly, L. (2002). Disabusing the definition of domestic abuse: How women batter men and the role of the feminist state. *Florida State University Law Review, 30*, 791–856.

Kelly, R. J., Wood, J. J., Gonzalez, L. S., MacDonald, V., & Waterman, J. (2002). Effects of mother–son incest and positive perceptions of sexual abuse experiences on the psychosocial adjustment of clinic-referred men. *Child Abuse & Neglect, 26*(4), 425–441.

Kempe, S., et al. (1962). The battered-child syndrome. *Journal of the American Medical Association, 181*(1), 17–24.

Kendell, R., Chalmers, J., & Platz, C. (1987). Epidemiology of puerperal psychosis. *British Journal of Psychiatry, 150*(5), 662–673.

Kernsmith, P., & Kernsmith, R. (2009a). Treating female perpetrators: State standards for batterer intervention services. *Social Work, 54*(4), 341–349.

Kernsmith, P. D., & Kernsmith, R. M. (2009b). Female pornography use and sexual coercion perpetration. *Deviant Behavior, 30*(7), 589–610.

Kierski, W. (2002). Female violence: Can we therapists face up to it? *Counselling and Psychotherapy Journal, 13*(10), 32–35.

Kirschner, D. (1990). The adopted child syndrome: Considerations for psychotherapy. *Psychotherapy in Private Practice, 8*(3), 93–100.

Kite, D., & Tyson, G. A. (2004). The impact of perpetrator gender on male and female police officers' perceptions of child sexual abuse. *Psychiatry, Psychology and Law, 11*(2), 308–318.

Kjellgren, C., Priebe, G., Svedin, C. G., Mossige, S., & Långström, N. (2011). Female youth who sexually coerce: Prevalence, risk, and protective factors in two national high school surveys. *The Journal of Sexual Medicine, 8*(12), 3354–3362.

Klahr, A., McGue, M., Iacono, W., and Burt, S. (2011). The association between parent–child conflict and adolescent conduct problems over time: Results from a longitudinal adoption study. *Journal of Abnormal Psychology, 120*(1), 46–56.

Klein, M. W. (2005). The value of comparisons in street gang research. *Journal of Contemporary Criminal Justice, 21*(2), 135–152.

Kleiss, K. (June 23, 2009). Mistrial rejected: Alberta mother who killed baby gets life. *National Post.* Retrieved from www.nationalpost.com/related/topics/Mistrial+rejected+Alberta+mother+killed+baby+gets+life/1725168/story.html

Knoll, J. L. (2010). The 'pseudocommando' mass murderer: Part I, the psychology of revenge and obliteration. *Journal of the American Academy of Psychiatry and the Law Online, 38*(1), 87–94.

Kohm, L. M., & Liverman, T. S. (2002). Prom mom killers: The impact of blame shift and distorted statistics on punishment for neonaticide. *Wm. & Mary J. Women & L., 9*, 43.

Kolko, D. J. (1996). Individual cognitive behavioral treatment and family therapy for physically abused children and their offending parents: A comparison of clinical outcomes. *Child Maltreatment, 1*(4), 322–342.

Korbin, J. E. (1986). Childhood histories of women imprisoned for fatal child maltreatment. *Child Abuse & Neglect, 10*(3), 331–338.

Korbin, J. E. (1987). Incarcerated mothers' perceptions and interpretations of their fatally maltreated children. *Child Abuse & Neglect, 11*(3), 397–407.

Korbin, J. E. (1989). Fatal maltreatment by mothers: A proposed framework. *Child Abuse & Neglect, 13*(4), 481–489.

Korn, M. L., Botsis, A. J., Kotler, M., Plutchik, R., Conte, H. R., Finkelstein, G., et al. (1992). The Suicide and Aggression Survey: A semistructured instrument for the measurement of suicidality and aggression. *Comprehensive Psychiatry, 33*(6), 359–365.

Krahe, B., Waizenhöfer, E., & Möller, I. (2003). Women's sexual aggression against men: Prevalence and predictors. *Sex Roles, 49*(5–6), 219–232.

Kramer, S. (2010). *Discourse and power in the self-perceptions of incarcerated South African female sexual offenders* (doctoral dissertation). University of South Africa Institute for Social and Health Sciences, Lenasia, South Africa.

Kramer, S., & Bowman, B. (2011). Accounting for the 'invisibility' of the female paedophile: An expert-based perspective from South Africa. *Psychology & Sexuality, 2*(3), 244–258.

Krob, M. J., Johnson, A., & Jordan, M. H. (1986). Burned-and-battered adults. *Journal of Burn Care & Research, 7*(6), 529–531.

Krug, R. S. (1989). Adult male report of childhood sexual abuse by mothers: Case descriptions, motivations and long-term consequences. *Child Abuse & Neglect, 13*(1), 111–119.

Kubik, E. K., & Hecker, J. E. (2005). Cognitive distortions about sex and sexual offending: A comparison of sex offending girls, delinquent girls, and girls from the community. *Journal of Child Sexual Abuse, 14*(4), 43–69.

Kubik, E. K., Hecker, J. E., & Righthand, S. (2003). Adolescent females who have sexually offended: Comparisons with delinquent adolescent female offenders and adolescent males who sexually offend. *Journal of Child Sexual Abuse, 11*(3), 63–83.

Kumar, C., McIvor, R., Davies, T., Brown, N., Papadopoulos, A., et al. . . . (2003). Estrogen administration does not reduce the rate of recurrence of affective psychosis after childbirth. *The Journal of Clinical Psychiatry, 64*(2), 112–118.

Kumar, R., & Robson, K. (1984). A prospective study of emotional disorders in childbearing women. *The British Journal of Psychiatry, 144*(1), 35–47.

Kunz, J., & Bahr, S. J. (1996). A profile of parental homicide against children. *Journal of Family Violence, 11*(4), 347–362.

Kupelian, D. (2006, March 3). What's behind today's epidemic of teacher–student sex? *World News Daily.* Retrieved from http://www.wnd.com/2006/03/35370/

Kurland, N. B., & Pelled, L. H. (2000). Passing the word: Toward a model of gossip and power in the workplace. *Academy of Management Review, 25*(2), 428–438.

Lagerspetz, K. M., Björkqvist, K., & Peltonen, T. (1988). Is indirect aggression typical of females? Gender differences in aggressiveness in 11-to-12-year-old children. *Aggressive Behavior, 14*(6), 403–414.

Laker, B. (2010, February 3). Killer of eight babies now alone. *Philadelphia Daily News.* Retrieved from www.philly.com

Lambert, P. M. (2002). The archaeology of war: A North American perspective. *Journal of Archaeological Research, 10*(3), 207–241.

Lambert, S., & O'Halloran, E. (2008). Deductive thematic analysis of a female paedophilia website. *Psychiatry, Psychology and Law, 15*(2), 284–300.

Langhinrichsen-Rohling, J., Turner, L. A., & McGowen, M. (2007). Family therapy and interpersonal violence: Targeting at-risk adolescent mothers. In T. L. Nicholls & J. Hamel (Ed.), *Family Interventions in Domestic Violence* (pp. 477–498). New York: Springer.

Large, M., Nielssen, O., Lackersteen, S., & Smith, G. (2010). The associations between infant homicide, homicide, and suicide rates: An analysis of world health organization and centers for disease control statistics. *Suicide and Life-Threatening Behavior, 40*(1), 87–97.

Laroche, D. (2005). *Aspects of the Context and Consequences of Domestic Violence – Situational Couple Violence and Intimate Terrorism in Canada in 1999*. Quebec City: Government of Quebec, Table 8, p. 16.

Law Commission (2004). *The Law Commission Report on Partial Defences to Murder*, Part 4.

Lawrence, R. (2004). Understanding fatal assault of children: A typology and explanatory theory. *Child and Youth Service Review, 26*(9), 837–852.

LeDoux, J. E. (1994). Emotion, memory and the brain. *Scientific American, 270*(6), 50–57.

Lee, A., Li, C., Kwong, N., & So, K. (2006). Neonaticide, newborn abandonment and denial of pregnancy – newborn victimisation associate with unwanted motherhood. *Hong Kong Medical Journal, 12*(1), 61–64.

Leschied, A. W., Cummings, A., Van Brunschot, M., Cunningham, A., & Saunders, A. (2000). *Female Adolescent Aggression: A Review of the Literature and the Correlates of Aggression*. Quebec: Canada Minister of Public Works and Government Services.

Lester, D. (1991). Murdering babies. *Social Psychiatry and Psychiatric Epidemiology, 26*(2), 83–85.

Letendre, J. (2007). 'Sugar and spice but not always nice': Gender socialization and its impact on development and maintenance of aggression in adolescent girls. *Child and Adolescent Social Work Journal, 24*(4), 353–368.

Leung, D. W., & Slep, A. M. S. (2006). Predicting inept discipline: The role of parental depressive symptoms, anger, and attributions. *Journal of Consulting and Clinical Psychology, 74*(3), 524–534.

Levene, S., & Bacon, C. J. (2004). Sudden unexpected death and covert homicide in infancy. *Archives of Disease in Childhood, 89*(5), 443–447.

Levitzky, S., & Cooper, R. (2000). Infant colic syndrome – maternal fantasies of aggression and infanticide. *Clinical Pediatrics (July), 39*(7), 395–400.

Lewis, C. F. (2010). Childhood antecedents of adult violent offending in a group of female felons. *Behavioral Sciences & the Law, 28*(2), 224–234.

Lewis, C. F., & Bunce, S. C. (2003). Filicidal mothers and the impact of psychosis on maternal filicide. *Journal of the American Academy of Psychiatry and the Law Online, 31*(4), 459–470.

Liang, B. A., & Macfarlane, W. L. (1999). Murder by omission: Child abuse and the passive parent. *Harvard Journal on Legislation, 36*(2), 397–450.

Lie, G. Y., & Gentlewarrier, S. (1991). Intimate violence in lesbian relationships: Discussion of survey findings and practice implications. *Journal of Social Service Research, 15*(1–2), 41–59.

Lie, G. Y., Schilit, R., Bush, J., Montagne, M., & Reyes, L. (1991). Lesbians in currently aggressive relationships: How frequently do they report aggressive past relationships? *Violence and Victims, 6*(2), 121–135.

Liem, J. H., O'Toole, J. G., & James, J. B. (1992). The need for power in women who were sexually abused as children: An exploratory study. *Psychology of Women Quarterly, 16*(4), 467–480.

Lindberg, N., Tani, P., Sailas, E., Virkkala, J., Urrila, A. S., & Virkkunen, M. (2008). Sleep in conduct-disordered adolescents – a polysomnographic and spectral power analysis study. *Psychiatry Research, 159*(3), 339–345.

Liu, C. (2000, August 2). Ex-husbands testify in penalty phase of Nieves trial. *Los Angeles Times*. Retrieved from articles.latimes.com

Lodge, E., (2010, November 9). The Campione confession and interrogation. *National Post*. Retrieved from news.nationalpost.com

Logan, T. K., Leukefeld, C., & Walker, B. (2000). Stalking as a variant of intimate violence: Implications from a young adult sample. *Violence and Victims, 15*(1), 91–111.

Loomis, M. J. (1986). Maternal filicide: A preliminary examination of culture and victim sex. *International Journal of Law and Psychiatry, 9*, 503–6.

Lorber, M. F., O'Leary, S. G., & Kendziora, K. T. (2003). Mothers' over-reactive discipline and their encoding and appraisals of toddler behavior. *Journal of Abnormal Child Psychology, 31*(5), 485–494.

Lorber, M. F., & Slep, A. M. S. (2005). Mothers' emotion dynamics and their relations with harsh and lax discipline: Microsocial time series analyses. *Journal of Clinical Child and Adolescent Psychology, 34*(3), 559–568.

Lottes, I. L., & Weinberg, M. S. (1997). Sexual coercion among university students: A comparison of the United States and Sweden. *Journal of Sex Research, 34*(1), 67–76.

Lou, L. (2008, September 14). Faded, but not forgotten. *San Diego Union Tribune*. Retrieved from http://www.utsandiego.com/uniontrib/20080914/news_1mc14 eubanks.html

Lounds, J. J., Borkowski, J. G., & Whitman, T. L. (2006). The potential for child neglect: The case of adolescent mothers and their children. *Child Maltreatment, 11*(3), 281–294.

Loy, E., Machen, L., Beaulieu, M., & Greif, G. L. (2005). Common themes in clinical work with women who are domestically violent. *The American Journal of Family Therapy, 33*(1), 33–44.

Lysova, A.V., & Douglas, E. M. (2008). Intimate partner violence among male and female Russian university students. *Journal of Interpersonal Violence, 23*(11), 1579–1599.

Magdol, L., Moffitt, T. E., Caspi, A., Newman, D. L., Fagan, J., & Silva, P. A. (1997). Gender differences in partner violence in a birth cohort of 21-year-olds: Bridging the gap between clinical and epidemiological approaches. *Journal of Consulting and Clinical Psychology, 65*(1), 68–78.

Makepeace, J. M. (1986). Gender differences in courtship violence victimization. *Family Relations, 35*(3), 383–388.

Mallett, S., & Rosenthal, D. (2009). Physically violent mothers are a reason for young people's leaving home. *Journal of Interpersonal Violence, 24*(7), 1165–1174.

Malloy, K. A., McCloskey, K. A., Grigsby, N., & Gardner, D. (2003). Women's use of violence within intimate relationships. *Journal of Aggression, Maltreatment & Trauma, 6*(2), 37–59.

Mann, C. R. (1988). Getting even? Women who kill in domestic encounters. *Justice Quarterly, 5*(1), 33–51.

Mann, C. R. (1996). *When Women Kill.* Albany, NY: Suny Press.

Margolin, L. (1990). Fatal child neglect. *Child Welfare, 69*(4), 309–319.

Marks, M. N., & Kumar, R. (1993). Infanticide in England and Wales. *Medicine, Science and the Law, 33*(4), 329–339.

Marks, M. N., & Kumar, R. (1996). Infanticide in Scotland. *Medicine, Science and the Law, 36*(4), 299–305.

Marks, V., & Richmond, C. (2008). Beverly Allitt: The nurse who killed babies. *Journal of the Royal Society of Medicine (March), 101*(3), 110–115.

Marleau, D. J., Dube, M., & Leveillee, S. (2004). Neonaticidal mothers: Are more boys killed? Medicine, Science and the Law, *44*(4), 311–316.

Marshall, W. L., & Kennedy, P. (2003). Sexual sadism in sexual offenders: An elusive diagnosis. *Aggression and Violent Behavior, 8*(1), 1–22.

Marvesti, J. (1986). Incestuous mothers. *American Journal of Forensic Psychiatry, 7*, 63–69.

Mash, E. J., Johnston, C., & Kovitz, K. (1983). A comparison of the mother–child interactions of physically abused and non-abused children during play and task situations. *Journal of Clinical Child Psychology, 12*(3), 337–346.

Matthews, J., Matthews, R., & Speltz, K. (1991). Female sex offenders: A typology. In M. Patton (Ed.), *Family Sexual Abuse: Frontline Research and Evaluation* (pp. 199–219). Newbury Park, NJ: Sage Publications.

May-Chahal, C., & Cawson, P. (2005). Measuring child maltreatment in the United Kingdom: A study of the prevalence of child abuse and neglect. *Child Abuse & Neglect, 29*(9), 969–984.

Mayer, A. (1992). *Women Sex Offenders: Treatment and Dynamics.* Holmes Beach, FL: Learning Publications, Inc.

McCartan, F. M., Law, H., Murphy, M., & Bailey, S. (2011). Child and adolescent females who present with sexually abusive behaviours: A 10-year UK prevalence study. *Journal of Sexual Aggression, 17*(1), 4–14.

McCarty, L. M. (1986). Mother–child incest: Characteristics of the offender. *Child Welfare, 65*(5), 447–458.

McClain, P. D. (1982). Black female homicide offenders and victims: Are they from the same population? *Death Education, 6*(3), 265–278.

McConaghy, N., Zamir, R., & Manicavasagar, V. (1993). Non-sexist sexual experiences survey and scale of attraction to sexual aggression. *Australian and New Zealand Journal of Psychiatry, 27*(4), 686–693.

McCrae, R. R., & Costa Jr, P. T. (1989). Different points of view: Self-reports and ratings in the assessment of personality. In J. P. Forgas & M. J. Innes (Eds.), *Recent Advances in Social Psychology: An International Perspective* (pp. 429–439). Amsterdam: Elsevier.

McCurdy, K., & Daro, D. (1994). Child maltreatment: A national survey of reports and fatalities. *Journal of Interpersonal Violence, 9*(1), 75–94.

McDonald, M. (2003, October 24). Chechnya's eerie rebels: black widows – the 19 black-clad female terrorists in Moscow's theater siege – are still shrouded in mystery, one year later. *Gazette (Montreal, Quebec)*, sec. A, p. 4.

McDonald, R., Jouriles, E. N., Ramisetty-Mikler, S., Caetano, R., & Green, C. E. (2006). Estimating the number of American children living in partner-violent families. *Journal of Family Psychology, 20*(1), 137–142.

McKee, G. R. (2006). *Why Mothers Kill*. New York: Oxford University Press.

McKee, G. R., Shea, S. J., Mogy, R. B., & Holden, C. E. (2001). MMPI-2 profiles of filicidal mariticidal, and homicidal women. *Journal of Clinical Psychology, 57*(3), 367–374.

McLachlin, B. M. (1991). Crime and women: Feminine equality and the criminal law. *University of British Columbia Law Review, 25*, 1–22.

McLeod, M. (1984). Women against men: An examination of domestic violence based on an analysis of official data and national victimization data. *Justice Quarterly, 1*(2), 171–193.

Mechem, C. C., Shofer, F. S., Reinhard, S. S., Hornig, S., & Datner, E. (1999). History of domestic violence among male patients presenting to an urban emergency department. *Academic Emergency Medicine, 6*(8), 786–791.

Mellor, D., & Deering, R. (2010). Professional response and attitudes toward female-perpetrated child sexual abuse: A study of psychologists, psychiatrists, probationary psychologists and child protection workers. *Psychology, Crime & Law, 16*(5), 415–438.

Meloy, J. R. & Boyd, C. (2003). Female stalkers and their victims. *Journal of the American Academy of Psychiatry and the Law Online, 31*(2), 211–219.

Menard, K. S., Anderson, A. L., & Godboldt, S. M. (2009). Gender differences in intimate partner recidivism: A 5-year follow-up. *Criminal Justice and Behavior, 36*(1), 61–76.

Mendlowicz, M., Rapaport, M., Fontenelle, L., Jean-Louis, G., & De Moraes, T. (2002). Amnesia and neonaticides. *American Journal of Psychiatry, 159*(3), 498–9.

Mendlowicz, M., Rapaport, M., Mecler, K., Golshan, S., & De Moraes, T. (1998). A case controls study on the socio-demographic characteristics of 53 neonaticidal mothers. *International Journal of Law and Psychiatry, 21*(2), 209–219.

Mellor, D., & Deering, R. (2010). Professional response and attitudes toward female-perpetrated child sexual abuse: A study of psychologists, psychiatrists, probationary psychologists and child protection workers. *Psychology, Crime & Law, 16*(5), 415–438.

Mercer, R. T. (2004). Becoming a mother versus maternal role attainment. *Journal of Nursing Scholarship, 36*(3), 226–232.

Merrill, L. L., Crouch, J. L., Thomsen, C. J., & Guimond, J. M. (2004). Risk for intimate partner violence and child physical abuse: Psychosocial characteristics of multirisk male and female navy recruits. *Child Maltreatment, 9*(1), 18–29.

Merrill, L. L., Hervig, L. K., & Milner, J. S. (1996). Childhood parenting experiences, intimate partner conflict resolution, and adult risk for child physical abuse. *Child Abuse & Neglect, 20*(11), 1049–1065.

Merrill, L. L., Newell, C. E., Milner, J. S., Koss, M. P., Hervig L .K., Gold, S. R., . . . & Thornton, S. R. (1998). Prevalence of pre-military adult sexual victimization and aggression in a navy recruit sample. *Military Medicine, 163*(4), 209–212.

Messing, J. T., & Heeren, J. W. (2004). Another side of multiple murder: Women killers in the domestic context. *Homicide Studies, 8*(2), 123–158.

Messing, J. T., & Heeren, J. W. (2009). Gendered justice domestic homicide and the death penalty. *Feminist Criminology, 4*(2), 170–188.

Meyer, C. L., & Oberman, M. (2001). *Mothers Who Kill Their Children: Understanding the Acts of Moms from Susan Smith to the 'Prom Mom'*. New York University Press.

Miller, L. J. (1990). Psychotic denial of pregnancy: Phenomenology and clinical management. *Hospital and Community Psychiatry, 41*(11), 1233–1237.

Milner, J. S. (2003). Social information processing in high-risk and physically abusive parents. *Child Abuse & Neglect, 27*(1), 7–20.

Milner, J. S. et al. (2010). Do trauma symptoms mediate the relationship between childhood physical abuse and adult child abuse risk? *Child Abuse & Neglect, 34*(5), 332–344.

Moffitt, T. E. (2005). The new look of behavioural genetics in developmental psychopathology: Gene–environmental interplay in antisocial behaviours. *Psychological Bulletin, 131*(4), 533–554.

Moffitt, T. E., Caspi, A., Rutter, M., & Silva, P. A. (2001). Sex differences in physical violence and sex similarities in partner abuse. *Sex Differences in Antisocial Behavior. Conduct Disorder, Delinquency, and Violence in the Dunedin Longitudinal Study*, 53–70.

Moffitt, T. E., Krueger, R. F., Caspi, A., & Fagan, J. (2000). Partner abuse and general crime: How are they the same? How are they different? *Criminology, 38*(1), 199–232.

Moise, J. F., & Huesmann, L. R. (1996). Television violence viewing and aggression in females. *Annals of the New York Academy of Sciences, 794*(1), 380–383.

Möller-Leimkühler, A. M., & Yücel, M. (2010). Male depression in females? *Journal of Affective Disorders, 121*(1), 22–29.

Money, J. (1990). Forensic sexology: Paraphilic serial rape (biastophilia) and lust murder (erotophonophilia). *American Journal of Psychotherapy, 44*(1), 26–36.

Montaldo, C. (2011). Women who kill their children: 11 women are on death row for killing their kids. *Crime.* Retrieved from http://crime.about.com/od/female_offenders/a/mother_killers.htm

Moore, M. (2007). Is it really so different for girls? Challenging misconceptions about young offenders and aggression. *Safer Communities, 6*(3), 44–49.

Moretti, M. M., Obsuth, I., Odgers, C. L., & Reebye, P. (2006). Exposure to maternal vs paternal partner violence, PTSD, and aggression in adolescent girls and boys. *Aggressive Behavior, 32*(4), 385–395.

Moretti, M. M., Penney, S., Obsuth, I., & Odgers, C. (2007). Family lessons in attachment and aggression: The impact of interparental violence on adolescent adjustment (pp. 191–214). In J. Hamel and T. L. Nicholls (Eds.), *Family Interventions in Domestic Violence.* New York: Springer Publishing Company.

Morgan, E. (1972). *The Descent of Woman.* Souvenir Press: London.

Morris, D. (1967). *The Naked Ape: A Zoologist's Study of the Human Animal.* London: Cape.

Morton, R. J., & Hilts, M. A. (2005). Serial murder: Multi-disciplinary perspectives for investigators. *US Department of Justice, 8.*

Moulden, H. M., Firestone, P., & Wexler, A. F. (2007). Child care providers who commit sexual offenses: A description of offender, offense and victim characteristics. *International Journal of Offender Therapy and Comparative Criminology, 51*(4), 384–406.

Muehlenhard, C. L., & Cook, S. W. (1988). Men's self-reports of unwanted sexual activity. *Journal of Sex Research, 24*(1), 58–72.

Mugavin, M. (2008). Maternal filicide theoretical framework. *Journal of Forensic Nursing, 4*(2), 68–79.

Mulryan, N., Gibbons, P., & O'Conner, A. (2002). Infanticide and child murder: Admissions to the Central Mental Hospital 1850–2000. *Irish Journal of Psychological Medicine, 19*(1), 8–12.

Munoz-Rivas, M. J., Graña, J. L., O'Leary, K. D., & González, M. P. (2007). Aggression in adolescent dating relationships: Prevalence, justification, and health consequences. *Journal of Adolescent Health, 40*(4), 298–304.

Murphy, J. E. (1988). Date abuse and forced intercourse among college students. In G. T. Hotaling, D. Finkelhor, J. T. Kirkpatrick, & M. A. Strauss (Eds.), *Family Abuse and its Consequences: New Directions in Research* (pp. 285–296). Beverly Hills, CA: Sage.

Muskens, M., Bogaerts, S., van Casteren, M., & Labrijn, S. (2011). Adult female sexual offending: A comparison between co-offenders and solo offenders in a Dutch sample. *Journal of Sexual Aggression, 17*(1), 46–60.

Myers, W. C., Gooch, E., & Meloy, J. R. (2005). The role of psychopathy and sexuality in a female serial killer. *J Forensic Sci, 50*(3), 652–657.

Nathan, P., & Ward, T. (2002). Female sex offenders: Clinical and demographic features. *The Journal of Sexual Aggression, 8*(1), 5–21.

National Center for Health Statistics (2007). *Health, United States, 2007: With Chartbook on Trends in the Health of Americans.* Retrieved from www.cdc.gov/nchs/data/hus/hus07.pdf#032

Nelson, R., & Trainor, B. (2007). Neural mechanisms of aggression. *Nature Reviews Neuroscience, 8,* 536–546.

New York Times (1997). December 27: Killer of Girl, 8, Gets Up to 19 Years in Prison. *Metro News Briefs.* Retrieved from http://query.nytimes.com/gst/fullpage.html?res=9500E0DD123EF930A15751C1A961958260

Newby, J. H., Ursano, R. J., McCarroll, J. E., Martin, L. T., Norwood, A. E., & Fullerton, C. S. (2003). Spousal aggression by US army female soldiers toward employed and unemployed civilian husbands. *American Journal of Orthopsychiatry, 73*(3), 288–293.

News 24 (2003). Mother admits killing babies. Retrieved from www.news24.com

Niaz, U., Hassan, S., & Tariq, Q. (2002). Psychological consequences of intimate partner violence: Forms of domestic abuse in both genders. *Pakistan Journal of Medical Sciences, 18*(3), 205–214.

Nix, R. L., et al. (1999). The relation between mothers' hostile attribution tendencies and children's externalizing behavior problems: The mediating role of mothers' harsh discipline practices. *Child Development, 70*(4), 896–909.

NSPCC (2009). *More Children Telling Childline about Female Sex Abusers.* Press release.

Nydell, M. (2006). *Understanding Arabs: A Guide for Modern Times.* Boston: Intercultural Press.

O'Dougherty-Wright, M.., Norton, D. L., & Matusek, J. A. (2010). Predicting verbal coercion following sexual refusal during a hookup: Diverging gender patterns. *Sex Roles, 62*(9–10), 647–660.

O'Hara, M. W., Schlechte, J. I., Lewis, D., & Varner, M. (1991). Controlled prospective study of postpartum mood disorders: Psychological, environmental and hormonal variables. *Journal of Abnormal Psychology, 100*(1), 63–73.

O'Leary, K. D., Tintle, N., Bromet, E. J., & Gluzman, S. F. (2008). Descriptive epidemiology of intimate partner aggression in Ukraine. *Social Psychiatry and Psychiatric Epidemiology, 43*(8), 619–626.

Oldershaw, L., Walters, G. C., & Hall, D. K. (1989). A behavioral approach to the classification of different types of physically abusive mothers. *Merrill-Palmer Quarterly (1982–),* 255–279.

Olson, L. N., & Lloyd, S. A. (2005). 'It depends on what you mean by starting': An exploration of how women define initiation of aggression and their motives for behaving aggressively. *Sex Roles, 53*(7–8), 603–617.

Osterman, K., Bjorkqvist, K., Lagerspetz, K. M., Kaukiainen, A., Landau, S. F., Fraczek, A., & Caprara, G. V. (1998). Cross-cultural evidence of female indirect aggression. *Aggressive behavior, 24*(1), 1–8.

Overpeck, M., Brenner, R., Trumble, A., Trifiletti, L., & Berendes, H. (1998). Risk factors for infant homicide in the United States. *New England Journal of Medicine, 339*(17), 1211–1216.

Owens, L., Shute, R., & Slee, P. (2000). 'Guess what I just heard!': Indirect aggression among teenage girls in Australia. *Aggressive Behavior, 26*(1), 67–83.

Palmstierna, T., & Wistedt, B. (1987). Staff observation aggression scale, SOAS: Presentation and evaluation. *Acta Psychiatrica Scandinavica, 76*(6), 657–663.

Parker-Pope, T. (2010, September 8). New parents at risk for depression. *The New York Times*. Retrieved from well.blogs.nytimes.com

Patkin, T. (2004). Explosive baggage: Female Palestinian suicide bombers and the rhetoric of emotion. *Women and Language, 27*(2), 79–89.

Paulozzi, M., & Sells, M. (2002). Variations in homicide risk during infancy: US 1989–1998. *Morbidity and Mortality Weekly Report, 51*(9), 187–189.

Pearson, P. (1997). *When She was Bad: Violent Women and the Myth of Innocence*. New York: Viking.

People vs Wernick (1996). 674 NE2d 322 NY Legal Information Institute Database. Retrieved from www.law.cornell.edu/nyctap/196_0227.htm

Perez-Albeniz, A., & de Paul, J. (2003). Dispositional empathy in high-and low-risk parents for child physical abuse. *Child Abuse & Neglect, 27*(7), 769–780.

Perri, F. S., & Lichtenwald, T. (2010). Last frontier: Myths and the female psychopathic killer. *Forensic Examiner, 19*(2), 50–67.

Peter, T. (2006). Mad, bad, or victim? Making sense of mother–daughter sexual abuse. *Feminist Criminology, 1*(4), 283–302.

Peter, T. (2008). Speaking about the unspeakable: Exploring the impact of mother–daughter sexual abuse. *Violence against Women, 14*(9), 1033–1053.

Petersen, M. L., & Farrington, D. P. (2007). Cruelty to animals and violence to people. *Victims and Offenders, 2*, 21–43.

Petrovich, M., & Templer, D. I. (1984). Heterosexual molestation of children who later became rapists. *Psychological Reports, 54*(3), 810.

Pillemer, K., & Finkelhor, D. (1988). The prevalence of elder abuse: A random sample survey. *The Gerontologist, 28*(1), 51–57.

Pitts, J. (2009). Youth gangs, Ethnicity and the politics of estrangement. *Youth and Policy, 102* (Spring).

Poels, V. (2007). Risk assessment of recidivism of violent and sexual female offenders. *Psychiatry, Psychology and Law, 14*(2), 227–250.

Poitras, M., & Lavoie, F. (1995). A study of the prevalence of sexual coercion in adolescent heterosexual dating relationships in a Quebec sample. *Violence and Victims, 10*(4), 299–313.

Polaschek, D. L., & Ward, T. (2002). The implicit theories of potential rapists: What our questionnaires tell us. *Aggression and Violent Behavior, 7*(4), 385–406.

Popper, K. R. (1959). *The Logic of Scientific Discovery.* London: Hutchinson.

Porter, T., & Gavin, H. (2010). Infanticide and neonaticide: A review of 40 years of research literature on incidence and causes. *Trauma, Violence, & Abuse, 11*(3), 99–112.

Post, J. M. (2007). *The Mind of the Terrorist: The Psychology of Terrorism from the IRA to al-Qaeda.* New York: Palgrave Macmillan.

Powers, J. L., Eckenrode, J., & Jaklitsch, B. (1990). Maltreatment among runaway and homeless youth. *Child Abuse & Neglect, 14*(1), 87–98.

Pozzulo, J. D., Dempsey, J., Maeder, E., & Allen, L. (2010). The effects of victim gender, defendant gender, and defendant age on juror decision making. *Criminal Justice and Behavior, 37*(1), 47–63.

Prentky, R., Burgess, A., Rokous, F., & Lee, A. (1989). The presumptive role of fantasy in serial sexual homicide. *The American Journal of Psychiatry, 146*(7), 887–891.

Pron, Nick (2005). *Lethal Marriage: The Uncensored Truth Behind the Crimes of Paul Bernardo and Karla Homolka* (updated ed.). Berkeley, CA: Seal Books.

Pronk, R. E., & Zimmer-Gembeck, M. J. (2010). It's 'mean,' but what does it mean to adolescents? Relational aggression described by victims, aggressors, and their peers. *Journal of Adolescent Research, 25*(2), 175–204.

Purcell, R., Pathé, M., & Mullen, P. E. (2001). A study of women who stalk. *American Journal of Psychiatry, 158*(12), 2056–2060.

Purely, D., & Frank, E. (1996). Should postpartum mood disorders be given a more prominent or distinctive place in the DSM IV? *Depression and Anxiety, 1*(2), 59–70.

Putallaz, M., & Bierman, K. L. (Eds.) (2004). *Aggression, Antisocial Behavior and Violence Among Girls: A Developmental Perspective.* New York: Guilford.

Putkonen, H., Amon, S., Almiron, M. P., Cederwall, J.Y., Eronen, M., Klier, C., Kjelsberg, E., & Weizmann-Henelius, G. (2009). Filicide in Austria and Finland – A register-based study on all filicide cases in Austria and Finland 1995–2005. *BMC Psychiatry, 9*(1), 74.

Putkonen, H., Collander, J., Weizmann-Henelius, G., & Eronen, M. (2007). Legal outcomes of all suspected neonaticides in Finland 1980–2000. *International Journal of Law and Psychiatry 30*(3), 248–254.

Quas, J. A., Bottoms, B. L. Haegerich, T. M., & Nysse-Carris, K. L. (2002). Effects of victim defendant, and juror gender on decisions in child sexual assault cases. *Journal of Applied Social Psychology, 32*(10), 1993–2021.

Querido, J. G., Bearss, K., & Eyberg, S. M. (2002). Parent/child interaction therapy. In F. Kaslow and T. Patterson (Eds.), *Comprehensive Handbook of Psychotherapy: Cognitive-Behavioral Approaches* (pp. 91–113). New York: Wiley-Blackwell.

Quinsey, V. L., Ketsetzis, M., Earls, C., & Karamanoukian, A. (1996). Viewing time as a measure of sexual interest. *Ethology and Sociobiology, 17*(5), 341–354.

Raine, A., Lenz, T., Bihrle, S., Lacasse, L., & Colletti, P. (2000). Reduced grey matter volume and reduced autonomic activity in antisocial personality disorder. *Arch Gen Psychiatry, 57*(2), 119–127.

Ramirez, J. (2009). Some dychotomous classifications of aggression according to its function. *Journal of Organisational Transformation and Social Change, 6*(2), 85–101.

Rand, D. C., & Feldman, M. D. (2001). An explanatory model for Munchausen by proxy abuse. *International Journal of Psychiatry in Medicine, 31*(2), 113–126.

Rantala, M. J. (2007). Evolution of nakedness in Homo sapiens. *Journal of Zoology, 273*(1), 1–7.

Ray, A. E. (1996). Shame of it: Gender-based terrorism in the former Yugoslavia and the failure of international human rights law to comprehend the injuries. *The American University Law Review, 46*, 793–840.

Reeves, K. A., Desmarais, S. L., Nicholls, T. L., & Douglas, K. S. (2007). Intimate partner abuse of older men: Considerations for the assessment of risk. *Journal of Elder Abuse & Neglect, 19*(1–2), 7–27.

Reich, T., & Winokur, G. (1970). Postpartum psychosis in patients with manic depressive disease. *The Journal of Nervous and Mental Disease, 151*(1), 60–68.

Renzetti, C. (1999). The challenge to feminism posed by women's use of violence in intimate relationships. In S. Lamb (Ed.), *New Versions of Victims: Feminists Struggle with the Concept* (pp. 42–56). New York: NY University Press.

Resnick P. J. (1970). Murder of the newborn: A psychiatric review of neonaticide. *American Journal of Psychiatry, 126*, 1414–20.

Resnick, P. J., & Hatters-Friedman, S. (2003). Review of Infanticide: Psychosocial and Legal Perspectives on Mothers who Kill. *Psychiatric Services, 54*(8), 1172.

Ressler, R., & Shachtman, T. (1992). *Whoever Fights Monsters*. New York: Pocket Books.

Richards, C. E. (2000). *The Loss of Innocents: Child Killers and Their Victims*. Rowman & Littlefield.

Richardson, D. S. (2005). The myth of female passivity: Thirty years of revelations about female aggression. *Psychology of Women Quarterly, 29*(3), 238–247.

Richardson, D. S., & Hammock, G. S. (2007). Social context of human aggression: Are we paying too much attention to gender? *Aggression and Violent Behavior, 12*(4), 417–426.

Robbins, T. (2003). *Tender Murderers: Women Who Kill*. York Beach, ME: Conari Press.

Robling, S., Paykel, E., Dunn, V., Abbott, R., & Katona, C. (2000). Long-term outcome of severe puerperal psychiatric illness: A 23-year follow-up study. *Psychological Medicine, 30*(6), 1263–1271.

Roe-Sepowitz, D. E. (2009). Comparing male and female juveniles charged with homicide child maltreatment, substance abuse, and crime details. *Journal of Interpersonal Violence, 24*(4), 601–617.

Rogde, S., Hougen, H. P., & Poulsen, K. (2001). Asphyxial homicide in two Scandinavian capitals. *The American Journal of Forensic Medicine and Pathology, 22*(2), 128–133.

Rougé-Maillart, C., Jousset, N., Gaudin, A., Bouju B., & Penneau, M. (2005). Women who kill their children. *The American Journal of Forensic Medicine and Pathology, 26*(4), 320–326.

Rousseau, M. M., & Cortoni, F. (2010). The mental health needs of female sexual offenders. In T. A. Gannon & F. Cortoni (Eds.), *Female Sexual Offenders: Theory, Assessment, and Treatment* (pp. 73–86). West Sussex: Wiley-Blackwell.

Roys, D. T., & Timms, R. J. (1995). Personality profiles of adult males sexually molested by their maternal caregivers: Preliminary findings. *Journal of Child Sexual Abuse, 4*(4), 63–77.

Rudin, M. M., Zalewski, C., & Bodmer-Turner, J. (1995). Characteristics of child sexual abuse victims according to perpetrator gender. *Child Abuse & Neglect, 19*(8), 963–973.

Rumney, P. (2007). In defense of gender neutrality within rape. *Seattle Journal of Social Justice, 6*, 481.

Russell, G. W., & Baenninger, R. (1996). Murder most foul: Predictors of an affirmative response to an outrageous question. *Aggressive Behavior, 22*(3), 175–181.

Rutter, M. (2005). *Genes and Behavior: Nature–Nurture Interplay Explained*. Oxford: Blackwell Publishing.

Salekin, R., Rogers, R., Ustad, K., & Sewell, K. (1998). Psychopathy and recidivism among female inmates. *Law and Human Behavior, 22*(8), 109–128.

Salter, D., McMillan, D., Richards, M., Talbot, T., Hodges, J., Bentovim, A., . . . Skuse, D. (2003). Development of sexually abusive behaviour in sexually victimised males: A longitudinal study. *The Lancet, 361*(9356), 471–476.

Samaniego, S. (2009). Outed model blogger plans to sue Google. *CNN*. Retrieved from http://www.cnn.com/2009/TECH/08/25/new.york.model.blogger/index.html?_s=PM:TECH .

Sandberg, G., Jackson, T. L., & Petretic-Jackson, P. (1987). College students' attitudes regarding sexual coercion and aggression: Developing educational and preventive strategies. *Journal of College Student Personnel, 28*(4), 302–311.

Sandler, J. C., & Freeman, N. J. (2007). Topology of female sex offenders: A test of Vandiver and Kercher. *Sexual Abuse: A Journal of Research and Treatment, 19*, 73–89.

Sandler, J. C., & Freeman, N. J. (2009). Female sex offender recidivism: A large-scale empirical analysis. *Sexual Abuse: A Journal of Research and Treatment, 21*(4), 455–473.

Sandler, J., & Freeman, N. J. (2011). Female sex offenders and the criminal justice system: A comparison of arrests and outcomes. *Journal of Sexual Aggression, 17*(1), 61–76.

Saradjian, D. (2010). Understanding the prevalence of female-perpetrated sexual abuse impact of that abuse on victims. In T. A. Gannon & F. Cortoni (Eds.), *Female Sexual Offenders: Theory, Assessment, and Treatment* (pp. 9–30). West Sussex: Wiley-Blackwell.

Sarantakos, S. (2004). Deconstructing self-defense in wife-to-husband violence. *The Journal of Men's Studies, 12*(3), 277–296.

Sarlar, S., Dsouza, R., Dasgupta, A., & Fiebert, M. S. (2008). *Men as Victims of Domestic Violence in India.* Poster session presented at annual meeting of the Western Psychological Association, Irvine, CA.

Sarrel, P. M., & Masters, W. H. (1982). Sexual molestation of men by women. *Archives of Sexual Behavior, 11*(2), 117–131.

Saunders, D. G. (1986). When battered women use violence: Husband-abuse or self-defense? *Violence and Victims, 1*(1), 47–60.

Schank, R. C., & Abelson, R. (1977). *Scripts, Goals, Plans, and Understanding: An Inquiry Into Human Knowledge Structures* (Artificial Intelligence Series). New Jersey: Lawrence Erlbaum Associates.

Schloesser, P., Pierpont, J., & Poertner, J. (1992). Active surveillance of child abuse fatalities. *Child Abuse & Neglect, 16*(1), 3–10.

Schmidt, S. R. (2008). Adolescent girls with illegal sexual behavior. *APSAC Advisor 20*(2), 12–13.

Schmidt, P., Grass, H., & Madea, B. (1996). Child homicide in Cologne (1985–1994). *Forensic Science International, 79*(2), 131–144.

Schmidt, S., & Pierce, K. (2004). What research shows about female adolescent sex offenders. Fact Sheet. National Center on Sexual Behavior of Youth.

Schmitt, D. P., & Pilcher, J. J. (2004). Evaluating evidence of psychological adaptation: How do we know one when we see one? *Psychological Science, 15*(10), 643–649.

Schpoliansky, C., & Childs, D. (2009, June 18). When parents kill their kids. *ABC News.* Retrieved from http://abcnews.go.com

Schwartz, J., Steffensmeier, D. J., & Feldmeyer, B. (2009). Assessing trends in women's violence via data triangulation: Arrests, convictions, incarcerations, and victim reports. *Social Problems, 56*(3), 494–525.

Schwartz, M., O'Leary, S. G., & Kendziora, K. T. (1997). Dating aggression among high school students. *Violence and Victims, 12*(4), 295–305.

Scott, P. D. (1973). Parents who kill their children. *Medicine, Science and the Law, 13*, 120–126.

Sears, D. J. (1991). *To Kill Again: The Motivation and Development of Serial Murder.* Wilmington, Delaware: Scholarly Resources.

Sedlak, A., & Broadhurst, D. D. (1996). *Third National Incidence Study of Child Abuse and Neglect: Final Report.* US Department of Health and Human Services.

Seng, A. C., & Prinz, R. J. (2008). Parents who abuse: What are they thinking? *Clinical Child and Family Psychology Review, 11*(4), 163–175.

Serin, R. (1991). Psychopathy and violence in criminals. *Journal of Interpersonal Violence, 6*(4), 423–431.

Serran, G., & Firestone, P. (2004). Intimate partner homicide: A review of the male proprietariness and the self-defense theories. *Aggression and Violent Behavior, 9*(1), 1–15.

Sheehan, V., & Sullivan, J. (2010). A qualitative analysis of child sex offenders involved in the manufacture of indecent images of children. *Journal of Sexual Aggression, 16*(2), 143–167.

Shelton, J. L. E., Muirhead, Y., & Canning, K. E. (2010). Ambivalence towards mothers who kill: An examination of 45 US cases of maternal neonaticide. *Behavioral Sciences and the Law, 28*(6), 812–831.

Shepherd G., & Ferslew, B. C. (2009). Homicidal poisoning deaths in the United States 1999–2005. *Clinical Toxicology, 47*(4), 342–347.

Sheridan, M. S. (2003). The deceit continues: An updated literature review of Munchausen syndrome by proxy. *Child Abuse & Neglect, 27*(4), 431–451.

Shilling, E., & Geller, A. (2008, November 13). 43 years for Ma of Nixzmary. *New York Post.* Retrieved from http://nypost.com/2008/11/13/43-years-for-ma-of-nixzmary/

Siegel, A., & Victoroff, J. (2009). Understanding human aggression: New insights from neuroscience. *International Journal of Law and Psychiatry, 32*(4), 209–215.

Sigelman, C. K., Berry, C. J., & Wiles, K. A. (1984). Violence in college students' dating relationships. *Journal of Applied Social Psychology, 14*(6), 530–548.

Silverman, R., & Kennedy, L. (1988). Women who kill their children. *Violence & Victims, 3*(2), 113–27.

Silvio, H., McCloskey, K., & Ramos-Grenier, J. (2006). Theoretical consideration of female sexual predator serial killers in the United States. *Journal of Criminal Justice, 34*, 251–259.

Simmons, C. A., Lehmann, P., Cobb, N., & Fowler, C. R. (2005). Personality profiles of women and men arrested for domestic violence: An analysis of similarities and differences. *Journal of Offender Rehabilitation, 41*(4), 63–81.

Simonelli, C. J., & Ingram, K. M. (1998). Psychological distress among men experiencing physical and emotional abuse in heterosexual dating relationships. *Journal of Interpersonal Violence, 13*(6), 667–681.

Simons, D., Heil, P., Burton, D., & Gursky, M. (2008). Developmental and offense histories of female sexual offenders. *Symposium presented at the 27th Annual Association for the Treatment of Sexual Abusers Research and Treatment Conference.* Atlanta, GA.

Sit, D., Rothschild, A., & Wisner, K. (2006). A review of postpartum psychosis. *Journal of Women's Health, 15*(4), 352–368.

Slep, A. M. S., & O'Leary, S. G. (1998). The effects of maternal attributions on parenting: An experimental analysis. *Journal of Family Psychology, 12*(2), 234–243.

Sloan, L., & Edmond, T. (1996). Shifting the focus: Recognizing the needs of lesbian and gay survivors of sexual violence. *Journal of Gay & Lesbian Social Services, 5*(4), 33–52.

Slotboom, A. M., Hendriks, J., & Verbruggen, J. (2011). Contrasting adolescent female and male sexual aggression: A self-report study on prevalence and predictors of sexual aggression. *Journal of Sexual Aggression, 17*(1), 15–33.

Smarty, S. (2009). Battered child syndrome. In the *Wiley Encyclopedia of Forensic Science*.

Smith, L. (2010). Call for female child sex offenders to go on programme. *BBC News.* Retrieved from www.bbc.co.uk/news/uk-england-humber-11760445

Smith, H., & Thomas, S. P. (2000). Violent and nonviolent girls: Contrasting perceptions of anger experiences, school, and relationships. *Issues in Mental Health Nursing, 21*(5), 547–575.

Snyder, J. K., Fessler, D. M., Tiokhin, L., Frederick, D. A., Lee, S. W., & Navarrete, C. D. (2011). Trade-offs in a dangerous world: Women's fear of crime predicts preferences for aggressive and formidable mates. *Evolution and Human Behavior, 32*(2), 127–137.

Solomon, J. C. (1992). Child sexual abuse by family members: A radical feminist perspective. *Sex Roles, 27*(9–10), 473–485.

Southall, D. P., Plunkett, M. C., Banks, M. W., Falkov, A. F., & Samuels, M. P. (1997). Covert video recordings of life-threatening child abuse: Lessons for child protection. *Pediatrics, 100*(5), 735–760.

Sperling, C. (2005). Mother of atrocities: Pauline Nyiramasuhuko's role in the Rwandan genocide. *Fordham Urban Law Journal, 33*(2), 637.

Spinelli, M. G. (2001). A systematic investigation of 16 cases of neonaticide. *American Journal of Psychiatry, 158*(5), 811–813.

Spinelli, M. G. (2003). Neonaticide: A systematic investigation of 17 cases. *Infanticide: Psychosocial and Legal Perspectives on Mothers who Kill, 105*, 106–107.

Spitzberg, B. H. (1999). An analysis of empirical estimates of sexual aggression victimization and perpetration. *Violence and Victims, 14*(3), 241–260.

Stangle, H. (2008). Murderous Madonna: Femininity, violence, and the myth of postpartum mental disorder in cases of maternal infanticide and filicide. *William & Mary Law Review 50*(2), 699–734.

Stanko, E. A., & Hobdell, K. (1993). Assault on men: Masculinity and male victimization. *British Journal of Criminology, 33*(3), 400–415.

Stanton, J., & Simpson, A. (2001). Murder misdiagnosed as SIDS: A perpetrator's perspective. *Archives of Disease in Childhood, 85,* 454–459.

Stanton, J., & Simpson, A. (2006). The aftermath: Aspects of recovery described by perpetrators of maternal filicide committed in the context of severe mental illness. *Behavior Sciences and the Law, 24,* 103–112.

Stanton, J., Simpson, A., & Wouldes, T. (2000). A qualitative study of filicide by mentally ill mothers. *Child Abuse & Neglect, 24*(11), 1451–1460.

Staples, D. (2006, November 12). Revisiting Canada's infanticide law. *The Edmonton Journal.* Retrieved from www.canada.com/edmontonjournal/news/sundayreader/story.html?id=60527175-b3dc-4002-a27d-e9cf2f1ddd62

Steans, J. (1999). *Gender and International Relations: An Introduction.* New Jersey: Rutgers University Press.

Steinmetz, S. K. (1977). The battered husband syndrome. *Victimology, 2*(3–4), 499–509.

Stets, J. E., & Pirog-Good, M. A. (1989). Patterns of physical and sexual abuse for men and women in dating relationships: A descriptive analysis. *Journal of Family Violence, 4*(1), 63–76.

Stets, J. E., & Straus, M. A. (1990). Gender differences in reporting marital violence and its medical and psychological consequences. In M. A. Straus & R. J. Gelles (Ed.), *Physical Violence in American Families: Risk Factors and Adaptations to Violence* (pp. 151–165). New Brunswick, NJ: Transaction Press.

Stincelli, R. A. (2004). *Suicide by Cop.* Interviews & Interrogations Institute.

Stone, M. (2001). Serial sexual homicide: Biological, psychological, and sociological aspects. *Journal of Personality Disorders, 15*(1), 1–18.

Straus, M. A. (1986). Domestic violence and homicide antecedents. *Bulletin of the New York Academy of Medicine, 62*(5), 446–465.

Straus, M. A. (2007). Processes explaining the concealment and distortion of evidence on gender symmetry in partner violence. *European Journal on Criminal Policy and Research, 13*(3), 227–232.

Straus, M. A. (2008). Dominance and symmetry in partner violence by male and female university students in 32 nations. *Children and Youth Services Review, 30*(3), 252–275.

Straus, M. A., & Gelles, R. J. (1985). Is family violence increasing? A comparison of 1975 and 1985 national survey rates. *American Society of Criminology, San Diego, CA,* 1–6.

Straus, M. A., Hamby, S. L., Boney-McCoy, S., & Sugarman, D. B. (1996). The revised conflict tactics scales (CTS2) development and preliminary psychometric data. *Journal of Family Issues, 17*(3), 283–316.

Struckman-Johnson, C., & Struckman-Johnson, D. (1998). The dynamics and impact of sexual coercion of men by women. *Sexually Aggressive women: Current Perspectives and Controversies,* 121–143.

Struckman-Johnson, C., Struckman-Johnson, D., & Anderson, P. B. (2003). Tactics of sexual coercion: When men and women won't take no for an answer. *Journal of Sex Research, 40*(1), 76–86.

Struckman-Johnson, D., & Struckman-Johnson, C. (1991). Men and women's acceptance of coercive sexual strategies varied by initiator gender and couple intimacy. *Sex Roles, 25*(11/12), 661–676.

Stuart, G. L., Moore, T. M., Gordon, K. C., Ramsey, S. E., & Kahler, C. W. (2006). Psychopathology in women arrested for domestic violence. *Journal of Interpersonal Violence, 21*(3), 376–389.

Suetonius (2007). *The Twelve Caesars.* Project Gutenberg. Retrieved from http://history-world.org/suetonius.pdf

Sullivan, T., Cavanaugh, C., Ufner, M., Swan, S., & Snow, D. (2009). Relationships among women's use of aggression, their victimization, and substance use problems: A test of the moderating effects of race/ethnicity. *Journal of Aggression, Maltreatment & Trauma, 18*(6), 646–666.

Suris, A., Lind, L., Emmett, G., Borman, P. D., Kashner, M., & Barratt, E. S. (2004). Measures of aggressive behavior: Overview of clinical and research instruments. *Aggression and Violent Behavior, 9*(2), 165–227.

Swan, S. C., & Snow, D. L. (2003). Behavioral and psychological differences among abused women who use violence in intimate relationships. *Violence Against Women, 9*(1), 75–109.

Swan, S. C., & Snow, D. L. (2006). The development of a theory of women's use of violence in intimate relationships. *Violence Against Women, 12*(11), 1026–1045.

Sykes, G., & Matza, D. (1957). Techniques of neutralization: A theory of delinquency. *American Sociological Review, 22*(6), 664–670.

Taguchi, H. (2007). [Maternal filicide in Japan: Analyses of 96 cases and future directions for prevention.] *Seishin shinkeigaku zasshi= Psychiatria et neurologia Japonica, 109*(2), 110–127.

Takahashi, A., Quadros, I. M., de Almeida, R. M., & Miczek, K. A. (2011). Brain serotonin receptors and transporters: Initiation vs termination of escalated aggression. *Psychopharmacology, 213*(2–3), 183–212.

Tatar, M. (1998). *The Classic Fairy Tales: Texts, Criticism.* New York: W. W. Norton.

Taylor, C. (2006, December 26). Turning the tables. *ABC News.* Retrieved from http://abcnews.go.com/Primetime/story?id=2741047&page=1

Tedeschi, J. T., & Felson, R. B. (1994). *Violence, Aggression, and Coercive Actions.* American Psychological Association.

Tilbrook, E., Allan, A. & Dear, G. (2010). *Intimate Partner Abuse of Men.* Perth: ECU.

Timmer, S. G., Urquiza, A. J., Zebell, N. M., & McGrath, J. M. (2005). Parent–child interaction therapy: Application to maltreating parent–child dyads. *Child Abuse & Neglect, 29*(7), 825–842.

Tjaden, P. & Thoennes N. (2000). National Violence Against Women Survey. Department of Justice. National Institute of Justice.

Torniero, C., Bernardina, B. D., Fontana, E., Darra, F., Danesino, C., & Elia, M. (2011). Electroclinical findings in four patients with karyotype 47, XYY. *Brain and Development, 33*(5), 384–389.

Toro, K, Feher, S., Farkas, K., & Dunay, G. (2010). Homicides against infants, children and adolescents in Budapest (1960–2005). *Journal of Forensic and Legal Medicine 17*(8), 407–411.

Townsend, M., & Syal, R. (2009, October 3). Up to 64,000 women in UK 'are child-sex offenders'. *The Observer.*

Tremblay, R. E., Hartup, W. W., & Archer, J. (Eds.). (2005). *Developmental Origins of Aggression.* New York: Guilford Press.

Trocmé, N. et al. (2001). *Canadian Incidence Study of Reported Child Abuse and Neglect: Final Report.* Ottawa, Canada: Health Canada.

Troutman, B. R., & Cutrona, C. E. (1990). Nonpsychotic postpartum depression among adolescent mothers. *Journal Abnormal Psychology, 99*(1), 69–78

Tschinkel, S., Harris, M., Le Noury, J., & Healy, D. (2007). Postpartum psychosis: Two cohorts compared, 1875–1924 and 1994–2005. *Psychological Medicine, 37*(4), 529–536.

Tursz, A., Crost, M., Gerbouin-Rerolle, P., & Cook, J. M. (2010). Underascertainment of child abuse fatalities in France: Retrospective analysis of judicial data to assess underreporting of infant homicides in mortality statistics. *Child Abuse & Neglect, 34*(7), 534–544.

Tyler, K. A., & Cauce, A. M. (2002). Perpetrators of early physical and sexual abuse among homeless and runaway adolescents. *Child Abuse & Neglect, 26*(12), 1261–1274.

UK Home Office (2012). British Crime Survey datasets. *GovUK.* Retrieved from https://www.gov.uk/government/publications/british-crime-survey-datasets

Underwood, M. K. (2003). *Social Aggression in Girls.* New York: Guilford.

US Bureau of Justice Statistics (2009). Prisoners in 2009. US Department of Justice. Retrieved from www.bjs.gov/content./pub/pdf/p09.pdf

US Bureau of Justice Statistics (2014). Statistical reports. Office of Justice Programs. Retrieved from www.ojp.usdoj.gov.

Vanamo, T., Kauppi, A., Karkola, K., Merkanto, J., & Rasanen, E. (2001). Intra-familial child homicide in Finland 1970–1994: Incidence causes of death and demographic characteristics. *Forensic Science International 117*(3), 199–204.

Vandello, J. A., Ransom, S., Hettinger, V. E., & Askew, K. (2009). Men's misperceptions about the acceptability and attractiveness of aggression. *Journal of Experimental Social Psychology, 45*(6), 1209–1219.

Vandiver, D. (2006). Female sex offenders: A comparison of solo offenders and co-offenders. *Violence and Victims, 21*, 339–354.

Vandiver, D. M. (2010). Assessing gender differences and co-offending patterns of a predominantly 'male-oriented' crime: A comparison of a cross-national sample of juvenile boys and girls arrested for a sexual offense. *Violence and Victims, 25*(2), 243–264.

Vandiver, D., & Kercher, G. (2004). Offender and victim characteristics of registered female sexual offenders in Texas: A proposed typology of female sexual offenders. *Sexual Abuse, 16*(2), 121–137.

van Mastrigt, S. B., & Farrington, D. P. (2009). Co-offending, age, gender and crime type: Implications for criminal justice policy. *British Journal of Criminology, 49*(4), 552–573.

Värnik, A., Kõlves, K., van der Feltz-Cornelis, C., Marusic, A., Oskarsson, H., Palmer, A., Reisch, T., Scheerder, G., Arensman, E., Aromaa, E., Giupponi, G., Gusmäo, R., Maxwell, M., Pull, C., Szekely, A., Sola, V., & Hegerl, U. (2008). Suicide methods in Europe: A gender-specific analysis of countries participating in the 'European Alliance Against Depression'. *Journal of Epidemiology and Community Health, 62*(6), 545–551.

Vess, J. (2011). Risk assessment with female sex offenders: Can women meet the criteria of community protection laws? *Journal of Sexual Aggression, 17*(1), 77–91.

Videbech, P., & Gouliaev, G. (1995). First admission with puerperal psychosis: 7–14 years of follow-up. *Acta Psychiatrica Scandinavica 91*(3), 167–173.

Vronsky, P. (2007). *Female Serial Killers: How and Why Women Become Monsters.* Berkley Books.

Wagner, G. C., Beuving, L. J., & Hutchinson, R. R. (1980). The effects of gonadal hormone manipulations on aggressive target-biting in mice. *Aggressive Behavior, 6*(1), 1–7.

Waldner-Haugrud, L. K., Gratch, L. V., & Magruder, B. (1997). Victimization and perpetration rates of violence in gay and lesbian relationships: Gender issues explored. *Violence and Victims, 12*(2), 173–184.

Walker, J., & Gavin, H. (2011). Interpretations of domestic violence: Defining intimate partner abuse. *The Twelfth Conference of the International Academy of Investigative Psychology, Crime, Criminalistics & Criminal Psychology: New Directions in Investigative Behavioural Science.* Amsterdam, 31 March–2 April 2011.

Walker, L. (2006). Battered woman syndrome. *Annals of the New York Academy of Sciences, 1087,* 142–157.

Walker, L. E., & Meloy, J. R. (1998). Stalking and domestic violence. In J. R. Meloy (Ed.), *The Psychology of Stalking: Clinical and Forensic Perspectives* (pp. 131–161). San Diego, CA: Academic Press.

Walker, P. L. (2001). A bioarchaeological perspective on the history of violence. *Annual Review of Anthropology, 573–596.*

Walker, S., Richardson, D. S., & Green, L. R. (2000). Aggression among older adults: The relationship of interaction networks and gender role to direct and indirect responses. *Aggressive Behavior, 26*(2), 145–154.

Waller, J. (2002). *Becoming Evil: How Ordinary People Commit Genocide and Mass Killing* Oxford: Oxford University Press.

Walley-Jean, J. C., & Swan, S. (2009). Motivations and justifications for partner aggression in a sample of African American college women. *Journal of Aggression, Maltreatment & Trauma, 18*(7), 698–717.

Wanamaker, C. E., & Reznikoff, M. (1989). Effects of aggressive and nonaggressive rock songs on projective and structured tests. *The Journal of Psychology, 123*(6), 561–570.

Warren, J., & Hislop, J. (2001). Female sex offenders: A typological and etiological overview. In R. Hazelwood & A. Burgess (Eds.), *Practical Aspects of Rape Investigation: A Multidisciplinary Approach* (pp. 421–434). Boca Raton, FL: CRC Press.

Waterman, C. K., Dawson, L. J., & Bologna, M. J. (1989). Sexual coercion in gay male and lesbian relationships: Predictors and implications for support services. *Journal of Sex Research 26*(1), 118–124.

Weekes-Shackelford, V. A., & Shackelford, T. K. (2004). Methods of filicide: Stepparents and genetic parents kill differently. *Violence and Victims, 19*(1), 75–81.

Weinhardt, L. S., Forsyth, A. D., Carey, M. P., Jaworski, B. C., & Durant, L. E. (1998). Reliability and validity of self-report measures of HIV-related sexual behavior: Progress since 1990 and recommendations for research and practice. *Archives of Sexual Behavior, 27*(2), 155–180.

Werner, N. E., & Crick, N. R. (2004). Maladaptive peer relationships and the development of relational and physical aggression during middle childhood. *Social Development, 13*(4), 495–514.

Wessel, J., & Buscher, U. (2002). Denial of pregnancy: Population based study. *British Medical Journal, 324*(7335), 458.

Wessel, J., Endrika, J., & Buscher,U. (2002). Frequency of denial of pregnancy: Results and epidemiological significance of a 1-year prospective study in Berlin. *Acta Obstetricia et Gynecologica Scandinavica, 81*(11), 1021–1027.

Wessel, J., Gauruder-Burmester, A., & Gerlinger, C. (2007). Denial of pregnancy – characteristics of women at risk. *Acta Obstetricia et Gynecologica Scandinavica, 86*(5), 542–546.

West, C. M. (2008). 'A thin line between love and hate'? Black men as victims and perpetrators of dating violence. *Journal of Aggression, Maltreatment & Trauma, 16*(3), 238–257.

West, S. G., & Feldsher, M. (2010). Parricide: Characteristics of sons and daughters who kill their parents. *Current Psychiatry 18*(11), 20–38.

West, S. G., & Friedman, S. H. (2008). These boots are made for stalking: Characteristics of female stalkers. *Psychiatry, 5*(8), 37–42.

Whalley, L. J., Roberts, D. F., Wentzel, J., & Wright, A. F. (1982). Genetic factors in puerperal affective psychosis. *Acta Psychiatrica Scandinavica, 65*(3), 180–193.

White, J. W., & Kowalski, R. M. (1994). Deconstructing the myth of the nonaggressive woman: A feminist analysis. *Psychology of Women Quarterly, 18*(4), 487–508.

White, G., & Mullen, P. (1989). *Jealousy, Theory, Research & Clinical Strategies.* New York: Guildford Press.

White, H. R., & Widom, C. S. (2003). Intimate partner violence among abused and neglected children in young adulthood: The mediating effects of early aggression, antisocial personality, hostility and alcohol problems. *Aggressive Behavior, 29*(4), 332–345.

Wiegel, M. (2009, June). Adult women who sexually abuse minors: Self-reported characteristics and objectively measured sexual interest. *Paper presented at the Eleventh Annual Joint Conference, MASOC/MATSA.* Marlborough, Massachusetts.

Wijkman, M., Bijleveld, C., & Hendriks, J. (2011). Female sex offenders: Specialists, generalists and once-only offenders. *Journal of Sexual Aggression, 17*(1), 34–45.

Wilczynski, A. (1997). Prior agency contact and physical abuse in cases of child homicide. *British Journal of Social Work, 27*(2), 241–253.

Williams, S. (1996). *The Strange Case of Paul Bernardo and Karla Homolka.* Toronto, Canada: Little Brown and Co.

Wilson, C., Gardner, F., Burton, J., & Leung, S. (2007). Maternal attributions and observed maternal behaviour: Are they linked? *Behavioural and Cognitive Psychotherapy, 35*(2), 165–178.

Winton, M. A., & Unlu, A. (2008). Micro–macro dimensions of the Bosnian genocides: The circumplex model and violentization theory. *Aggression and Violent Behavior, 13*(1), 45–59.

Wisner, K. L., & Stowe, Z. N. (1997, February). Psychobiology of postpartum mood disorders. *Seminars in Reproductive Endocrinology, 15*(1), 77–89.

Wistedt, B., Rasmussen, A., Pedersen, L., Malm, U., Träskman-Bendz, L., Wakelin, J., & Bech, P. (1990). The development of an observer-scale for measuring social dysfunction and aggression. *Pharmacopsychiatry.*

Wolfe, D. A. (1999). *Child Abuse: Implications for Child Development and Psychopathology.* Thousand Oaks, CA: Sage Publications.

Wolfner, G. D., & Gelles, R. J. (1993). A profile of violence toward children: A national study. *Child Abuse & Neglect, 17*(2), 197–212.

World Health Organization and London School of Hygiene and Tropical Medicine (2010). *Preventing Intimate Partner and Sexual Violence against Women: Taking Action and Generating Evidence*. Geneva: World Health Organization.

Wright, L. W., Jr & Adams, H. E. (1994). Assessment of sexual preference using a choice reaction time task. *Journal of Psychopathology and Behavioral Assessment*, *16*(3), 221–231.

Yasumi, K., & Kageyama, J. (2009). Filicide and fatal abuse in Japan, 1994–2005: Temporal trends and regional distribution. *Journal of Forensic Legal Medicine*, *16*(2), 70–75.

Yin, S. (2010). Malicious use of pharmaceuticals in children. *The Journal of Pediatrics*, *157*(5), 832–836.

Yudofsky, S. C., Silver, J. M., Jackson, W., Endicott, J., & Williams, D. (1986). The Overt Aggression Scale for the objective rating of verbal and physical aggression. *The American Journal of Psychiatry*, *143*(1), 35–39.

Zoccolillo, M., Paquette, D., Azar, R., Cote, S., & Tremblay, R. (2004). Parenting as an important outcome of conduct disorder in girls. In M. Putallaz, & K. L. Bierman (Eds.), *Aggression, Antisocial Behavior and Violence Among Girls: A Developmental Perspective* (pp. 242–261). New York: Guilford.

Zoroya, G. (2002, 22 April). Woman describes the mentality of a suicide bomber. *USA Today*, *22*, 1. Retrieved from http://usatoday30.usatoday.com/news/world/2002/04/22/cover.htm

Index

Female Aggression, First Edition. Helen Gavin and Theresa Porter.
© 2015 John Wiley & Sons, Ltd. Published 2015 by John Wiley & Sons, Ltd.

This index was prepared by Neil Manley.